iPad® and iPhone® Digital Photography
Tips and Tricks

Jason R. Rich

iPAD® AND iPHONE® DIGITAL PHOTOGRAPHY TIPS AND TRICKS

COPYRIGHT © 2014 BY PEARSON EDUCATION, INC.

ISBN-13: 978-0-7897-5312-0

ISBN-10: 0-7897-5312-X

Library of Congress Control Number: 2014931710

Printed in the United States of America

First Printing: March 2014

TRADEMARKS

WARNING AND DISCLAIMER

SPECIAL SALES

For information about buying this title in bulk quantities, or for special sales opportunities (which may include electronic versions; custom cover designs; and content particular to your business, training goals, marketing focus, or branding interests), please contact our corporate sales department at corpsales@pearsoned.com or (800) 382-3419.

For government sales inquiries, please contact governmentsales@pearsoned.com.

For questions about sales outside the U.S., please contact international@pearsoned.com.

EDITOR-IN-CHIEF
Greg Wiegand

SENIOR ACQUISITIONS EDITOR
Laura Norman

DEVELOPMENT EDITOR
Todd Brakke

MANAGING EDITOR
Sandra Schroeder

SENIOR PROJECT EDITOR
Tonya Simpson

COPY EDITOR
Karen Annett

INDEXER
Erika Millen

PROOFREADER
Debbie Williams

TECHNICAL EDITOR
Paul Sihvonen-Binder

EDITORIAL ASSISTANT
Cindy Teeters

INTERIOR DESIGNER
Anne Jones

COVER DESIGNER
Mark Shirar

COMPOSITOR
Trina Wurst

CONTENTS AT A GLANCE

TABLE OF CONTENTS

ABOUT THE AUTHOR

Jason R. Rich (www.JasonRich.com) is the best-selling author of more than 55 books as well as a frequent contributor to a handful of major daily newspapers, national magazines, and popular websites. He's also an accomplished photographer, blogger, and an avid Apple iPhone, iPad, Apple TV, and Mac user.

Jason R. Rich is the author of the books *Your iPad at Work*, Fourth Edition, as well as *iPad and iPhone Tips and Tricks*, Third Edition, both published by Que Publishing. He has also written *How to Do Everything MacBook Air, How to Do Everything iCloud*, Second Edition, and *How to Do Everything iPhone 5* for McGraw-Hill, and *Ultimate Guide to YouTube for Business* for Entrepreneur Press.

Jason R. Rich has written more than 160 feature-length how-to articles, covering the Apple iPhone and iPad, which you can read free online at the Que Publishing website. Visit www.iOSArticles.com and click on the Articles tab. You can also follow Jason R. Rich on Twitter (@JasonRich7) or read his blog, called Jason Rich's Featured App of the Week, to learn about new and useful iPhone and iPad apps (www.FeaturedAppOfTheWeek.com).

DEDICATION

This book is dedicated to the late Steve Jobs as well as to my niece, Natalie.

ACKNOWLEDGMENTS

Thanks once again to Laura Norman at Que Publishing for inviting me to work on this book and for all of her guidance as I've worked on this project. My gratitude also goes out to Tonya Simpson, Todd Brakke, Greg Wiegand, and Cindy Teeters as well as everyone else at Que Publishing and Pearson who contributed their expertise, hard work, and creativity to the creation and publication of *iPad and iPhone Digital Photography Tips and Tricks*.

Thanks also to my friends and family for their ongoing support. Finally, thanks to you, the reader. I hope this book helps you take full advantage of the digital photography capabilities of your iPhone or iPad.

WE WANT TO HEAR FROM YOU!

As the reader of this book, *you* are our most important critic and commentator. We value your opinion and want to know what we're doing right, what we could do better, what areas you'd like to see us publish in, and any other words of wisdom you're willing to pass our way.

We welcome your comments. You can email or write to let us know what you did or didn't like about this book—as well as what we can do to make our books better.

Please note that we cannot help you with technical problems related to the topic of this book.

When you write, please be sure to include this book's title and author as well as your name and email address. We will carefully review your comments and share them with the author and editors who worked on the book.

Email: feedback@quepublishing.com

Mail: Que Publishing
ATTN: Reader Feedback
800 East 96th Street
Indianapolis, IN 46240 USA

READER SERVICES

Visit our website and register this book at www.quepublishing.com/register for convenient access to any updates, downloads, or errata that might be available for this book.

PREPARE YOUR iPHONE OR iPAD TO TAKE AWESOME PHOTOS

Apple's iPhone smartphones and iPad tablets have become the most widely used digital cameras in the world. With each new iPhone and iPad model that's been released, the picture-taking capabilities of these devices have been improved.

At the same time, hundreds of third-party photography apps are available from the App Store that further expand your digital photography toolset. Plus, there are a handful of accessories you can purchase that give you even more options when it comes to taking, viewing, organizing, editing, enhancing, printing, and sharing digital photos from just about anywhere.

NOTE Chapter 9, "Photography Apps That Expand Your Photo Editing and Enhancement Capabilities," showcases just some of the more popular and powerful third-party apps that offer features and functions that go beyond what's possible using just the Camera and Photos apps that come preinstalled with iOS 7.

Thanks to the technology built in to your iPhone or iPad, as well as the Camera and Photos apps that come preinstalled with iOS 7, you have the equivalent of a full-featured, point-and-shoot digital camera, a mobile photo editing workstation (see Figure 1-1), and an Internet-enabled device that enables you to immediately share your photos available at your fingertips.

FIGURE 1-1
Wherever you are, whatever you're doing, if you have your iPhone or iPad handy, you can photograph what's happening and, if you choose, immediately edit or share those photos with friends and family.

Using the rear-facing camera that's built in to your iPhone or iPad, you can easily take photos that are as detailed, clear, vibrant, and visually interesting as any photo you could otherwise take using a standalone point-and-shoot digital camera. And, because most people carry around an iPhone or iPad just about everywhere they go, taking lots of pictures as events in life unfold has become more convenient than ever. Thus, you're able to capture memories, edit them almost instantly from your mobile device, and then share moments in your life with other people via email (see Figure 1-2), instant message, AirDrop, or by uploading images to a popular online social networking service (like Facebook, Twitter, Snapchat, or Instagram) or an online photo sharing service (like Shutterfly.com, Smugmug.com, or Snapfish.com).

FIGURE 1-2

Using the Photos or Mail app, both of which come preinstalled with iOS 7, you can share photos taken on your iOS mobile device with other people via email.

Figure 1-3 shows a photo as it's about to upload to Facebook via the Photos app that comes with iOS, which is one of many options available in that app. The official Facebook app, however, enables you to create, upload, and manage entire online galleries from your iOS mobile device. From this app, you can share groups of photos with all of your online-based Facebook friends.

FIGURE 1-3

Uploading photos taken on an iPhone or iPad directly to Facebook is easy using the Facebook option available from the Share menu of the Photos app.

THERE'S A LOT MORE YOU CAN DO WITH THE PHOTOS YOU TAKE USING YOUR iPHONE OR iPAD

After you've taken and edited digital photos using your iPhone or iPad, it's possible to create traditional prints from those images. This can be done using a home photo printer or a one-hour photo lab (a service available at most pharmacies and mass-market retail superstores) or by uploading your digital image files to a professional photo lab (which then creates the prints and mails them to you within a few business days).

For example, if you have the Costco app installed on your iPhone or iPad, before heading to your local Costco store to do your shopping, you can select and upload images that you've shot on your mobile device and order prints to be made from them (see Figure 1-4).

After choosing the images from within the Costco app, selecting what size prints you want, and selecting the quantity of prints for each image, within an hour or so, your prints will be available for pickup at the Costco Photo counter. Similar apps are available from Walgreens, CVS, Target, and Wal-Mart.

FIGURE 1-4

With the Costco app, for example, you can quickly select specific images stored on your iPhone or iPad, upload them to Costco's one-hour photo-processing service, and then pick up your prints when you arrive at the store.

> **NOTE** You can learn more about creating prints from your iPhone or iPad in Chapter 11, "Create Prints from Your iPhone/iPad Photos."

As you'll soon discover, you can also showcase your digital photos on your high-definition (HD) television set or online in the form of an online gallery or animated digital slideshow. You can also incorporate those same images into professionally bound hardcover or softcover photo books (or photo eBooks), or create all sorts of photo gifts that feature your images. These items include everything from T-shirts, refrigerator magnets, and mouse pads, to canvas enlargements and customized iPhone or iPad covers/cases (see Figure 1-5).

FIGURE 1-5

Using the Shutterfly app (shown here on the iPad), you can create and order a wide range of photo products and gifts, including a custom iPhone case.

Meanwhile, if you opt to share your photos on the Instagram online service, you can use the independent StickyGram service (https://stickygram.com) to order two-inch square magnets that feature your photos. Each StickyGram sheet ($14.99) includes nine photo magnets featuring your individual photos. You can use them to decorate your refrigerator, for example (see Figure 1-6).

Right out of the box, you can use your iPhone or iPad camera to snap photos and shoot HD video clips. You can then view, edit, enhance, organize, print, and share those images using the Photos app. The fact is, using the Camera app, just about anyone with the most rudimentary understanding of how your iOS mobile device works can take decent quality photos.

However, if you're more serious about consistently capturing high-quality, in-focus, well-lit, and professional-quality images using your iPhone or iPad, which you'll be proud to show off to your friends and family, you can acquire the skills and information you'll need from this book.

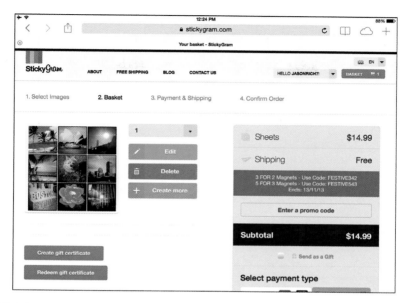

FIGURE 1-6

The StickyGram service enables you to create colorful and inexpensive magnets from digital photos that you have published on Instagram via your iPhone or iPad.

DIGITAL PHOTOGRAPHY IS BOTH A SKILL AND AN ART FORM

Whether you're taking pictures with a $5,000 digital Single Lens Reflex (SLR) camera from Nikon or Canon, a $400 point-and-shoot digital camera, or your iOS mobile device, the basic skills and knowledge you need as a photographer to take consistently good pictures are basically the same.

What you should understand right from the start is that digital photography is both a skill and an art form. To shoot good-quality photos, you must first learn how to properly use your camera—in this case, your iPhone or iPad, with a photography app. This means knowing how to operate your iOS mobile device and its built-in cameras, as well as being able to launch and use a photography app.

Just like using a computer or another cutting-edge technological gadget, this requires knowledge and a particular skill set. However, there is a second part to the equation, which is understanding that digital photography is also an art form that requires creative decision making and the ability to look at the world through the camera's viewfinder and be able to capture visually interesting images that can convey a message or emotion or capture a moment in time in a meaningful way.

The art form aspect of digital photography requires you, as the photographer, to determine what to shoot, when to shoot, and how to best shoot your intended subject(s) in order to wind up with a visually interesting digital photograph. In addition to choosing your primary subject, as the photographer, you need to frame your shots utilizing what's in the foreground, in the background, and to the sides of your intended subject in a way that creates a more compelling image that is visually pleasing to the eye.

At the same time, you must pay attention to and work with your primary light source, and sometimes overcome challenges that come from having too much or too little light shining on your intended subject(s). As you're working with natural (ambient) light and/or artificial light (including light generated by the iPhone's flash, for example), it's your job as the photographer to watch out for unwanted shadows, glares, and other challenges that imperfect lighting often creates.

A good digital photographer also pays attention to the shooting angle or perspective, as well as how the subject is posed or positioned within the frame. Then, as all of these elements come together to create what will be a single photograph that's captured when you tap on the Shutter button, determining exactly when to press that Shutter button to take a photo is another part of the creative decision process involved with being a digital photographer.

As you'll soon discover—especially if you're taking pictures of people or animals or your intended subject is in motion—developing a good sense of timing is important.

From this book, you'll learn how to use the Camera and Photos apps that come preinstalled with the iPhone and iPad, so that you can begin taking, viewing, organizing, printing, and sharing digital photos almost immediately. You'll also learn a wide range of photography techniques and strategies that are commonly used by professional photographers, but you'll discover how to utilize them when taking pictures with your iOS mobile device.

Then, you'll focus on how to use some of the third-party photography apps that greatly expand what's possible, giving you more creative freedom as you take pictures in a wide range of situations and later edit, showcase, and share them.

What you'll soon discover is that taking pictures using your iPhone or iPad is not only convenient, but it's also fun. Plus, digital photography offers a powerful and versatile way to express yourself creatively, and at the same time, capture moments in your life that you can later reminisce about and/or share with others.

WHAT YOU NEED TO GET STARTED AS A MOBILE DIGITAL PHOTOGRAPHER

This book focuses on teaching you how to take consistently high-quality, in-focus, and visually interesting digital pictures using the front- and rear-facing cameras that are built in to the iPhone or iPad. To take full advantage of what you're about to learn, you definitely need an iPhone or iPad model updated to run iOS 7 or the most recently released version of the Apple operating system.

> **TIP** If you're serious about taking the best-quality pictures possible using an iOS mobile device (instead of having to carry around your smartphone and a separate point-and-shoot digital camera), you should definitely consider upgrading to the Apple iPhone 5s.
>
> This latest iPhone model offers an 8MP high-resolution, rear-facing camera, plus a better-quality image sensor and lens than other iPhone models (including the iPhone 5c, iPhone 5, and iPhone 4s). Plus, because the iPhone 5s uses a faster and more powerful processor (Apple's A7 chip), it enables you to utilize camera features, such as burst shooting and an improved HDR (High Dynamic Range) shooting mode, that other iPhone models don't support. Both of these features are explained in Chapter 2, "Snap Photos Using the Camera App."
>
> Although the latest iPad models, including the iPad Air and iPad mini with Retina display, are also powered using Apple's A7 chip, the rear-facing camera that's built in to these tablets offers 5MP resolution. When used with the Camera app and other technology built in to the tablet, this allows for excellent-quality digital photos to be taken, but these cameras are not as high-quality as what the iPhone 5s offers.

MAKE SURE YOU HAVE POWER

Regardless of which iOS mobile device you wind up using to take pictures, in addition to choosing the best photography app(s) to meet your needs, it's essential that you keep your iPhone or iPad charged, so when you want to snap photos, you have the battery power to do so.

Keep in mind that using the iPhone or iPad's built-in cameras extensively, and then constantly uploading images to a cloud-based service or online social networking site, for example, depletes your device's battery charge a bit faster than using it for some other applications, such as listening to music. Plus, if you're using the iPhone's built-in flash when taking pictures, this drains your smartphone's battery even more quickly. So, plan accordingly and make sure you have an external battery pack and/or charging cable with you while on the go.

HAVE ADEQUATE STORAGE

Another consideration—especially if you're going on vacation, you plan to take a lot of photos, but you won't be able to transfer them to your primary computer or upload them to an online service—is the internal storage capacity of your device. Although a 16GB iPhone or iPad can store thousands of digital photos, if you're also storing lots of other files and content in your device (such as TV show episodes or movies acquired from the iTunes Store or other large files), that leaves less internal storage available for your images.

If you start running low on internal storage space, you might wind up needing to delete content from your iOS mobile device to make more room to store photos. Keep in mind that shooting HD video clips on your iPhone or iPad also utilizes a lot of internal storage space, so consider using this feature sparingly if available storage space is limited.

To determine how you're currently utilizing the internal storage space of your iOS mobile device, and to manage what's stored in it, launch Settings, tap on the General option, and then select the Usage option from the General submenu (see Figure 1-7). From this menu, under the Storage heading, you can see the total storage capacity of your smartphone or tablet, as well as how much of that storage is currently utilized.

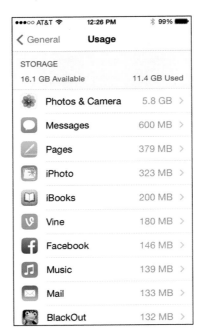

FIGURE 1-7

From Settings, you can easily determine how much internal storage space you have available on your iPhone or iPad, plus free up space by deleting apps or related app-specific content.

Below this information is a listing of all apps installed on your device, along with how much internal storage space the app and app-specific data use.

> **NOTE** Multimedia content, such as TV show episodes, movies, or music videos acquired from the iTunes Store, as well as HD video clips you've shot yourself using your iOS mobile device, tend to take up a lot of internal storage space within your device. Digital slide presentations created using Keynote (or PowerPoint presentations that are being used with Keynote) also tend to have large file sizes associated with them.

Tap on any app listing to see details about that app and its app-specific data. From the submenu screen that's displayed for each app, there is an option to delete the app and its related data. Keep in mind that if you delete an app and its related data without backing up the data first, that data will be lost, but you can always reload the app for free.

By tapping on the Photos & Camera option, for example, you can see how much internal storage space is being used by digital photos and video clips stored in the Camera Roll folder, Photo Library, and Photo Stream folders. You'll find specific tips for managing the Photos app in Chapter 6, "View, Organize, Edit, and Share Pictures Using the Photos App."

> **TIP** If you plan to rely heavily on the cameras built in to your iPhone or iPad, when purchasing your iOS mobile device, choose a hardware configuration with plenty of internal storage space. Also, keep in mind that although iCloud's Shared Photo Stream works only with a Wi-Fi Internet connection, other methods for uploading photos to various online services do work with a cellular data connection, which might be useful to you while you're out and about taking pictures. So, when choosing an iPad model, consider one with Wi-Fi plus cellular Internet connectivity.

ADD SOME APPS OR ACCESSORIES

Based on what you're trying to accomplish and how you want to share your images, you'll inevitably want to download and install some third-party photography apps that are available from the App Store. Some of these apps are free, whereas others have a fee associated with them. A handful of the most feature-packed and powerful photography apps, as well as strategies for how to best use them, are showcased in Chapter 9.

TIP   To discover all of the latest photography-related apps available from the App Store, launch the App Store app on your iPhone or iPad, and then tap on the Featured icon. On the iPhone, tap on the Categories option (displayed near the top-left corner of the screen), and then select the Photo & Video option.

On the iPad, after tapping the Featured icon, near the top center of the screen, tap on the More tab, and then select the Photo & Video option (shown in Figure 1-8).

To see a listing of the most popular photography apps available from the App Store, after launching the App Store app, tap on the Top Charts icon. Next, tap on the Categories option, and then select the Photo & Video option. A list of the current most popular Paid, Free, and Top Grossing photography-related apps is displayed.

FIGURE 1-8

The App Store offers hundreds of specialty digital photography apps that greatly expand the picture taking, as well as photo editing and sharing capabilities, of your iPhone or iPad.

You might also want to invest in a few digital photography accessories that you can use with your iPhone or iPad, such as optional clip-on lenses and/or a tripod. You'll learn more about these options in Chapter 10, "Use Optional Accessories to Improve Your Pictures."

PLACES TO SHOW OFF YOUR PHOTOS

Again, depending on what you plan to do with your photos, you might ultimately want to transfer them from your iOS mobile device to your Mac or PC, where they can be archived, viewed, printed, edited, and shared. This process can be done in a variety of ways, using Apple's iCloud service (or another cloud-based service, such as Dropbox), the iTunes Sync process, or via email, to name just a few.

Another option is to upload your photos from your iPhone or iPad to an online social networking service, such as Facebook, Twitter, or Instagram, to share them with your online friends and/or the general public. All of the popular online services have their own iPhone/iPad apps that make it very easy to upload and share images directly from your mobile device, as long as an Internet connection is available.

To use any of the online social networking services, or any of the online photo sharing services, you must set up a free account if you don't already have one. You learn how to do this in Chapter 12, "Share Your Digital Photos Online." You also learn in Chapter 12 how to share individual photos with specific people, as well as how to easily and quickly create online galleries or animated slideshows to show-case groups of images online.

> **CAUTION**   To ensure that only the people you want will be able to view the photos you publish online, whether you're using iCloud's Shared Photo Stream, Facebook, or an online gallery created on the Shutterfly.com service, for example, it's important that you correctly set up the service's privacy settings.
>
> Also, to protect your online privacy, you might opt to refrain from tagging photos and/or attaching location-based information to them. What precautions to take and how to take them are the subjects of Chapter 12.

DEVELOP YOUR PHOTOGRAPHER'S EYE

By combining your knowledge of how to operate your iPhone or iPad and the various digital photography apps available for it with the artistic and creative elements of being a digital photographer, with a bit of practice, you'll soon be taking amazing photos that you'll be excited to share with friends, family, co-workers, and even complete strangers.

As you gain experience taking pictures using your iOS mobile device, you'll begin to see things differently as you look at the viewfinder and plan your shots, and then frame or compose them before tapping the Shutter button to capture the image. How you see the world around you when looking at the viewfinder, and the creative decisions you make related to how to best capture your intended subject(s), is often referred to as using your "photographer's eye."

Instead of just pointing the camera lens at your intended subject, centering the subject in the frame, and then shooting from a head-on perspective, using your photographer's eye, you should be able to quickly come up with creative and artistic ways to take more visually interesting and imaginative photos. How to tap your creativity to achieve this objective is covered throughout this book.

It's important to understand that simply snapping a photo is only the first step before it's ready to be showcased or viewed by others. Using the photo editing and enhancement tools that are built in to many of the photography apps for the iPhone and iPad, in a few seconds, and with just a few taps on the screen, it's possible to quickly edit, enhance, crop, and work with your images, one at a time, to create true visual masterpieces.

> **TIP**   Even if you capture what looks like an ordinary, not-too-visually interesting photo, don't get discouraged right away. Try using the editing and enhancement tools available, as well as the image filters that are built in to many of the photography apps, and you'll often be pleasantly surprised at the quick image transformations that are possible.

Figure 1-9 is an image shot using the Camera app on an iPhone 5s. With no filter and without using HDR mode, the image looks pretty ordinary. However, using the tools offered in the Photos app, the image can quickly be enhanced, as you can see in Figure 1-10.

FIGURE 1-9

This photo was taken using an iPhone 5s but not yet enhanced or edited in any way.

FIGURE 1-10

In less than 10 seconds, the original image was edited and enhanced using the Instagram app to create a more visually compelling and professional-looking shot.

Not too shabby! However, using the more extensive and powerful image editing tools offered by a third-party photography app, like Mobli (see Figure 1-11) or Adobe's Photoshop Touch, even more incredible things can be done to enhance an image. Even if you are not at all technically savvy and don't consider yourself to be a creative individual, this kind of power is all within your reach.

FIGURE 1-11

Using the Mobli app, a photo can be transformed into black and white, with only a selected portion colorized.

START TAKING PICTURES USING THE CAMERA APP

Although many apps available from the App Store enable you to control the cameras that are built in to your iPhone or iPad, let's start by becoming acquainted with shooting photos using the Camera app already installed on your iOS mobile device.

Discovering how to use the various features and functions of the Camera app, in a wide range of shooting situations, is the primary focus of the next chapter. Start by learning the basic technical skill you'll need to take pictures, and then move on to developing your photographer's eye and focusing on the creative aspects of digital photography.

2

IN THIS CHAPTER

- Learn ways to activate the Camera app
- See an overview of the Camera app that comes preinstalled with iOS 7
- Use the Camera app's shooting modes
- Adjust the Camera app's settings

SNAP PHOTOS USING THE CAMERA APP

When it comes to taking pictures on your iPhone or iPad, the easiest thing to do is to launch the Camera app and start shooting. Using the Camera app, your smartphone or tablet literally transforms into a powerful and feature-packed point-and-shoot digital camera that's capable of shooting vibrant, colorful, highly detailed, and high-resolution images that immediately get saved on your iOS mobile device.

As you'll discover, the Camera app that comes preinstalled with iOS 7 is chock full of easy-to-access features, but not all of the app's features are available from all iOS mobile devices. In fact, if you want to see everything that the Camera app is capable of, you must use it with an iPhone 5s.

> **NOTE** The Camera app transforms your iPhone or iPad into a powerful point-and-shoot digital camera that can be used for snapping digital photos or shooting high-definition (HD) video. (If you're using an iPhone 5s, you can do both at the same time.) Because you probably carry your iPhone and/or iPad with you just about everywhere, you can now capture more moments in your life using the Camera app and preserve or share these memories with ease.

After you've taken some digital snapshots, it's possible to view, edit, enhance, print, or share them using the Photos app that also comes preinstalled with iOS 7. However, to gain access to additional photo editing tools and a greater selection of options for showcasing and sharing your images, consider using the optional iPhoto app or another optional third-party photography app that's available from the App Store.

> **NOTE** Although Camera and Photos are two separate apps, as you'll discover, they're nicely integrated with one another. You learn all about the Photos app in Chapter 6, "View, Organize, Edit, and Share Pictures Using the Photos App." Also developed by Apple is the optional iPhoto app, which is the focus of Chapter 7, "Expand Your Photo Editing Toolbox with iPhoto."

Getting back to the concept that digital photography is both a skill and an art form, this chapter focuses on the technical information you need in terms of how to use the Camera app. You learn the basic skills required to use this picture-taking app with your iPhone or iPad. Then, in Chapter 3, "Ten Strategies to Quickly Improve Your Picture-Taking Skills," and beyond, you'll discover digital photography techniques that enable you to use the Camera app with your own creativity to consistently capture visually interesting, artistic, and eye-capturing photos.

WAYS TO LAUNCH THE CAMERA APP

Sometimes you have very little advance notice when you're about to experience the perfect picture-taking opportunity. Knowing this, Apple has made it easy to launch the Camera app in a variety of different ways, regardless of what you're doing on your iOS mobile device. After you launch the Camera app, based on what and where you're shooting and the available light, for example, you might need to adjust various settings within the app before you begin snapping photos.

Regardless of what you're doing on your iPhone or iPad, use one of these methods to launch the Camera app to start taking pictures.

LAUNCH THE CAMERA APP FROM THE LOCK SCREEN

When you wake up your iOS mobile device from Sleep mode, the Lock screen always appears. Displayed in the bottom-right corner of the Lock screen (shown in Figure 2-1) is a Camera icon. To quickly launch the Camera app from the Lock screen (without first unlocking the device), place your finger on the Camera icon and swipe upward.

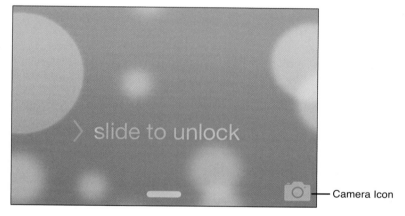

— Camera Icon

FIGURE 2-1
Launch the Camera app directly from the Lock screen.

> **NOTE** When you launch the Camera app from the Lock screen, you can snap photos but your access to your mobile device's other features and functions is limited. Exiting the Camera app returns you to the Lock screen, not the Home screen.

LAUNCH THE CAMERA APP FROM THE HOME SCREEN

App icons for all the apps you have installed on your iPhone or iPad are displayed on the Home screen. To launch the Camera app from the Home screen, tap the Camera app's icon (shown in Figure 2-2).

The Camera App icon

For faster access,
move the Camera icon
to the favorite apps area.

FIGURE 2-2

From the Home screen, tap on the Camera app's icon to launch the Camera app and begin taking pictures.

TIP   If you plan to use the Camera app often, consider moving it to one of the positions along the bottom row of app icons found on the Home screen. This makes it easier to access because the app icons on the bottom row appear regardless of which Home screen page you're viewing.

To save time when launching the Camera app from the Home screen, refrain from moving its app icon into a folder. If you do this, it requires additional screen taps (and valuable seconds) to ultimately find and launch the app.

LAUNCH THE CAMERA APP FROM THE CONTROL CENTER

Rather than go to the Home screen to launch the Camera app, you can save a few seconds by instead accessing the Control Center, and then launching the Camera app.

To launch the Control Center (which is a new feature in iOS 7), place your finger near the very bottom of the iPhone or iPad's screen, and swipe upward to open the Control Center.

On the iPhone, you find the Camera app icon at the bottom-right corner of the Control Center window (see Figure 2-3). Tap this icon to launch the Camera app. Whatever app you were previously using continues running in the background.

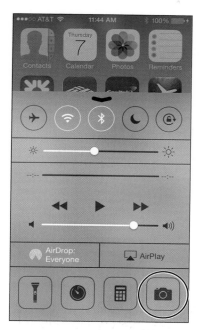

FIGURE 2-3

It's possible to launch the Camera app from the Control Center of your iPhone.

On the iPad, you can find the Camera app icon at the bottom-right side of the Control Center, just above the Screen Brightness slider (see Figure 2-4). Tap on this icon to launch the Camera app.

FIGURE 2-4

While using any app on an iPad, access the Control Center and then tap on the Camera icon to launch the Camera app.

LAUNCH THE CAMERA APP FROM MULTITASKING MODE

The iOS 7 operating system enables your iPhone or iPad to run many apps at the same time, although you use only one. To quickly switch between apps that are running, access Multitasking mode by pressing the Home button twice. Then, use your finger to swipe left or right and scroll through your device's currently running apps (see Figure 2-5). Tap on either the app's thumbnail screen or the app icon to relaunch and begin using a specific app.

FIGURE 2-5

Launch the Camera app while in Multitasking mode.

To shut down an app while in Multitasking mode (so it no longer runs in the background), swipe your finger in an upward direction over its thumbnail. Keep in mind that when you power down (turn off) your iPhone or iPad (as opposed to placing it in Sleep mode), this automatically shuts down all apps that were running in the background.

OVERVIEW OF THE CAMERA APP

After you've launched the Camera app and it's running on your iPhone or iPad, you can either adjust the app's settings or begin snapping photos. As you will see, the touch screen on your iOS mobile device transforms into your viewfinder. Anything you see in the viewfinder via the iPhone or iPad's camera lens is what will be captured when you snap a digital photo.

Based on whether you're using an iPhone or iPad, the appearance of the Camera app's viewfinder screen is slightly different. On the iPhone, shown in Figure 2-6, displayed along the top and bottom of the screen are a series of icons and options used to adjust the Camera app's settings and to snap photos.

HDR Mode Icon

Flash Icon

Camera Selection Icon

Viewfinder

Shooting Mode Menu

Image Preview Thumbnail

Filter Icon

Shutter Button

FIGURE 2-6

The main Camera app screen on the iPhone displays your viewfinder, along with a handful of command icons and options.

On the iPad, many of the same icons and options are available, but they're all displayed along the right margin of the Camera app's screen (see Figure 2-7). Compared with the iPhone, you'll notice the Camera app offers fewer options when it's used on an iPad.

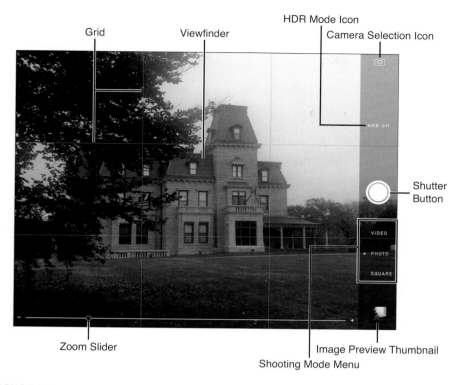

Grid   Viewfinder   HDR Mode Icon
                                   Camera Selection Icon

Shutter
Button

Zoom Slider   Image Preview Thumbnail
            Shooting Mode Menu

FIGURE 2-7

The main Camera app screen on the iPad displays all available command icons and options along the right margin.

NOTE   Depending on how you set up the Camera app (covered later in this chapter), you can opt to automatically display an onscreen grid. This grid can be used as a tool to help you frame your images, but the grid itself does not appear in your actual photos.

USING THE VIEWFINDER

Your iPhone or iPad has two built-in cameras. The front-facing camera is located on the front of the device, near the top center of the display. The rear-facing camera is located on the back of your device, near the top-left corner. What you see in your viewfinder when the Camera app is running depends on which camera you have selected.

When the Camera app is running, the main area of your iPhone or iPad's display becomes your viewfinder (refer to Figures 2-6 and 2-7). After you select your subject, position it within your viewfinder to frame your image, and then snap your picture by tapping on the Shutter button.

TIP When you're ready to snap a photo, you can either tap on the Shutter button that's displayed on the iPhone or iPad's screen, or press the Volume Up or Volume Down button that's located on the side of your device.

In the next chapter, you learn all about how to creatively frame your subjects within the viewfinder to capture professional looking, visually interesting, and/or creative photos using your iPhone or iPad.

Just like when using any point-and-shoot digital camera, as you're taking photos using the Camera app, you have a variety of tools at your disposal, such as the ability to zoom in on your subject.

TIP On the iPhone, while you're looking at your subject(s) in the viewfinder, you can activate the autoexposure/autofocus sensor (also referred to as the AE/AF sensor), switch shooting modes, activate and adjust the zoom, turn on or off the smartphone's built-in flash, add a filter, utilize the Camera app's HDR mode, or switch between the front- and rear-facing cameras—all of which you'll be learning more about shortly.

On the iPad, while you're looking at your subject(s) in the viewfinder, you have the option to activate the AE/AF sensor, turn on or off the HDR feature, switch shooting modes, activate the zoom, or switch between the front- or rear-facing cameras.

When all of the Camera app's features and functions are adjusted to your liking (which takes just a few seconds) and you've framed your image in the viewfinder, press the Shutter button to snap your photo. The digital image(s) you take are automatically stored in the Camera Roll folder, which is accessible from the Photos app, from the iPhoto app, from other apps that come preinstalled on your iOS mobile device, or from many third-party photography apps.

PREVIEW THE IMAGE YOU JUST SHOT

After shooting each image, a preview of the image you just shot appears as a tiny thumbnail at the bottom-left corner of the iPhone's screen or in the bottom-right corner on the iPad's screen. Tap this thumbnail to view a larger version of the image without having to open the Photos app.

Here you see a variety of icons and options, shown in Figure 2-8, including

- **Camera Roll**—Tap this option (displayed in the top-left corner of the preview screen) to view thumbnails of all images stored in the Camera Roll folder on your device. You learn more about using this option in Chapter 6.

FIGURE 2-8

Immediately after taking a photo, you can preview it on your iPhone or iPad's screen plus access a handful of tools from the Photos app by tapping on the Edit option.

- **Done**—Tap this option to immediately return to the Camera app so you can continue taking pictures. The Done option is displayed in the top-right corner of the image preview screen after edits to an image have been made.

- **Edit**—From within the Camera app, you can quickly use the photo editing and enhancement tools offered by the Photos app, including the Rotate, Enhance, Filters, Red-Eye, and Crop tools. After tapping on the Edit option, tap on an icon for the tool you want to use (see Figure 2-9). Upon using any of the edit or enhancement tools, additional onscreen options become available, including

- **Cancel**—Returns you to the previous image preview screen.
- **Undo**—Removes the last edit or enhancement you made to the image.
- **Revert to Original**—Returns the image you're editing/enhancing to its original form and removes all edits you've made.
- **Save**—Saves your newly edited or enhanced image in the Camera Roll folder. Doing this replaces the original image file.
- **Trash**—Deletes the image from your iPhone or iPad. Tap the Delete Photo option to confirm your decision.

Trash—To delete the image you just shot from your iPhoto or iPad, tap on the Trash icon. Tap the Delete Photo option to confirm your decision, or tap the Cancel option to keep the photo and return to the image preview screen.

Editing Tools

FIGURE 2-9

From the Camera app's Edit mode, you can rotate, enhance, or crop an image; add a filter; or fix red-eye.

> **TIP** While actually taking pictures with the iPhone, you have the option to tap on the Filters icon and incorporate a special effect filter to your image as you're shooting in real time. However, on the iPhone or iPad, if you snap a regular, filter-free image, you can always add one special effect filter after the fact, either when previewing an image in the Camera app or while using the Photos app to view and edit your images later. How to use filters is explained shortly.

SWITCH BETWEEN THE FRONT- AND REAR-FACING CAMERAS

Located on the front of the most recently released iPhone and iPad models is the built-in FaceTime HD Camera. This 1MP-resolution camera was designed for the FaceTime video calling application, but you can use it to take photos of yourself while you're using the iOS mobile device. It's important to understand, however, that the FaceTime HD Camera does not offer the high-quality resolution that the rear-facing camera offers.

Based on which model iPhone or iPad you're using, the rear-facing camera offers either 5MP or 8MP resolution. The resolution of the camera is then digitally enhanced thanks to other technology and hardware that's built in to the device.

> **NOTE** MP stands for megapixel, which is equivalent to one million pixels. Thus, when a 5MP camera takes a photo, that image is composed of five million colored pixels. An 8MP camera creates images composed of eight million colored pixels. The higher the resolution of a camera, the more detail and vibrancy you'll see within the images you shoot.

If you want to capture the highest-quality images currently possible using an iOS mobile device, you should use the rear-facing, 8MP camera that's built in to the iPhone 5s. Although the iPhone 5c and iPhone 4s, for example, also have 8MP cameras built in, the lens aperture, image sensor, and lens quality in these devices is inferior to the iPhone 5s.

The iPad Air, iPad mini, and iPad mini with Retina display all feature a 5MP rear-facing camera, while the iPad 2 offers a much-lower-resolution rear-facing camera that's capable of capturing images at just 960 by 720 pixel resolution (which is equivalent to less than 1MP resolution).

TIP   The Camera app works with both the front- and rear-facing cameras that are built in to your iPhone or iPad; however, the rear-facing camera on these devices is a much higher-resolution camera. Thus, you'll always be able to take better-quality pictures when you utilize the rear-facing camera.

In general, unless you want to hold your iPhone or iPad and simultaneously be in the photo (to take a selfie), you're always better off using the device's rear-facing camera. When the Camera app is running, to switch between the front- and rear-facing cameras, tap on the Camera Selection icon that's located in the top-right corner of the Camera app screen.

NOTE   A selfie is a digital photo taken on a smartphone or tablet that you take of yourself. It's captured either using the front-facing camera or by standing in front of a mirror and snapping a photo of yourself using the device's rear-facing camera. Publishing and sharing selfies with online friends is common on Facebook, Instagram, and other online social networking services.

SWITCH BETWEEN PORTRAIT AND LANDSCAPE MODES

You can hold the iPhone or iPad in either Portrait or Landscape mode when shooting pictures using the Camera app. Portrait mode, where you hold the iPhone or iPad vertically (see Figure 2-10), is ideal when the subject of your photo is intended to be the main focal point of the image and what's in the background is not as important. Choosing whether to use Portrait or Landscape mode when taking a picture is a matter of personal preference, based on what you're trying to accomplish.

FIGURE 2-10

To shoot in Portrait mode, hold your iPhone or iPad vertically, and frame your image so the subject is the main focal point.

When using Portrait mode, much less of what's in the background (behind your intended subject) is visible. So, as the name suggests, Portrait mode is ideal for taking portraits of people or pets or when taking close-up shots of your subject(s).

Landscape mode, which is activated by holding your iOS mobile device horizontally (see Figure 2-11), is better for taking pictures where the subject and the background are equally important, or when you want to showcase what's in the background as well. It's also useful for taking landscape shots, city skyline shots, group shots, or photos of large (wide) objects.

FIGURE 2-11

Simply rotate the iPhone or iPad horizontally to shoot an image in Landscape mode.

For example, if you're on vacation in Washington, D.C. and your kids are standing in front of the White House, use Landscape mode to showcase your kids as well as the White House in the background. On the other hand, if they're standing in front of the Washington Monument, you'll probably want the extra height that Portrait mode provides.

You'll notice that when you rotate the iPhone or iPad between Portrait and Landscape mode, the position of the onscreen icons and options rotates accordingly within the Camera app, and the field of view captured in the viewfinder widens dramatically.

> **TIP**   If you want to significantly increase your field of view and capture a panoramic shot from your iPhone, this is done by switching to the Pano shooting mode, which you'll learn about later in this chapter.

Keep in mind that digital photography is all about creativity. Instead of holding your iPhone or iPad in Portrait or Landscape mode, you always have the option of holding the device at another angle to create a more visually interesting shooting perspective. For example, you can literally hold your iPhone or iPad at a diagonal.

Chapter 3, "Ten Strategies to Quickly Improve Your Picture-Taking Skills," focuses more on the creative aspects of digital photography using your iPhone or iPad.

ACTIVATE THE AE/AF SENSOR AND SENSOR LOCK

Anytime you attempt to take a photo of a person using the Camera app, the camera's automatic Face Detection feature kicks in. This works for taking pictures featuring between 1 and 10 people. What you see in the viewfinder is an AE/AF sensor box superimposed over each subject's face. When one or more of these autofocus sensors kick in, this is what the Camera app focuses in on as an image is captured.

The Face Detection feature helps to ensure that the people in your photos are always in focus and properly exposed, while whatever other objects in that same image—located in front, to the sides, or behind your primary subject(s)—might not be in perfect focus.

If you're taking photos of objects or anything else besides people, the Camera app's AE/AF sensor might try to kick in, but the artificial intelligence built in to the app might not select the correct part of the image for your intended subject. Thus, you should manually activate the Camera app's AE/AF sensor. To do this, position your intended subject(s) within your viewfinder and frame your image accordingly. Then, using your finger, tap on the area where your main subject is located. The AE/AF sensor box appears superimposed over your intended subject in the viewfinder (see Figure 2-12). This square does not appear in your actual digital image.

The AE/AF Sensor Box

FIGURE 2-12

To manually set the Camera app's autofocus sensor, tap on the screen where your primary (intended) subject is positioned.

Whatever is displayed directly behind this AE/AF sensor box in the viewfinder is what will be in sharp focus when you press the Shutter button and capture the image.

CAUTION If there are several objects in your photo, and you fail to manually set the AE/AF sensor, the Camera app does this for you. The result could be that the Camera app winds up focusing on an object that isn't your intended subject.

For example, if the object on which it focuses is physically located in front of your intended subject, the depth of field in the image might make your intended subject appear blurry, while the object in front of it winds up in focus and crystal clear. Always make sure that the AE/AF sensor is positioned over your intended subject(s).

TIP If you plan to take multiple photos and want the AE/AF sensor to stay locked onto your intended subject, press and hold down your finger on the viewfinder, directly over your intended subject, until the AE/AF Lock banner appears on the screen and the sensor square pulses. You can then take multiple photos without having to reactivate the AE/AF sensor. To deactivate the AE/AF lock, simply tap anywhere on the viewfinder, or tap on a new intended subject.

ZOOM IN ON YOUR SUBJECT

The rear-facing camera that's built in to your iPhone or iPad has a digital zoom feature built in that's controlled from within the Camera app as you're taking pictures. When you're looking at the viewfinder, to zoom in on your intended subject(s), use your thumb and index finger to perform a pinch gesture on the touch screen. The Camera app's Zoom slider appears near the bottom center of the screen (see Figure 2-13).

Drag Dot to Adjust ——————   —— The Zoom Slider

FIGURE 2-13

Use a pinch finger gesture on the touch screen to make the Zoom slider appear when using the Camera app. Here, the Zoom slider is activated but positioned to the extreme left, so no digital zoom is actually being used.

Place one finger on the slider dot and drag it to the right to zoom in on your subject, or move the slider to the left to zoom out. With the iPhone physically kept at the same distance from the subject, Figure 2-13 shows the viewfinder with the Zoom slider slid to the extreme left (so no zoom was used). Figure 2-14 shows the zoom slider positioned near its halfway point, demonstrating a partial zoom, while Figure 2-15 shows the same subject with the zoom fully utilized.

FIGURE 2-14

In this image, the digital zoom is being used at half its possible intensity. The iPhone 5s was not physically moved from its original location.

FIGURE 2-15

In this image, the zoom is being fully utilized. The Zoom slider has been moved to the extreme right.

TIP Anytime you use the zoom or attempt to shoot in a low-light situation, it becomes more important to hold your iPhone or iPad extremely still when taking a photo. Not doing so may cause blur or an out-of-focus image.

To avoid unnecessary movement, as you're about to take a photo while holding your iOS mobile device in your hands, lock your elbows against your body and hold your breath for a second or two as you tap the Shutter button. Other options are to lean against a wall or post to help steady your entire body, stand the iPhone or iPad on a stable table or ledge, or use a tripod or mobile device stand.

ENHANCE IMAGES AS YOU SHOOT USING HDR MODE

HDR stands for High Dynamic Range. This is a shooting mode that's built in to the Camera app and that should be used when taking pictures in low-light situations or when the ambient lighting where you're taking photos isn't ideal.

NOTE HDR mode is used instead of the iPhone's flash to capture ambient (natural) light.

When HDR mode is turned on, every time you press the Shutter button to take a photo, your iPhone or iPad captures either three or four images simultaneously (depending on which model device you're using). Each image is taken at a slightly different exposure and captures the ambient light slightly differently. Then, within a fraction of a second, the three or four images are digitally combined into one image that offers better clarity and a truer representation of the natural colors and lighting.

To turn on HDR mode while you're shooting, tap the HDR On/Off option that's displayed on the viewfinder screen of the Camera app. On the iPhone, it's located near the top center of the screen. On the iPad, this option is located immediately above the Shutter button.

TIP Depending on how you set up this feature from within Settings, when HDR mode is turned on, your iPhone or iPad can either save just one image (captured with HDR mode turned on), or it can store two of the same images in the Camera Roll folder (one with and one without HDR mode turned on).

To adjust this setting, from the Home screen, launch Settings. Then, from the main Settings menu, tap on the Photos & Camera option. Scroll toward the bottom of the Photos & Camera submenu and turn on or off the virtual switch that's associated with Keep Normal Photo.

NOTE In some situations when you compare an image shot using HDR mode with a similar shot taken with HDR mode turned off, the differences between the images can be very subtle, and the "better" image will be a matter of personal preference. However, in certain circumstances, particularly in low-light situations, the image shot with HDR mode turned on offers more detail, better lighting, and improved contrast.

Thus, for more options and control over the appearance of your photos, it's better to turn on the Keep Normal Photo option from within Settings, manually compare the two saved images, and then choose the best one using the Photos app (or when you transfer the images to your computer or an online service).

HOW TO UTILIZE THE GRID FEATURE

Another feature you can turn on or off from within Settings is the Camera app's Grid feature. This feature simply superimposes a grid (which looks like a tic-tac-toe board) over your viewfinder as you're taking pictures. This grid is a useful tool when it comes to framing your images and incorporating a shooting technique called the "Rule of Thirds," which you'll learn about in the next chapter.

When turned on, the grid appears in your viewfinder but does not appear in your actual photos (see Figure 2-16). To turn on this feature, launch Settings. From the main Settings menu, tap the Photos & Camera option. Then, from the Photos & Camera submenu, turn on the virtual switch associated with the Grid option if you want the grid to appear in your viewfinder anytime you use the Camera app.

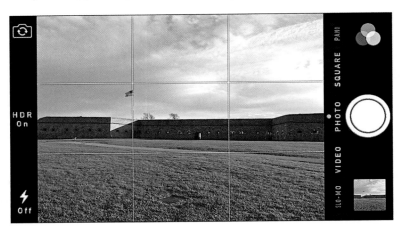

FIGURE 2-16

Shown here is the Camera app with the Grid feature turned on. This is a useful tool when utilizing the "Rule of Thirds" framing technique as you're taking pictures.

If you turn off the virtual switch associated with the Grid option, the grid does not display at all in the Camera app.

THE CAMERA APP'S SHOOTING MODES

Depending on which model of iPhone or iPad you're using, the Camera app offers several different shooting modes, each of which is used for a different purpose.

When using the Camera app on any model iPhone, the Shooting Mode menu is displayed directly above the Shutter button. Place your finger over this menu and swipe to the left or right to select the shooting mode you want to use. The mode that's displayed in yellow, directly over the Shutter button, is the one that's currently active.

On the iPad, the available shooting modes are all displayed simultaneously below the Shutter button, near the bottom-right corner of the screen. Tap on the mode you want to use. When selected, the active shooting mode is displayed in yellow.

The following sections offer a summary of the shooting modes built in to the Camera app. However, all of these shooting modes are available to you only when used with an iPhone 5s.

> **NOTE** When using the Camera app on an iPad, only the Video, Photo, and Square shooting modes are available. On the newer iPad models that run using Apple's A7 chip (including the iPad Air and iPad mini with Retina display), the Burst shooting mode is also available.

SLO-MO (iPHONE 5S ONLY)

This is a slow-motion shooting mode used when capturing HD video on your iPhone 5s. It's not used for taking still images.

VIDEO

When selected, the Video shooting mode allows an iPhone or iPad to shoot 1080p HD-quality video at up to 30 frames per second. You can then view, clip, and share video clips using the Photos app. You can also fully edit, view, and share them using the optional iMovie app.

> **TIP** If you're shooting video using the iPhone 5/5s/5c, it's possible to simultane-ously take digital photos using the rear-facing camera. To do this, tap the red button to begin shooting your video. The timer appears near the top center of the screen. Then, as you're filming video, tap the white circle (displayed to the left of the red circle icon) to snap individual photos, which are automatically saved in the Camera Roll folder. Tap the red circle icon again to stop filming the video.

PHOTO

Use the Photo shooting mode to capture regular (rectangular-shaped) digital images using the Camera app. This is the shooting mode smartphone or tablet digital photographers use most often.

SQUARE

The Square shooting mode works just like the Photo shooting mode; however, the viewfinder displays a smaller, square-shaped image (see Figure 2-17). What you wind up capturing with this mode are digital photos that are automatically cropped into a square shape. This is ideal if you plan to upload your images to an online photo sharing service, like Instagram, that utilizes only square-shaped images.

FIGURE 2-17

Images are auto-cropped into a square shape when Square mode is selected.

TIP   You can always shoot a regular-shaped image using the Photo mode and then manually use the Crop tool to transform the image into a square shape after it's been taken. This can be done when previewing an image with the Camera app, while using the Photos app, or with another photo editing app. The official Instagram app also offers a cropping and repositioning/resizing tool for transforming regular images into square-shaped ones.

PANO (iPHONE ONLY)

Using the rear-facing camera of the iPhone 4/4s/5/5c/5s, it's possible to shoot panoramic images. These are extremely wide-angle shots that enable you to capture a vast landscape, a city skyline, or a large group of people, for example. See "Taking Panoramic Photos from Your iPhone," later in this chapter, to learn how to use this Camera app feature.

> **TIP** Instead of taking panoramic shots from your iPhone, the optional Cycloramic app (available for free from the App Store) enables you to easily capture 360-degree panoramic shots from any iPhone or iPad's rear-facing camera. Thus, you can take panoramic shots from an iPad and more visually impressive 360-degree panoramic shots from an iPhone. You can view these images using this app, or convert them into short movie clips and then share them with others via email or any online social networking or photo sharing service. You can also embed the 360-degree panoramic movie clips into web pages or blogs, for example.
>
> The Cycloramic app also offers enhancements specifically for use with the iPhone 5s. You'll learn more about the Cycloramic app in Chapter 9, "Photography Apps That Expand Your Photo Editing and Enhancement Capabilities."

BURST (iPHONE 5S, iPAD AIR, AND iPAD MINI WITH RETINA DISPLAY ONLY)

Typically, when you press the Shutter button in the Camera app once (or press the Volume Up or Volume Down button), one image is captured and saved. However, if you're photographing a fast-moving subject and you want to shoot a specific movement or instant that can't easily be replicated, or that would otherwise require extremely precise timing to capture, consider using the Burst shooting mode.

To activate this shooting mode on any iOS mobile device that utilizes an Apple A7 processor chip, including the iPhone 5s, iPad Air, or iPad mini with Retina display, instead of tapping the Shutter button, press and hold your finger down on it. This enables you to shoot up to 10 frames (pictures) per second.

The Camera app automatically groups together and stores these images in the Camera Roll folder. You can then review the collection of photos and pick and choose your favorites, and at the same time, quickly delete the unwanted images. You'll learn how to do this in Chapter 6.

TIP   If you're taking pictures at a sporting event, for example, and a player is about to make a basket, score a touchdown, or shoot a goal, the Burst shooting mode enables you to capture images leading up to, during, and after that split-second event, ensuring you ultimately capture the perfect shot you're looking for. Keep in mind that, when shooting sports, sometimes the athlete's facial expression immediately after scoring, for example, makes for a more impactful image than a shot of the scoring action itself. The Burst shooting mode enables you to capture it all, without having to worry about achieving perfect timing when pressing the Shutter button.

WORK WITH FILTERS

When using the Camera app with any iPhone model, it's possible to activate and incorporate one of eight special effect filters in real time as you're actually taking pictures. To do this, as you're looking through the viewfinder, tap on the Filters icon that's displayed near the bottom-right corner of the Camera app's display. When you do this, the main viewfinder screen is replaced by a nine-box grid (see Figure 2-18). Each box displays a different special effect filter. To select one of the filters, tap it. The original viewfinder screen reappears, but the filter you selected is displayed and automatically incorporated into your image(s) as you're shooting.

Available filters include Mono, Tonal, Noir, Fade, Chrome, Process, Transfer, and Instant. When you select a filter, to deactivate it, press the Filters icon again. When the filter screen appears, tap the None box (displayed in the center of the screen).

Instead of selecting and utilizing a filter when shooting in real time, on either the iPhone or iPad, it's possible to add a filter after the fact, either when using the Image Preview option that's built in to the Camera app or when editing images later using the Photos app. To do this, after snapping a normal image using the Camera app (on an iPhone or iPad), tap the Image Preview thumbnail. When the image you just shot appears, tap the Edit option. Then, tap on the Filters icon and select which filter you want to apply to the image you're previewing. Tap on the Apply option to save your changes and store the "edited" image in the Camera Roll folder.

FIGURE 2-18

The Camera app, when used on an iPhone, includes eight special effect filters that can be added in real time when taking pictures.

NOTE You'll find more information about adding filters when editing and enhancing photos after they're shot using the Photos app in Chapter 6.

TIP In addition to the special effect filters available to you in the Camera app (iPhone) and the Photos app (iPhone or iPad), a variety of different special effect filters are available from third-party apps that you can add before sharing your photos online. For example, both the official Facebook and Instagram apps (which you'll learn more about in Chapter 12, "Share Your Digital Photos Online") have their own image filter options.

USE THE iPHONE'S FLASH

All of the more recent iPhone models, including the iPhone 4s/5/5c/5s, have a built-in, rear-facing camera flash. However, instead of just a bright white, single-color LED flash, the iPhone 5s offers what Apple calls a True Tone flash, which works much better. None of the iPad models currently have a flash built in.

As you're using the Camera app on the iPhone, you have the option to have the iPhone automatically turn on or off the flash as needed (based on the available light where you're taking pictures), or you can manually turn on or off the flash. To adjust the flash settings, tap on the Flash icon that's displayed in the top-left corner of the Camera app's screen. There are three options: Auto, On, or Off.

The Auto mode tells the Camera app to automatically decide when and whether the flash is needed and then activate it accordingly as you're taking pictures. However, if you select the On option, every time you snap a photo, the flash is automatically used (regardless of the ambient lighting conditions). Likewise, if you select the Off option, the flash never activates as you're taking photos.

Each of these flash modes has pros and cons. For example, the Auto mode kicks in and emits a bright burst of light, aimed directly at your subject, if the iPhone determines you're taking pictures in a low-light situation. However, if your subject is too close to you (the photographer), this could result in an overexposed, washed-out image, or your human subject could display red-eye in the photo. Or if your subject is standing in front of a window or a reflective surface, you might discover unwanted glares within your images caused by the flash.

Deciding whether to utilize a flash when taking pictures is both a creative and technical decision, based on what you're trying to accomplish. The entire focus of Chapter 4, "Taking Awesome Pictures in Low Light," deals specifically with how and when to use the iPhone's built-in flash to consistently capture the best images possible, without capturing unwanted glares, shadows, or red-eye or winding up with overexposed or underexposed images.

NOTE   The True Tone flash that's built in to the iPhone 5s is really composed of two different-colored LED flashes that work simultaneously to more accurately match the color of the ambient light while brightening up the area where you're taking pictures. By automatically adjusting the color and intensity of the light emitted by the True Tone flash, many of the common problems that occur when using a bright white flash are reduced or eliminated altogether.

TIP To avoid overexposed images or red-eye when standing close to your subject and using the iPhone's built-in flash, try taking several steps away from your subject and then compensating for the distance using the zoom. Also, make sure your subject is not standing in front of a window, mirror, or another reflective surface that the light emitted from the flash will bounce off of.

TAKE PANORAMIC PHOTOS FROM YOUR iPHONE

The Camera app when used with the iPhone features the Pano shooting mode for taking visually impressive panoramic shots. To utilize this shooting mode, select it from the Shooting Mode menu. The look of the viewfinder will change slightly (see Figure 2-19).

FIGURE 2-19

The Pano shooting mode built in to the Camera app (when used with an iPhone) enables you to capture visually stunning panoramic images.

Displayed near the center of the viewfinder screen you'll see a yellow line upon which is a large, white, right-pointing arrow. Position your iPhone to the extreme left of your subject, and then tap the Shutter button. Upon doing this, slowly move the iPhone from left to right, in a steady horizontal motion. Make sure you keep the iPhone level.

As you're doing this, pan across the landscape, city skyline, or group of people you want to capture in the panoramic shot. Keep this steady panning motion going until the white arrow reaches the right side of the screen or you've captured your entire subject matter. If you want to stop capturing the panoramic image before the arrow reaches the right side of the screen, tap on the Shutter button again to save your image.

Once a panoramic image is taken (see Figure 2-20), you can edit, enhance, view, print, or share it just like any other digital photo taken on the iPhone.

FIGURE 2-20

A panoramic shot enables you to capture a vast landscape, a city skyline, or a large group of people within a single shot.

A tripod that enables you to rotate the iPhone while holding it steady and level can be a useful tool when shooting panoramic images. However, thanks to the artificial intelligence built in to the Camera app, a tripod is not necessary as long as you pay attention to the warning messages that appear on the screen if you begin panning too fast or don't hold the iPhone steady as you're panning.

> **TIP** Be sure to hold your iPhone in Portrait mode (vertically) when shooting in Pano mode.

> **TIP** If, for whatever reason, you want or need to shoot a panoramic shot by panning the camera from right to left (instead of from left to right), before pressing the Shutter button in Pano shooting mode, tap on the white arrow icon once. Its starting position changes to the opposite side of the screen.

CUSTOMIZE THE CAMERA APP FROM WITHIN SETTINGS

In addition to being able to turn on or off various Camera app-related features and functions from within the app itself, you can adjust several additional app-specific functions in Settings that relate to the Grid and Keep Normal Photo options already discussed.

Every time you snap a photo, the Camera app also records metadata related to that image, and then stores that metadata as part of the image file. This automatically includes the exact date and time each photo was taken.

Based on how you set up the Location Services feature in your iPhone or iPad, the metadata information captured with each image can also include the exact location where it was shot. When you include geotagging information with your photos, and then use the Photos or iPhoto app on your iOS mobile device or the iPhoto app on your Mac, you can automatically display a detailed map that shows exactly where you took the photos. You can also automatically sort and group images by location.

The potential downside to geotagging is that if you publish your photos online and opt to display this information, the exact location where your photos were taken is displayed with the photos themselves. If you're publishing photos online for the public to see, you might not want strangers seeing your photos to know exactly where they were taken or where you are.

> CAUTION When publishing photos on Facebook, Instagram, or Twitter, for example, use common sense before opting to display geotagging details about the photos you publish online.

TURN ON/OFF PHOTO GEOTAGGING

From within Settings, you have the option to turn on or off the Camera app's Geotagging feature. To adjust this setting, launch Settings and tap on the Privacy option. From the Privacy submenu, tap the Location Services option. Then, from the Location Services submenu, you can leave the main Location Services feature turned on but turn on or off the Camera app's capability to determine your location and store it with your digital photos. To do this, scroll down and turn on or off the virtual switch associated with the Camera option (see Figure 2-21).

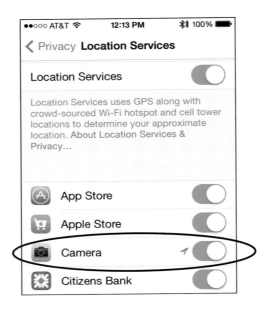

FIGURE 2-21

Turn off the virtual switch associated with the Camera option to prevent the Camera app from determining your location and saving this information with each image you take.

THE 10-STEP CAMERA APP RECAP

Much of what you just learned about using the Camera app to take photos can be summed up if you follow these 10 steps each time you want to snap a photo using the app:

1. Launch the Camera app.
2. Choose a shooting mode.
3. Select either the front- or rear-facing camera.
4. Turn on or off the flash (iPhone) and/or HDR mode.
5. Turn on or off the Grid feature.
6. Add an optional filter as you're shooting in real time (iPhone only).
7. Zoom in or out as needed.
8. Focus on your subject(s) and activate the AE/AF sensor by tapping on the screen where your subject is positioned in the viewfinder.
9. Hold the iPhone/iPad very still.
10. Tap the Shutter button (or the Volume Up or Volume Down button) to snap the photo and have it saved in the Camera Roll folder.

TIP After taking a photo, you can then tap on the Preview icon to view that image, and/or choose to edit or enhance it using the tools offered by the Photos app (while still working within the Camera app).

As you're viewing an image in Preview mode, it's possible to zoom in using a reverse-pinch finger gesture or by double-tapping on the screen in the area where you want to zoom. To zoom back out, double-tap again or use a pinch finger gesture.

NOTE In addition to following these steps when using the Camera app, you should use some of the picture-taking strategies outlined in the next chapter to adopt a more creative or artistic approach to your picture taking. Doing this results in your photos being more visually interesting and professional looking.

YOU NOW HAVE THE SKILL; LET'S GET CREATIVE

Knowing how to use the Camera app and adjust its settings based on your shooting conditions and available light plays a huge role in your ability to take professional-quality photos using your iPhone or iPad. Now that you've acquired the core knowledge needed to properly use the Camera app and its many features and functions, let's focus on developing your creative skills.

Starting in the next chapter, you learn how to use the Camera app, with your own creativity, as you develop your photographer's eye, to consistently capture visually interesting, artistic, in-focus, and meaningful images. Don't worry: It's not at all difficult, and it can actually be rather fun as you challenge yourself to look at everyday things from a new perspective as you're seeing them through the Camera app's viewfinder.

As you're about to discover, how you compose and frame your shots, utilize light, adjust your shooting angle, and showcase your subject(s) within each photo will help you capture more professional looking pictures, regardless of what or where you're shooting.

IN THIS CHAPTER

- Discover ways to enhance your photographer's eye to take better pictures
- Learn to use the "Rule of Thirds" when framing shots
- Make the best use of available light
- Choose the best shooting angle and perspective

3

TEN STRATEGIES TO QUICKLY IMPROVE YOUR PICTURE-TAKING SKILLS

Back in Chapter 1, "Prepare Your iPhone or iPad to Take Awesome Photos," you read that becoming a good digital photographer is both a skill and an art form. Then, in Chapter 2, "Snap Photos Using the Camera App," you started to develop the skill and knowledge needed to best use the Camera app to take pictures using your iPhone or iPad. Now, let's focus on some of the artistic and creative aspects of picture taking.

One core concept you should understand is that when it comes to using creativity in photography, there are very few rules. Instead, there is plenty of opportunity to make your own creative or artistic decisions. In fact, every time you take a picture, you can adopt a slightly different strategy to wind up with an ever-growing personal photo library that contains images you'll enjoy looking at again and again, and that you'll be proud to share with others.

Whether you're using an iOS mobile device to take pictures or you've invested thousands of dollars in a cutting-edge digital SLR camera, the concepts and strategies you'll want to incorporate as you take photos are virtually the same. In fact, what you're about to discover are core picture-taking strategies that professional photographers use every day in a wide range of shooting situations.

By implementing some or all of the strategies you're about to discover, whenever you take digital photos using your iPhone or iPad, you'll quickly notice a dramatic improvement in the quality and professionalism of your shots. Now, let's take a look at 10, easy-to-implement photography strategies that will quickly enable you to improve your picture-taking abilities.

> **NOTE** Throughout the book, numerous references to the *focal point* of particular images are made. This refers to the area or subject of the photo that the photographer intended for the photo's viewer(s) to focus in on first and pay the most attention to. It's the part of the image that captures the attention of its viewers. Thus, it's the focal point within your images that should always be in focus, even if what's in the foreground or background, for example, is slightly blurred.

LET YOUR PHOTOS TELL A STORY

One goal you should have as a digital photographer is that each of your photos should tell its own story to the people looking at it. A photo should not require a long explanation or wordy caption to communicate a message or emotion.

Likewise, if you're putting together a photo album, photo book, scrapbook, online gallery collage, or animated slideshow to showcase your images, those images together should tell a story with a beginning, middle, and end—whether it's a wedding album, a recap of your vacation, your child's soccer game, or photos from the day you spent at the zoo.

As you're taking pictures, each photo, or your collection of images that will be shown together, should speak for itself and answer questions like who?, what?, where?, when?, why?, and how?.

There are many ways to communicate this; for example, through the expressions on your subjects' faces, what you showcase in the backgrounds in your photos, the actions of your subjects, the interactions between your subjects, the props your subjects are holding, the poses of your subjects, and your use of light and shadows.

In some cases, your photos might take on a purely artistic approach and not neces-sarily have an obvious message. They might simply be beautiful to look at or evoke some emotion or thought in the viewer's mind. It all comes down to what your goals are as the photographer and how you want to use each of your photos to communicate with the people who will ultimately view them.

> **TIP** Don't forget, once you take photos and they're stored in your iPhone or iPad, you have a wide range of options when it comes to editing and enhanc-ing those images. Often, with a few taps on the smartphone or tablet's screen when using a photo editing or enhancing app, it's possible to dramatically alter or improve the look and quality of an image.
>
> Before sharing your photos, it's also possible to transfer them to your Mac or PC and then use full-featured photo editing software, such as iPhoto, Aperture, Photoshop Elements, Windows Photo Gallery, Google's Picasa, or the software that makes up Adobe's Creative Cloud suite, to edit and/or enhance your images.

TEN STRATEGIES USED BY PROFESSIONAL PHOTOGRAPHERS THAT YOU CAN QUICKLY LEARN

Simply by implementing some or all of the strategies you're about to discover, whenever you take digital photos using your iPhone or iPad, you'll quickly notice a dramatic improvement in the quality and professionalism of your shots. Now, let's take a look at 10 easy-to-implement photography strategies that will quickly enable you to improve your picture-taking abilities.

> **NOTE** Some of the sample photos featured in this chapter were shot using a digital SLR camera and then transferred to an iPhone 5s to be edited and shared using the Photos app.

#1—AVOID THE MOST COMMON MISTAKE MADE BY AMATEUR PHOTOGRAPHERS

Most amateur photographers pick up their digital camera—in this case, their iPhone or iPad—and continuously adopt the same shooting strategy to each and every one of the photos they take. This strategy includes standing directly in front of the intended subject, centering the subject in the viewfinder, and taking a photo of that subject from a head-on perspective. Does this sound familiar?

Later, when that same photographer goes back to look at his or her images, the images might, in fact, all be in focus, but they also all look exactly the same, even though the subject(s) might be different. As a result, the photos are extremely boring to look at, especially if they're presented in a photo album, online gallery, digital slideshow, or photo book, where dozens of images are shown together.

Step one to becoming a more skilled digital photographer is to break this habit! There are many ways to do this. For example, you can change your shooting angle as the photographer; utilize the Rule of Thirds; frame your subject using objects in the foreground, background, and/or to the sides; utilize your camera's zoom; and make full use of the available light.

Regardless of which strategies you ultimately adopt, the one thing you definitely want to do, in the majority of the photos you take from this point forward, is to avoid always centering your subject in the viewfinder and shooting that subject from a head-on perspective (although once in a while, this is perfectly okay).

> **TIP**   When holding your iPhone or iPad and preparing to snap a photo, make sure your fingers are not accidentally covering the camera lens (and on the iPhone, the flash). This might seem obvious, but it's also one of the most common mistakes photographers make when using a smartphone or tablet. Practice holding your iPhone or iPad in a way that's comfortable and that allows you to keep the device very steady, without obstructing the lens or flash.

#2—USE THE RULE OF THIRDS WHEN FRAMING YOUR SHOTS

One quick and easy way to get out of the habit of centering your subject(s) in the dead center of the viewfinder and then snapping photos from a head-on perspective is to utilize the Rule of Thirds. The goal behind this photography strategy is simply to force you, the photographer, to frame your shots so that your subject does not wind up in the dead center of the frame.

To best utilize the Rule of Thirds, turn on the Camera app's Grid feature so that the tic-tac-toe board grid is superimposed on the viewfinder. How to do this when using the Camera app was covered in the previous chapter. However, if you're using another app to take photos, you might need to imagine the grid displayed in your viewfinder, if this feature isn't built in to the app you're using to take or edit your photos.

Now, as you look at the grid displayed in the viewfinder, it's easy to see that the center box is the dead center of the frame (see Figure 3-1).

FIGURE 3-1

Utilizing the Rule of Thirds when taking pictures is easier when the Grid feature of the Camera app is turned on.

The grid is composed of two horizontal lines and two vertical lines, each of which is off-center. Within this grid, the lines intersect at four distinct points, each of which is also off-center.

Each time you frame your image (after choosing your subject and positioning yourself as the photographer to be able to capture your shot from the best possible shooting angle and perspective), position your subject along one of the horizontal or vertical lines, or make the intended focal point of your image one of the grid's intersection points, and position your subject within the frame (viewfinder) accordingly. Keep in mind that this involves moving or repositioning the camera (your iPhone/iPad) just slightly. Your intended subject does not have to move. By placing your intended subject off-center, your images almost always immediately become more interesting.

Now, get into the habit of figuring out the best way to frame your images using the Rule of Thirds, while constantly choosing what will be the image's best main focal point as you're shooting. This might be aligning your subject(s) along one of the horizontal or vertical lines of the grid, or positioning the subject(s) at one of the grid lines' intersection points.

The Rule of Thirds can and should be used when taking pictures of anything—people, places, or things (or any combination thereof). You'll also definitely want to combine this shooting strategy with the others that are described in this chapter.

Let's take a look at a few examples of how the Rule of Thirds can be put into practice.

In Figure 3-2, the main subject in the photo is the Atlantis Resort, located in the Bahamas. As you can see, the building itself is positioned along the rightmost vertical line of the grid, whereas the rest of the image helps set the scene and shows that this resort is located along a tropical beach.

> **TIP**   Using the Crop tool that's built in to the Editing mode of the Camera app, as well as in to the Photos app, you can sometimes reframe an image after it's been shot so that you can better utilize the Rule of Thirds. To demonstrate this, have a look at Figure 3-2, Figure 3-3, Figure 3-4, Figure 3-5, and Figure 3-6, which all have the Crop tool turned on in the Photos app.
>
> As you'll see, when you activate the Crop tool, a movable grid is automatically superimposed over your image. Chapter 6, "View, Organize, Edit, and Share Pictures Using the Photos App," explains how to properly use this tool.

In Figure 3-3, the giraffe is also positioned off-center within the frame. This image shows how the subject is facing into the frame, not out of it, which is another useful photography strategy to utilize.

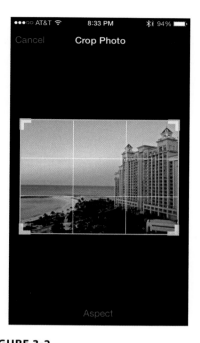

FIGURE 3-2

The Atlantis Resort is positioned along the rightmost vertical line of the grid.

FIGURE 3-3

Here, the giraffe is also positioned along the rightmost vertical line of the grid.

> **TIP** Whenever possible, you want to position your primary subject in the frame so if any motion is involved, the subject is looking or moving into the frame, toward the person viewing the image. The subject should not be moving or facing out of the frame.

If you look at Figure 3-4, the child is positioned within the bottom-right corner of the image, near one of the grid's intersection points.

The dog in Figure 3-5 might look centered (which is a no-no), but when you take a closer look, his eyes, which are the focal point of the image, are positioned along the topmost horizontal line of the grid.

FIGURE 3-4

The child in this photo is positioned near the bottom-right corner of the image.

FIGURE 3-5

The dog's eyes are the focal point of this image. Here, they're positioned along the topmost horizontal line of the grid.

Figure 3-6 also shows how to use an animal's eyes as the focal point of your image. Here, the koala bear's eyes are lined up with the top horizontal line on the grid, plus the majority of the subject is lined up along the rightmost vertical grid line.

> **TIP** Anytime you're taking photos of an animal, whether it's a pet, a wild animal, or a creature from the zoo, always try to focus in on its eyes, as opposed to its face. Unlike people who showcase facial expressions, animals convey emotion through their eyes. Thus, when it comes to shooting animals so they are looking directly into the camera, timing and patience are essential.

Taken at Waikiki Beach in Honolulu, Hawaii, the photo in Figure 3-7 uses the lifeguard station (which is positioned off-center, along the leftmost vertical line of the grid) to add a sense of depth to the beach image. The palm trees in the foreground are also used to frame the image.

FIGURE 3-6

As you can see here, the koala bear's eyes are lined up with the top horizontal line on the grid, plus the majority of the subject is lined up along the rightmost vertical grid line.

FIGURE 3-7

This image showcases the lifeguard station offset to the left, along the leftmost vertical line of the grid. Combined with the palm trees, the lifeguard station also adds a sense of depth to the image.

TIP Using your subject's surroundings to frame the image can help add a sense of depth to a photo.

#3—PAY ATTENTION TO YOUR PRIMARY LIGHT SOURCE AND USE IT TO YOUR ADVANTAGE

Whether you're taking photos outside in the sun or indoors, there's always a primary light source. As the photographer, it's your responsibility to pinpoint the primary light source and use it to your advantage, while at the same time, not allowing unwanted light to ruin an otherwise great photo.

As a general rule, your primary light source, whether it's the sun outside, overhead indoor lighting, a lamp, or even a candle, should be positioned in front of your primary (intended) subject (and potentially behind you, the photographer), so that the light is shining evenly over your subject with little or no annoying shadows being cast.

> TIP   Sometimes, it's possible to trick the Camera app's AE/AF sensor to make better use of lighting situations that are less than optimal if you lock in the AE/AF sensor on your intended subject, but then tap randomly on the screen, and then tap again near (not directly on) your intended subject. This causes the AE/AF sensor to refocus, often with slightly different results.
>
> Remember, you can also enhance the lighting and contrast within images as you're shooting by turning on the HDR mode of the Camera app.

If the primary light source winds up being positioned in front of the camera, it's likely that too much light will be captured in your photo. This can easily cause an overexposed and washed-out image, or it can cause unwanted and annoying glares (as shown in Figure 3-8).

Based on the position of the primary light source, it can also cause unwanted shadows over your subject or around your subject, which detracts from the professional quality of the image and ultimately is annoying to look at for people viewing your photos. As you're framing your shots, pay attention to the location of your primary light source, and position yourself and your subjects accordingly to capture the best possible shot in the best available light.

> TIP   In situations where you can't control the position of the primary light source, you can often reduce the amount of light being captured by the camera's lens by placing your hand or an object over the iPhone/iPad to deflect some of the light.

FIGURE 3-8

When the sun, for example, is positioned in front of you (the photographer), you'll often wind up with distracting glares in your shots. These glares could easily wash out or overexpose your image altogether.

Watch out for glares, but at times, you can use them to your advantage, for artistic purposes. As you can see in Figure 3-9 of the Golden Gate Bridge in San Francisco, the glare from the sun works well in this photo, although too much glare can easily become a distraction. How much is too much glare is a matter of your own personal taste as the photographer.

FIGURE 3-9

In this image, the glare from the sun was used for artistic purposes.

There are two situations when you want to break the rule of having your primary light source behind you. First, when you want to capture a sunrise or sunset, you want to position yourself so your camera lens is pointed directly at the primary light source—the rising or setting sun. Second, when you want to incorporate silhouettes into your photo for artistic reasons, you want the primary light source to be behind your subject and in front of you, the photographer.

As you can see in Figure 3-10, the primary light source is the setting sun; the couple on the beach and the photographer are in front of the sun, which results in the silhouette effect.

FIGURE 3-10

Sometimes, utilizing a silhouette effect can be used for creative and artistic purposes to your advantage as the photographer. Here, both the subjects and the photographer were in front of the primary light source.

> **TIP** While a silhouette can be used for artistic purposes, if you take a picture of someone standing in front of a window (during daylight hours), for example, this often causes the person you're photographing to appear as a silhouette because the primary light source is behind them. Be mindful of what causes this silhouette effect and use it when you want to, but know how to prevent it when it's unwanted in your photos.

CONSIDER USING A POLARIZING LENS OR FILTER WHEN SHOOTING OUTSIDE

When shooting outside, one way to rid yourself of unwanted glares caused by the sun, and at the same time enhance the vibrancy of the natural colors in your photos, is to utilize an optional polarizing filter or lens.

Several companies, including OlloClip (www.olloclip.com), offer optional polarizing lens accessories for the various iPhone models. One of OlloClip's offerings is the OlloClip Telephoto + Circular Polarizing Lens ($99.99), for example. You'll learn more about this useful accessory in Chapter 10, "Use Optional Accessories to Improve Your Pictures."

Some photo-editing and enhancement apps also include a digital polarizing filter, which can be added after the fact to digital images shot with an iPhone or iPad. Whether you use an actual polarizing lens or add a digital filter that offers a polarizing effect to your images, the end result is crisper and more colorful outdoor images, with less sun-induced glare and reflection.

> **NOTE** The camera built in to your iPhone or iPad is designed to detect and capture whatever light is in the area when you're taking pictures. Thus, it's your job to identify the light sources and use them to your advantage, eliminate unwanted light as needed, or reposition yourself to capture your subjects in the best possible light.

#4—CHANGE YOUR SHOOTING ANGLE AND/OR PERSPECTIVE

Using the Rule of Thirds is one way you can get out of the habit of centering your subjects(s) in the viewfinder and shooting them from a head-on perspective in all of your photos. However, in addition to utilizing the Rule of Thirds, you also have the option to alter your shooting angle and perspective.

In other words, instead of standing directly in front of your subjects when snapping photos, you can shoot them from an angle. For example, as the photographer, you can crouch down and shoot in a slightly upward direction. You can climb up on something so that you're higher than your subject and then shoot in a downward direction, or you can take one or two steps to the side and take photos from a slight angle.

Of course, it's also possible to mix and match shooting perspectives and angles, along with using the Rule of Thirds, to take visually more interesting photos. As you do this, pay attention to what's surrounding your subject(s), as well as the position of the primary light source.

In Figure 3-11, this area of Faneuil Hall in Boston was too large to capture simply by standing in front of the building and taking a photo in Portrait mode with the iPhone. However, by standing at a diagonal to the building and then crouching down and shooting in an upward direction (see Figure 3-12), not only is it possible to capture more of this historic landmark within a photo, it also makes for a more interesting photo to look at.

FIGURE 3-11

This image was shot using an iPhone 5s while standing directly in front of Faneuil Hall and taking a picture of this historic landmark from a head-on perspective.

FIGURE 3-12

By standing at a diagonal to the building and then crouching down and shooting in a slightly upward direction, a more visually interesting photo is easily taken.

> **TIP** The strategy of adjusting your shooting angle or perspective also works with people, and just about anything else you might want to photograph. Be creative as you take more visually interesting pictures by shooting your subject(s) from either a slight angle, or by purposely shooting from a sharp angle to create a more dramatic visual.

#5—TAKE ADVANTAGE OF WHAT'S IN THE FOREGROUND, THE BACKGROUND, AND TO THE SIDES OF YOUR INTENDED SUBJECT

Sometimes, the visual impact of a photo that would otherwise just feature your intended subject in the frame can be dramatically enhanced by taking advantage of what's in the foreground, the background, and to the sides of your intended subject and somehow framing your subject using those surroundings.

In some cases, purposely adding objects into the foreground or background of an image, for example, can also add a sense of depth to a photo. Once again, these are situations when your creativity comes into play, in terms of how you utilize what surrounds your subject(s) in your photos. Keep in mind that your subject doesn't necessarily need to interact with his or her surroundings to add this sense of depth or to make the image more visually interesting. This strategy can be used when taking photos involving people or when taking pictures of objects or landscapes, for example.

Refer to Figure 3-7, and notice how the palm trees in the photo help to naturally frame the lifeguard station and the Hawaiian beach.

You can see an additional example of how you can and should utilize what's in the foreground, the background, and/or to the sides of your intended subject in Figure 3-13.

FIGURE 3-13

The coin-operated binoculars add a sense of depth to this image of the Newport, Rhode Island, coastline.

#6—TIMING IS CRITICAL: BE AT THE RIGHT PLACE, AT THE RIGHT TIME, AND BE READY TO TAKE PICTURES

When it comes to taking pictures of people, if you want to capture their natural emotion or spontaneous reaction to something, you need to take a candid picture. This means that, as the photographer, you wait for something photoworthy to happen and you position yourself at the right place, at the right time, to catch the perfect shot. Timing is essential!

Candid photos are great because they're able to showcase natural and true emotions or responses, whereas posed pictures typically feature one or more people with a fake smile, in an uncomfortable or unnatural-looking pose. Most people become extremely self conscious when you put a camera in front of them with the intention of taking photos.

As a photographer, being able to take candid photos in a wide range of situations, and then mix and match those images with posed photos, makes for a much more compelling photo album, digital slideshow, photo book, or scrapbook, for example.

Being able to take really good candid photos requires planning and good timing. As the photographer, you must be extremely observant and anticipate when something that's photoworthy is about to happen. You also need to position yourself in the right place, at the right time, without being intrusive, to capture a truly candid image.

TIP One trick to capturing great candid photos is to stay at a distance from your intended subject and utilize the zoom that's built in to the Camera app (or whichever app you're using to take pictures). If you're not close to your intended subject, he or she is less apt to be aware of your presence and will continue acting naturally. This allows you, the photographer, to be less intrusive.

Candid images are all about spontaneity and capturing emotion—whether it's your kids at play, a couple having a romantic walk on the beach, or your dog doing something that's particularly adorable. Try to capture candid shots of real-life moments in creative and visually interesting ways.

NOTE Candid photos enable you to capture raw emotions and memories as they spontaneously happen; for example, if you snap a photo of the guest of honor at a surprise party and manage to capture his expression at the precise moment everyone in the room yells, "Surprise!"

Posed photos enable you to manufacture memories the way you want to remember them. For example, you can create a posed shot if you walk up to a group of friends and say, "Put your arms around each other, look at me, smile, and say cheese."

When working with a group of kids that need a little direction, it sometimes helps to let them take a couple of goofy photos first, under the condition they let you take a couple "nicer" photos afterward.

#7—TAKE PICTURES OF SIGNS TO SET THE SCENE AND SHOW WHERE YOU'VE BEEN

If you're on vacation, for example, and know you plan to put together a photo album, scrapbook, or photo book to showcase and share your vacation memories, one way you can set the scene and show where you've been, without having to utilize photo captions, is to take photos of interesting signs during your travels.

Once again, be creative as you take pictures of signs. For example, you can pose people in front of the signs to personalize them. Or, you can look for words that somehow describe your location on unusual objects. It's also possible to create your own signs. For example, if you're vacationing on a beach, you can take a stick and write your location in the sand (as shown in Figure 3-14).

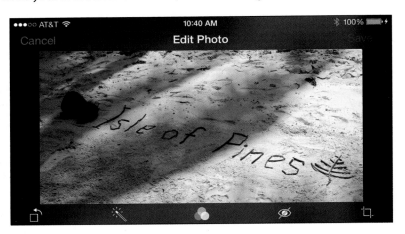

FIGURE 3-14

It's easy to create your own sign photos that can be used in slideshows, photo albums, photo books, or scrapbooks, for example, to set the scene and describe where you've been.

If you're putting together a group of photos taken at a birthday party, for example, the image you use as your "title" can be the birthday cake that clearly says, "Happy Birthday, Rusty."

As you explore your surroundings when you're out and about, you'll find all sorts of interesting signs that you can shoot creatively, and then incorporate into however you plan to present your photos.

#8—TAKE ADVANTAGE OF THE ZOOM

Often, a wide-angle shot can be used to show a location, just as taking a normal photo in Landscape mode enables you to showcase your subject but also see plenty of background in the image so the location is more obvious to the people viewing your photos. Sometimes, however, you'll be able to capture more visually interesting or compelling shots if you take full advantage of the zoom to get extremely close to your intended subject(s).

In situations when you have time to take lots of photos and experiment a bit, consider taking some wide-angle or even panoramic shots that can be used in a photo album, slideshow, online gallery, scrapbook, or photo book to set the scene, but then utilize the zoom at different intensities to capture images of the same subjects from a close-up perspective.

#9—WATCH OUT FOR UNWANTED SHADOWS

As a digital photographer, one of your worst enemies is often unwanted and annoying shadows. These shadows can be caused by the sun, by artificial lighting indoors, or by your iPhone's own flash. Depending on the cause, there are a variety of ways you can rid yourself of these photo menaces, or at least diminish the negative impact they have in your photos.

Typically, the easiest thing to do is adjust your lighting or the position of your primary light source. In some situations, adding more light to a situation helps get rid of shadows.

In other situations, repositioning yourself or your subject(s) can also go a long way toward ridding yourself of unwanted shadows. However, the time to be concerned about shadows is while you're actually taking pictures, not after the fact when it's too late to do anything about them.

NOTE   Chapter 4, "Take Awesome Pictures in Low Light," offers tips and strategies for using the iPhone's flash, while eliminating unwanted shadows and red-eye caused by the flash.

TIP Sometimes, when to use the flash and when to avoid using it can be counterintuitive. For example, if you're taking pictures outside on a bright and sunny day, but your subject is standing under a tree and is partially covered in annoying shadows, one way to reduce the negative impact of the shadows is to move your subject so he or she is not impacted by the shadows, or you can try turning on and using the iPhone's built-in flash to light up your subject and drown out the shadows.

Meanwhile, if you're taking photos inside and the lighting is dim, try taking photos using natural light, instead of turning on the flash and using it. (Also, take advantage of the HDR mode when using the Camera app.) Especially if your subject is positioned close to a wall behind them, for example, using the flash can cause unwanted shadows behind your subject, plus drown out the ambient light with a harsh bright light.

#10—USE THE AE/AF SENSOR TO YOUR ADVANTAGE

The autoexposure/autofocus sensor that's built in to the Camera app (and most other photography apps that can be used for taking pictures with the iPhone or iPad) is designed to ensure that the subject of your photo is captured in focus, utilizing the available light in the best possible way.

By default, the Camera app uses its artificial intelligence and attempts to automatically determine who or what your intended subject is within every photo you take. This is easier for the Camera app when you're taking pictures of people because the app is designed to recognize up to 10 faces at a time within a single picture.

However, as you begin to utilize the Rule of Thirds, take photos from different angles and perspectives and, at the same time, take advantage of what's in the foreground, the background, and/or to the sides of your subject to help frame your shots, the AE/AF sensor could easily get confused and automatically select the wrong object to be the subject of the image.

Keeping in mind that whatever the AE/AF sensor locks onto in your viewfinder is what will be in focus when a picture is taken, it's your responsibility to make sure this sensor knows what your intended subject is in every photo.

Especially if there are objects in front of or to the sides of your intended subject, it is often necessary to adjust the AE/AF sensor by framing your image in the viewfinder and then tapping on the screen on your intended subject. Otherwise, when you look closely at your photos after the fact, you might notice that the object to the side or in front of your intended subject is what's perfectly in focus, and your intended subject is actually slightly blurry.

CAUTION When using the AE/AF sensor, it's essential that when holding your iPhone or iPad, your fingers don't accidentally touch the screen (viewfinder) as you're about to snap a photo. Any unwanted contact with the touch screen could cause the AE/AF sensor to refocus on wherever your finger accidentally touches, resulting in your intended subject becoming out of focus.

AS THE PHOTOGRAPHER, BE AWARE OF EVERYTHING

To consistently capture well-lit, in-focus, visually interesting, and creative digital photos using your iPhone or iPad, as the photographer, you must pay careful attention to everything around you, tap your creativity, and at the same time, make sure you utilize the right features and functions of the photography app you're using to take pictures.

This might sound like an overwhelming task, but with just a little bit of practice, mastering the use of the Camera app, for example, while simultaneously using some or all of the strategies outlined in this chapter, will soon become second nature.

From a creative standpoint, here's a quick recap of what you need to do as you take each photo:

1. Remember to frame your shots using the Rule of Thirds. Avoid shooting your subject from a head-on perspective and always centering it within the frame.

2. Take advantage of an interesting shooting angle or perspective. This includes deciding whether to use Portrait or Landscape mode when taking a picture, and then positioning yourself at the best angle to capture your subject from an interesting point of view.

3. Pay attention to the primary light source and work with it.

4. Utilize what's in the foreground, the background, and to the sides of your subject, when possible, to frame your subject and add a sense of depth to each photo.

5. Watch out for unwanted and annoying shadows.

6. Make sure the AE/AF sensor locks on to your intended subject.

7. Be observant and ensure that you position yourself, as the photographer, in the right place, at the right time, to take the best possible photos as events unfold around you.

TIP Whether you're taking pictures of people, places, or things (or a combination of different subjects), you'll always be faced with challenges as a photographer.

Be sure to read Chapter 5, "Overcome Common Picture-Taking Challenges," to discover strategies for overcoming common obstacles, such as shooting through glass, taking pictures of fast-moving subjects, capturing in-focus images when you (the photographer) are in motion, taking pictures of animals, and capturing the perfect group photos when the people in the photo don't want to cooperate.

4

TAKE AWESOME PICTURES IN LOW LIGHT

Whether you want to take photos outside in the evening or at night, or just about any time indoors, you're going to be faced with one significant challenge—low light.

The good news is that the image sensor that's built in to your iPhone or iPad automatically captures as much light as possible when you press the Shutter button to take a picture. In addition, the iOS 7 edition of the Camera app is designed to work much better in low-light situations than previous versions of this app. This is particularly true when taking pictures using the iPhone 5s. However, it becomes your job as the photographer to make sure the available light is captured in the best way possible, or to decide when and if additional light (from the iPhone's flash, for example) is needed.

What you'll discover when you attempt to take pictures in low-light situations is that the cameras built in to your iPhone or iPad become much more sensitive to movement. As a result, even the slightest movement while you're taking a photo can result in a blurry image. Plus, images often wind up containing visual distortion, which is commonly referred to as *noise*. This means that instead of being vivid and sharp, images often appear slightly out of focus, a bit fuzzy, or display unwanted discoloration. The colors depicted within images are sometimes dull or washed out. In some cases, images appear grainy or pixelated (meaning the tiny dots that make up the image are visible).

> **TIP** To compensate for unwanted movement or a shaky hand, try holding your iPhone or iPad with both hands, lock your elbows to your body, and use the Volume Up or Volume Down button as your Shutter button, instead of the onscreen Shutter button. At the same time, hold your breath for the second or two while you press the Shutter button. This too can help steady your hands and body.

COMPENSATE FOR LOW LIGHT WHEN TAKING PICTURES

Unfortunately, there are only a few ways to compensate for the common problems that occur with all digital cameras when taking pictures in low light. These shooting strategies include the following:

- If possible, add more light to the scene where you're taking pictures. Achieving this might be as simple as turning on an additional lamp.
- Make sure you hold the iPhone or iPad perfectly still. Try propping the iOS mobile device on a flat and stable surface, as opposed to holding it in your hands, or use an optional tripod or stand.
- Turn on the Camera app's HDR (High Dynamic Range) shooting mode.
- Consider using the iPhone's built-in flash. (As you'll learn later in this chapter, there are pros and cons to using the iPhone's flash.)
- To achieve the sharpest images in low light, refrain from using the Zoom feature. Instead, use the Crop feature as you're editing your photos later, and then zoom in and reposition the image within the crop grid. You'll learn how to do this in Chapter 6, "View, Organize, Edit, and Share Pictures Using the Photos App." Also, while shooting with the iPhone, do not add a special effect filter. You can add one of the filters using the Photos app after

the fact or when using many other photography apps to edit or enhance your photos.

- Take advantage of a powerful photo editing app, or transfer the photos you take on your iPhone or iPad to your primary computer, and then use full-featured photo editing software to edit and enhance the image. Using photo editing software, you can easily fix the contrast, brightness, color saturation, and sharpness of an image, often using adjustable sliders.

> **TIP** In many cases, using the Enhance feature that's built in to the Photos app (or a similar editing feature offered by many third-party apps) helps sharpen and brighten a photo with a single onscreen tap. For more control when editing photos taken in low light, consider using Adobe Photoshop Touch.

- Use an alternative lighting option, such as a lamp or external light source, to shed more light on your intended subject(s).
- Try taking pictures using a third-party app as an alternative to the Camera app.

> **TIP** Some third-party photography apps, such as Pro HDR, are designed specifically for taking pictures in low-light situations using the iPhone or iPad. Actually snapping a photo using Pro HDR takes a few seconds longer than if you use the HDR mode in the Camera app, for example, but the results you'll achieve, particularly in low-light situations, are better. See Chapter 8, "Photography Apps That Enhance Your Picture-Taking Capabilities," for more information about Pro HDR.

As you'll discover, you can mix and match these strategies to achieve the best possible results. It's important to understand, however, that you'll rarely be able to capture the same high-quality photos on your iPhone or iPad in low-light situations as you can when shooting in bright light (such as outside on a sunny day). This is due to technological limitations with the image sensor and related digital photography technology that's built in to the iOS mobile devices (and most smartphones, tablets, and even standalone point-and-shoot digital cameras). With each new iPhone and iPad model that has been released, Apple has made great strides in improving the camera-related technology built in to these devices.

NOTE The iPhone 5s, compared with the iPhone 4s or the iPhone 5, for example, handles low-light shooting situations much better, thanks to its improved image sensor, its redesigned HDR shooting mode, and its True Tone flash.

KNOW WHEN AND HOW TO TAKE ADVANTAGE OF THE iPHONE'S BUILT-IN FLASH

All of the most recent iPhone models have a small LED flash that can be used with the device's rear-facing camera. On the iPhone 4/4s/5/5c, this is a bright white LED flash that, when activated, shines a burst of nonadjustable white light forward, directly onto your subject.

The iPhone's built-in flash does add extra light to a poorly lit shooting situation; however, if it's not used correctly, using this flash often results in unwanted shadows, red-eye, and potentially overexposed images. Unfortunately, there is no way to redirect, reflect, or diffuse this light. As you're about to discover, however, it's possible to compensate for some of these potential drawbacks while you're shooting.

NOTE With the iPhone 5s, Apple redesigned the smartphone's built-in flash and incorporated what the company calls a True Tone flash. In reality, this is actually two tiny LED flashes that are used simultaneously. Each flash emits a burst of slightly different colored light, and the iPhone 5s can adjust the intensity of each light so that it more closely matches the existing light where you're taking pictures.

As a result, the flash that's built in to the iPhone 5s is much more versatile, plus it automatically reduces the unwanted side effects that typically occur when using a flash, such as shadows, red-eye, pale-looking subjects, and/or overexposed images.

WHEN USING THE iPHONE'S FLASH, PAY ATTENTION TO ITS EFFECTIVE FLASH RANGE

When you use a flash with any camera, that flash has what's known as an *effective flash range*. This is the ideal distance range that the photographer should be from the intended subject to generate the best lighting results when using a camera's flash.

For example, if you stand too close to your subject when using the flash, the light emitted from it is too bright and your photo ends up overexposed. At the same time, the skin tones of your human subject(s) might look very pale and/or washed out. Meanwhile, if you stand too far away from your intended subject when using the flash, the light from the flash doesn't have the strength to reach your subject. As a result, what's in the foreground might be well lit, but the intended subject might be too dark or not visible.

TIP The effective flash range offered by the iPhone 4/4s/5/5c's built-in flash is limited. To achieve the best results when using the built-in flash, stay at least 2 to 3 feet away from your intended subject, but not more than 6 to 10 feet away. Thanks to the True Tone flash built in to the iPhone 5s, the effective flash range is a bit broader, although Apple has not published exact specifications.

CONSIDER OTHER HAZARDS OF USING THE iPHONE'S FLASH

Even if you stay within the effective flash range as you take pictures using the iPhone's built-in flash, you still run the risk of capturing unwanted shadows and red-eye.

NOTE To learn how to turn on or off the iPhone's built-in flash, refer to Chapter 2, "Snap Photos Using the Camera App."

To reduce unwanted shadows, try moving your subject away from his or her background and away from any reflective surfaces, such as windows or mirrors. If the subject is standing up against a wall, for example, have the subject take two or three steps forward.

At the same time, as the photographer, consider moving a few steps back (away) from your subject. You can compensate for this distance using the zoom, or better yet, using the Crop tool when editing your images after the fact. This strategy also works for reducing the occurrence or severity of red-eye.

With regard to shadows, remember that the light from the flash shines straight forward when you take a picture. So, if you're shooting from an angle, the light from your iPhone's flash hits your subject at an angle. Be aware of this, and pay careful attention to unwanted shadows caused by objects in your subject's surroundings and also from your subjects themselves.

For example, when taking photos of people using a flash, their hair (or the hats they're wearing) can often generate unwanted shadows that are cast over their foreheads and eyes. Meanwhile, their noses might cast unwanted shadows over their lips and mouths. If the subject is wearing earrings, a necklace, or eyeglasses, the light from the flash often reflects off of these objects and causes unwanted glares or visual distractions.

> **TIP** Sometimes, you can use the flash to create visually interesting shadow effects. For example, if you stand to the side or at a strong angle related to your subject, you can use the flash to light up only one portion of the subject. The angle from which you shoot is purely a creative decision on your part.

USE THE FLASH'S ON/OFF OR AUTO SETTINGS

To recap from Chapter 2, when the iPhone's built-in flash is set to Auto, the Camera app analyzes the light in the area where you're trying to take a photo and automatically decides when and if the flash is needed. When the flash is turned on, however, this causes the iPhone to activate the flash each time you take a photo.

If you discover your images are overexposed, this means you're too close to your subject. If the images are underexposed (too dark), you're standing too far away from your subject.

If you believe you're within the effective flash range for your iPhone, but the images you take aren't coming out as well as you'd like, as you're framing your shots, manually adjust the AE/AF sensor by tapping on the viewfinder (your device's touch screen) directly on your intended subject. This helps the Camera app adjust the exposure and how the light is utilized.

In situations when manually adjusting the AE/AF sensor still doesn't work as you'd hope, try manually activating the sensor but tapping somewhere within the viewfinder that is not directly on your intended subject. For example, tap on the lightest or darkest part of the image, based on what you see in the viewfinder.

TIP Instead of using the iPhone's flash, you always have the option of taking advantage of whatever existing light is in the area and then utilizing the Camera app's HDR shooting mode. This mode eliminates unwanted shadows and red-eye, for example, but can cause more noise within the image.

Instead of using the iPhone's built-in flash, a handful of companies offer external flash devices and/or continuous light sources that can be used with the iPhone or iPad to shed additional light on your intended subject(s) when taking pictures in low-light situations. These lighting options offer brighter light than what's possible using the iPhone's built-in flash. You learn about some of these external light source options, which are battery powered, portable, and typically connect to your iOS mobile device, in Chapter 10, "Use Optional Accessories to Improve Your Pictures."

TIP Another situation in which using the flash might be helpful is if you're outside on a sunny day but your subject is standing under a tree or another object that's casting an uneven shadow over your subject. In this case, if you turn on and use the flash, you can often reduce the impact the unwanted shadow has on the subject, while at the same time, fully utilizing the natural light.

THE CAMERA APP'S HDR SHOOTING MODE

In low-light situations when you want or need to capture the natural light in a scene, such as during a candlelit dinner or in front of a fireplace, using the flash is counterproductive. In these situations, when ambient light is needed to "set the scene," using the flash drowns out the natural light altogether.

To compensate for this, take advantage of your camera's HDR shooting mode. It enables the iPhone or iPad to make full use of the available light and capture as much of it as possible, while also preserving the colors (and your subject's skin tones, for example) within your photos.

HDR shooting mode can be used anytime, but it works best in low-light situations because it enables the iPhone or iPad's image sensor to capture the available light in a more efficient way. Refer to Chapter 2 for more information about how and why HDR shooting mode works.

TIP Be sure you hold the iPhone or iPad perfectly still when using HDR shooting mode in low-light situations. To have the most options available to you after the fact, when it comes to editing your images, be sure to set up the Camera app so that it automatically saves the regular and HDR-enhanced version of each photo you take in the Camera Roll folder. You can then compare the two images and, using an app for photo editing, ultimately work with the one that came out the best.

5

OVERCOME COMMON PICTURE-TAKING CHALLENGES

Even after you become proficient using the Camera and Photos apps on your iPhone or iPad, and simultaneously begin utilizing the shooting strategies described in Chapter 3, "Ten Strategies to Quickly Improve Your Picture-Taking Skills," as you go about your everyday life taking pictures, or when you go on vacation and want to chronicle your experiences by taking photos using your iOS mobile device, you are going to be faced with many different types of challenges that you'll need to overcome to consistently capture in-focus, well-lit, and great-looking shots.

This chapter offers tips and strategies for overcoming common problems you'll run into as you're using your iPhone or iPad to take pictures. By correctly dealing with these situations as you're actually snapping photos, you'll have much less work to do after the fact when attempting to edit or enhance the photos to compensate for the common problems, mistakes, or obstacles you encountered.

TIP If you find yourself facing a challenging situation, and the Camera app that comes preinstalled on your iOS mobile device isn't allowing you to achieve the photographic results you're striving for when taking pictures, consider using one of the third-party photography apps that also enable you to take pictures using the cameras built in to your iPhone or iPad.

For example, there's SmugMug's free Camera! Awesome app. You learn more about these optional Camera app alternatives in Chapter 8, "Photography Apps That Enhance Your Picture-Taking Capabilities."

TIP Throughout this chapter, multiple references are made about the necessity to hold the iPhone or iPad very steady, especially when taking pictures in low-light situations or when using the zoom. Consider using both hands to hold your iOS mobile device. Then, instead of tapping on the Shutter Button icon (that's displayed on the touch screen), use the Volume Up or Volume Down button on the side of your device as your Shutter button. Keep in mind that, whichever Shutter button you press, a photo isn't actually taken until you remove your finger from the button or icon.

STRATEGIES FOR TAKING PICTURES OF PEOPLE

There are many ways to capture people in pictures using your iPhone or iPad's camera. However, all of your picture-taking opportunities that involve humans can be categorized as either posed or candid shots, and the approach you'll take when capturing these two types of shots will vary greatly.

TAKE POSED PHOTOS OF PEOPLE

A posed photo involves you, as the photographer, telling your subject(s) how and where to sit or stand, where to look, and exactly what to be doing as you take the photo. These photos usually begin with the photographer saying, "Stand over here, look at me, smile, and say 'cheese'." The end result is hopefully a photo where you had full control over the staging of the image. In other words, because you told your subject(s) what to do and preplanned the shot, this is considered a posed shot.

As you're posing your subject and giving him or her direction, make sure no harsh light is shining on his or her face. This causes unflattering shadows to appear on the forehead, around eyes, and/or under the nose. If necessary, move your subject out of direct sunlight or away from a strong overhead light source.

TIP Many people become very self-conscious when a camera, even the camera built in to an iPhone or iPad, is pointed at them. As the photographer, it's your job to help your subjects feel at ease, so that their body language and facial expressions are relaxed, appear natural, and don't look forced.

For example, when someone is uncomfortable in front of a camera, you might see his or her body actually tense up. Telling the person to take a deep breath and to relax his or her shoulders often helps him or her to adopt a more relaxed pose. Many people also become less self-conscious if you give them some type of prop to hold or interact with while a photo is being taken.

As you're directing your subjects to take a posed photo or portrait, you'll need to make a handful of creative decisions, including the following:

- Whether your subject will be standing or sitting
- What your subject will be doing
- Where your subject will be looking
- What props your subject will be holding or interacting with
- What the subject's facial expression and pose will be
- How your subject will be interacting with his or her surroundings
- What will appear in the foreground, the background, and to the sides of your subject

NOTE Make sure there's nothing shiny or reflective in the photo that will distract attention from your intended subject when someone is looking at your photos. These distractions can include jewelry, a wristwatch, or even someone's eyeglasses that are reflecting light back into the iPhone or iPad's lens.

TIP   When taking posed portraits of people, your subjects do not necessarily need to be looking directly into the camera to capture a great shot. In some cases, you might discover that the photo is more thought provoking if the subject is staring off into the distance or looking at a particular object. If you're photograph-ing a couple in a romantic setting, a better shot might be acquired if the subjects are looking into each other's eyes instead of into the camera.

There's also no rule that says a subject must be smiling in a portrait. In some situa-tions, a more serious expression, or one that showcases some other emotion, might make for a better photo.

When posing and directing your subjects and, at the same time, making creative decisions relating to your intended subjects, you also need to determine the following:

- How you'll be holding the iPhone or iPad to utilize the Portrait or Landscape mode
- The location of your primary light source and how you'll utilize it
- How you'll position yourself, based on the location of your subject(s)
- The best shooting angle or perspective from which to take the shot
- Whether you want to utilize the digital zoom to get a close-up of your sub-ject, without physically moving in closer
- What camera-related features, functions, and/or filters you'll want to use as you take each shot

TIP   Don't forget to utilize the Rule of Thirds as you frame each shot. This becomes more important if you plan to incorporate your subject's surroundings in a photo.

TIP   If you're using the Camera app, or one of many other third-party app alter-natives that enable you to take photos using your iPhone or iPad's camera, be sure to take advantage of the Face Recognition feature. When your iOS mobile device determines you're taking pictures of people, the AE/AF sensor automatically focuses on each person's face, helping to ensure an in-focus and well-lit photo.

SHOOT CANDID SHOTS THAT FEATURE PEOPLE

Instead of directing your human subjects to create a posed photo, you often can capture more authentic emotions and actions by snapping candid pictures. The purpose of a candid photo is to capture a moment in time that happens spontaneously, with absolutely no direction from you, the photographer. Thus, you must take a different approach when taking candid pictures. In these situations, you want to be as unobtrusive and inconspicuous as possible, allowing your subjects to go about whatever it is they're doing.

While this is going on, as the photographer, be sure to position yourself in front of the action or subjects you want to capture, and make sure you're in the right place, at the right time, to snap a photo when the perfect opportunities arise.

> **TIP** When taking candid photos, you're typically better off staying at a distance from your intended subjects and utilizing the Zoom feature of the Camera app (or whichever app you're using) to get close-up shots of your subjects, without them being too conscious of your presence.

TIPS FOR CAPTURING THE PERFECT GROUP SHOT

The trick to capturing the perfect group shot is to make sure everyone can be clearly seen in your viewfinder as you get everyone to be doing the same thing, at the same time, each time you press the Shutter button. If someone is blocking someone else, or you can't see someone in the viewfinder because he or she is standing in the back of a group and is too short, then your group photo will not turn out as planned. It's your unenviable responsibility to position each person in the group so that everyone can be seen.

At the same time, you must make all of the same creative decisions as you would when taking a portrait of a single person, while also paying attention to the available light, avoiding unwanted shadows, and choosing the best shooting angle.

Next, tell the people in the group exactly what you want them to do and when. For example, say, "When I count to three, everyone look at me and smile." Make sure everyone is paying attention, and take a few practice shots.

When you're snapping group photos, always take several shots in a row. The fraction of a second difference between two or three shots taken in quick succession could mean the difference between capturing a photo where someone is blinking or looking in the wrong place, versus everyone doing exactly what they were instructed to do.

TIP If you're using the iPhone 5s, iPad Air, or iPad mini with Retina display, take advantage of the Burst shooting mode to capture a handful of similar shots in quick succession. Do this by holding down the Shutter button for two or three seconds at a time, as opposed to tapping it once. Then, go back and choose the one group photo where everyone is doing the same thing, and in which everyone can clearly be seen.

After taking several shots of your group, tell your group to stay put, but as the photographer, reposition yourself slightly, and then take a few more photos from a slightly different angle or perspective. For example, you could climb up on something and then shoot in a slight downward direction, or you could kneel down and shoot upward to create a more interesting group photo. Keep in mind that taking additional photos of the group increases your chances of capturing at least one perfect group shot, especially if one or more people in the group aren't fully cooperating.

Especially if you're taking a group photo featuring kids, it sometimes helps to ask them to make funny faces or pose in funny positions as you take a few initial shots, and then ask them to sit or stand still for a few more formal shots.

TIP If you want to add yourself to a group shot, prop up your iPhone or iPad on a nearby table or ledge (something stable and that's the appropriate height), or invest in a portable tripod or stand for your iOS device. (See Chapter 10, "Use Optional Accessories to Improve Your Pictures," for details about available tripods and stands, like the GorillaPod from Joby.com.)

Next, use an optional photography app, such as Camera+, TimerCam Pro, Self-Timer, Camera Timer, Self Photo Pro, or Camera Timer+, that offers a self-timer feature.

Set up the camera (the iPhone or iPad) and frame your shot as you normally would (using the other people in the group, but leave a spot for yourself), and then activate the timer. Set it for 15 or 20 seconds, and join the group about to be photographed.

CAPTURE ADORABLE BABY PICTURES

Depending on the age and alertness of the baby, it's sometimes easier to give a young child a rattle or toy as you attempt to capture a close-up, candid shot. The alternative is to have someone stand directly behind you (the photographer) and try to capture the baby's attention using keys or a rattle, or by making silly faces at the child.

When taking photos of a baby or young child, perfect timing and patience are essential because as the photographer, you can't direct your subject or tell the baby or young child how to act in front of the camera. Instead, what you can do is set up the perfect shot, and then be ready to snap photos when the young subject chooses to cooperate, does the action you want to capture, and/or looks directly into the camera, for example.

TIP To avoid scaring the child or making him or her upset, take advantage of your iPhone or iPad's HDR shooting mode, and utilize the ambient light. Don't use the iPhone's flash. Also, don't get too close to the child. Instead, rely on the zoom lens to get a close-up shot. Just make sure you're able to hold the iPhone or iPad perfectly steady, and that you take full advantage of the AE/AF sensor so that it locks in on your subject's face.

TAKE PROFESSIONAL LOOKING PICTURES OF ANIMALS

Pets, animals at a zoo or aquarium, and wild animals share the same challenges as taking photos of babies or young kids. As the photographer, you can't give animals much direction. Worse, there's no parent or loved one who can capture their attention or enthusiasm. Thus, it becomes your responsibility to be in the right place, at the right time, to capture great photos.

Sometimes, the best animal photos are extreme close-ups, or shots of the animal engaged in some type of action or activity. Remember, if you're utilizing the zoom, it's essential to hold the iPhone or iPad very still.

Instead of focusing in on an animal's face, when taking pictures of animals, its eyes should be the focal point of your image (if you want the animal looking at you when a photo is taken). Animals express their emotions through their eyes, not using facial expressions.

To avoid scaring the animal, refrain from using the iPhone's flash. If you're at a zoo or aquarium and need to take photos through glass, be sure to follow the tips outlined later in this chapter.

TIP   If an animal is in motion, make sure you frame the image so the animal is moving into the shot (or coming toward you), and not moving out of the view-finder as you're taking the picture. If the animal is standing still but being shot from an angle, once again, the animal should be facing into the frame, not out of it. (Remember your Rule of Thirds!) This is also true when taking pictures of people.

SHOOT IN-FOCUS IMAGES WHEN YOUR SUBJECT IS MOVING

The main challenge you'll face when your subject is moving is timing. If you're using an iPhone 5s, iPad Air, or iPad mini with Retina display, ideally, you want to use the Burst shooting mode in this situation to help ensure you capture the perfect shot, at just the right moment.

In addition to paying attention to the location of your primary light source, you also need to prepare for the action that's about to take place and preframe your shot. This means that in anticipation of your subject's action, you must be in the right place and have a preconceived idea of the shot you're about to take. Do everything that's necessary to have your iPhone or iPad ready, the Camera app (or whichever app you're using to snap pictures) running, and the zoom adjusted, so that when your subject moves into the frame and is exactly in the right spot, you can tap the Shutter button.

Figure 5-1 shows what your iPhone's viewfinder might look like as you're setting up a shot and waiting for your subject (in this case, a moving boat) to appear in the frame, whereas Figure 5-2 shows the intended subject moving across the frame, and moving rapidly.

Once again, from a photo composition standpoint, you want your subject to appear to be moving into the frame or directly toward you, which is why you need to position yourself accordingly, in advance.

FIGURE 5-1

When you know your subject will be moving quickly, preset everything related to your intended shot, and then wait for your subject to enter the frame.

FIGURE 5-2

As soon as your subject enters the frame as you anticipated, either use the Burst shooting mode or manually take several photos in quick succession.

STRATEGIES FOR TAKING PICTURES AT SPORTING EVENTS

Taking pictures at your child's soccer or Little League game is a lot easier than capturing awesome shots at a professional sporting event for a variety of reasons. For example, at a professional sporting event, you're probably required to stay in your seat, at a distance from the action. Thus, you must rely on the zoom lens to capture great photos because you can't move around and you have no control over your shooting angle or perspective. In this situation, hold your iPhone or iPad as stable as possible, especially when using the zoom, to avoid blurry images.

TIP If you know you want to take photos at a professional sporting event that's being held outdoors, when selecting your seat, choose wisely. Avoid being seated in an area that's directly facing the sun. Ideally, you want the sun behind you (the photographer) or directly overhead, but not in front of you. Attempting to shoot anything with the light from the sun shining directly into the iPhone or iPad's lens will result in glares, overexposed images, and/or your subjects looking like silhouettes.

When taking pictures of your child engaged in a sport, chances are you have a bit more freedom to move around and be closer to the action. To capture the best shots at these events, use the following strategies:

- Learn as much about the sport as possible, so you can anticipate what's about to happen.
- Position yourself at the best possible shooting location, so that you can capture the action as it's facing or coming toward you, not moving away from you. Be mindful of the location of your primary light source, ensuring that you won't be shooting directly into the sun, for example.
- Have a plan. Know what types of shots you want to get before the action/game/competition begins. Then be ready to capture those shots.
- In addition to capturing the action related to a sport, try to capture the facial expressions and emotions of the athletes themselves, particularly after something good or bad happens. You definitely want to utilize the zoom for this.

> **TIP** Although the zoom that's built in to the iPhone or iPad is good, if you're kept at a distance from the sports action, having better zoom capabilities will definitely be to your advantage. For any iPhone model, consider investing in the OlloClip Telephoto and Circular Polarizing Lens accessory ($99.99, www.olloclip.com). It easily clips onto the iPhone over its existing lens, and instantly doubles its zoom capabilities.
>
> When using the OlloClip Telephoto lens (or any optional zoom lens), holding the iPhone perfectly still when snapping photos becomes even more essential to avoid blurry images.

SHOOT IN-FOCUS IMAGES WHEN YOU (THE PHOTOGRAPHER) ARE IN MOTION

Especially if you're on vacation and being a tourist, taking photos while you, the photographer, are in motion is often a common necessity. You might also discover this need if you're on a boat, in a car (but not driving), or even when you're literally running around in your daily life.

> **TIP** When you (the photographer) are in motion, consider using a third-party photography app that offers image stabilization and a level gauge to help ensure your pictures come out in focus and don't appear crooked. Shown in Figure 5-3, the Camera+ app is one example of a third-party photography app that offers these two useful features.

In these situations, you will not be able to hold your iPhone or iPad perfectly steady. However, the technology that's built in to the photography app you're using and the iOS mobile device itself should be able to compensate for much of this movement, especially if you're taking pictures in a well-lit area.

That being said, while holding the iPhone or iPad in your hands, you still want to keep it as steady as possible, to avoid any additional movement as you're taking pictures. It also becomes more important than ever to rely on the AE/AF sensor and make sure it's centered over your intended subject as you're about to snap each photo.

The Level Gauge

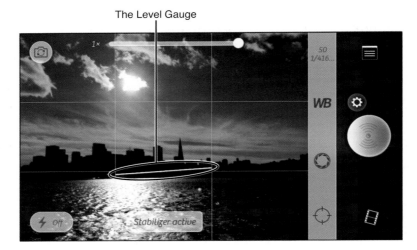

FIGURE 5-3

Turn on the Image Stabilization and Level Gauge features of the Camera+ app when taking pho-
tos while you, the photographer, are in motion and can't hold the iPhone or iPad perfectly still.

TIP Don't rely on the AE/AF sensor to kick in and lock on to your subject automatically while you're in motion. Instead, as you're about to take a picture, activate
the AE/AF sensor manually by tapping on the viewfinder (your iPhone or iPad's
screen), exactly where your subject is positioned in the frame. Make sure you see the
AE/AF sensor box displayed and centered on your intended subject before taking
the photo.

CAUTION This should be common sense, but never try to take photos
while you're actually driving. Also, if you're walking around or controlling any type
of moving vehicle (including a skateboard or bicycle), don't try to take photos
using your iOS mobile device at the same time.

OVERCOME PROBLEMS ASSOCIATED WITH SHOOTING THROUGH GLASS

As a passenger in a car, on a tour bus while sightseeing, or at an aquarium, these are just some of the situations where it might be necessary to take pictures through a window. This is actually a more common occurrence than you might think. When needing to take pictures with your iPhone or iPad while looking through glass, follow these steps:

1. Clean the window as much as possible. Get rid of fingerprints, dirt, and smudges.

2. Turn off the iPhone's flash.

3. Hold the iPhone or iPad directly up against the window so that no light can seep through between the window and the smartphone or tablet's camera lens (see Figure 5-4). All light to be captured in the photo should come from the opposite side of the glass. If necessary, use your hand or an article of clothing to block the unwanted light.

4. Hold the iOS mobile device as steady as possible, and tap the Shutter button to take the picture.

FIGURE 5-4

When shooting through glass, hold the iPhone or iPad right up to the glass so that no light (on your side of the glass) seeps between the glass and the camera lens.

CAUTION   If you leave the iPhone's flash turned on when taking a photo through glass, you end up with an unwanted reflection that bounces off of the glass (see Figure 5-5). Likewise, if the iPhone or iPad's camera picks up any light on your side of the glass because the iOS mobile device was not held directly up to the glass, this results in unwanted glares on the glass, causing what's behind the glass to be out of focus, washed out, or not visible.

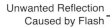
Unwanted Reflection
Caused by Flash

FIGURE 5-5

When taking pictures through glass using an iPhone, make sure the flash is turned off.

To take the image that's shown in Figure 5-6, the optional Pro HDR app was used. This app offers an enhanced version of the Camera app's HDR shooting mode and is ideal for taking photos in low-light situations. As you can see, the result is a clearer image that depicts the subject in more detail. Plus, there's more visible background detail. Once a shot is taken using the Pro HDR app, it's possible to manually adjust the brightness, contrast, saturation, warmth, and tint to bring out even more detail and color from the image (see Figure 5-7).

FIGURE 5-6

The Pro HDR app takes a few seconds longer to capture a photo, but this optional app enables you to capture more detailed images, especially in low-light situations.

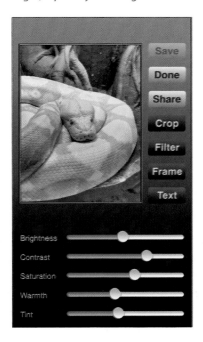

FIGURE 5-7

Immediately after you take a photo with the Pro HDR app, you can manually edit the image using sliders to control the brightness, contrast, saturation, warmth, and tint.

NOTE More information about the Pro HDR app can be found in Chapter 8.

USE YOUR CREATIVITY WHEN SHOOTING LANDMARKS, BUILDINGS, AND INANIMATE OBJECTS

Landmarks, buildings, and inanimate objects all have one thing in common—they can't pose for your photos. Thus, it becomes your sole responsibility as the photographer to capture these subjects in a creative and visually interesting way.

If the subject is large, shooting from a head-on perspective using Portrait or Landscape mode might not enable you to fit the entire object into the frame. Even if you utilize the Rule of Thirds, the image might still look uninteresting.

Instead, take a creative approach to shooting inanimate objects. In addition to adopting the Rule of Thirds when composing your shots, try shooting from a different perspective or angle. In other words, shoot from above your subject in a downward direction, from below your subject in an upward direction, from the side of your subject, or from a diagonal.

In addition, as necessary, take advantage of the app's zoom or panoramic functions to either get really close to your subject or capture the widest angle shot possible. Using the optional OlloClip 4-in-1 lens accessory, you can add a fisheye lens to your iPhone (see Figure 5-8), which offers the opportunity to capture larger subjects from a visually unique perspective.

Just as when taking photos of anything else, also try to utilize what's in the foreground, the background, and to the sides of your intended subject to frame your subject visually and/or add a sense of depth to each photo.

CAUTION You can see the shadow of the photographer in the foreground of Figure 5-8. By paying attention to what's happening in your viewfinder, you can avoid capturing unwanted shadows that can ultimately be distracting or take away from the professional look of your shots.

Unwanted
Shadows

FIGURE 5-8

Using an optional fisheye lens (such as what's offered by the OlloClip 4-in-1 lens) with your iPhone can create interesting visual effects.

CAPTURE THE BEST PANORAMIC SHOTS POSSIBLE WITH YOUR iPHONE

When taking digital photos using any iPhone model and the Camera app, instead of turning your smartphone sideways to take Landscape shots, you have the opportunity to use the Pano shooting mode to shoot panoramic images. The Pano shooting mode is ideal for capturing vast landscapes, city skylines, or large groups of people, for example.

The trick to capturing the best possible panoramic shots is to pay careful attention to your primary light source, and make sure that as you're panning the iPhone from left to right (or right to left), at no point does the camera lens get pointed directly into the sun (or the primary light source).

Also, make sure your horizontal panning motions are smooth and steady. It's essential that you hold the iPhone level as a panoramic shot is being taken. Once you start panning sideways, keep the fluid motion going until the white arrow on the screen crosses from the left to right side, or until you press the Shutter button a second time to stop the image capture process.

TIP   If your panning motions are too fast or shaky, a warning message appears on the screen (see Figure 5-9). Now, you have two options. You can follow the directions and continue taking the shot, or stop the process and start again (this time correcting the error). Some people find it useful to use a tripod to capture panoramic shots, but this requires carrying around extra equipment.

FIGURE 5-9

Watch for onscreen warning messages as you're taking panoramic photos. If one appears, make the necessary adjustments to your shooting technique to ensure the best possible photo.

STRATEGIES FOR TAKING CLOSE-UP IMAGES USING THE ZOOM

When you use the Zoom feature while taking pictures with an iPhone or iPad, the biggest challenge is holding the device very still as you press the Shutter button. The higher-intensity zoom you're using, the more sensitive the built-in cameras are to even the slightest movement. This is particularly relevant when using the zoom to take an extreme close-up of a tiny subject (thus utilizing the iPhone or iPad as a camera with a macro lens).

You'll often find that the Zoom feature works better when plenty of light is available and you utilize the HDR shooting mode.

> **TIP** If taking close-up images of tiny subjects, such as flowers or insects, is important to you, consider investing in the OlloClip 4-in-1 clip-on lens for the iPhone ($69.99, www.olloclip.com). It includes a 10x and 15x macro lens.

Instead of using the digital zoom built in to the Camera app (and many other photography apps for the iPhone or iPad), take a regular photo of your subject, and then use the Photos app's Crop tool to reframe your image and simulate a photo that used the zoom.

Figure 5-10 shows a photo taken without the Zoom feature used. Then, using the Crop tool offered by the Photos app, the same image was edited and repositioned after the fact to make the intended subject the focal point of the image, and to simulate the use of the zoom (see Figure 5-11).

FIGURE 5-10

This shot was taken on an iPhone 5s using the Photo shooting mode with no zoom.

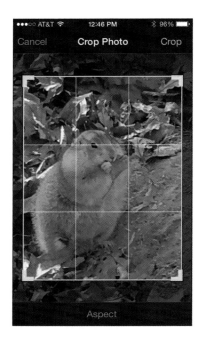

FIGURE 5-11

Using the image from Figure 5-10, I loaded the photo into the Photos app and used the Crop tool to reframe the image and simulate the Zoom feature.

Using the Crop tool when possible, instead of the zoom, helps to ensure you capture a clearer and more in-focus image, especially in low-light situations. Figure 5-12 shows the cropped and repositioned photo.

> **NOTE** There is more information about how to use the Photos app's Crop tool in Chapter 6, "View, Organize, Edit, and Share Pictures Using the Photos App." A similar Crop tool is also available in many other photography apps, including iPhoto.

FIGURE 5-12

As you can see, using the Crop tool, you can zoom in on your subject after the fact, plus reframe the image—in this case, taking the subject out of the direct center of the frame.

NOTE The Zoom feature is much more sensitive to movement. Thus, a shaky hand could result in a blurry image. Try to utilize the zoom only when you can hold the iPhone or iPad very still, there's plenty of light, and your subject is stationary. This is how you'll get the best results using the Zoom feature.

USE REFLECTIONS TO YOUR ADVANTAGE

When taking pictures that involve lakes, oceans, rivers, or any type of water, take advantage of the reflections in the water (or created by the water) to capture more visually interesting images. For example, if your intended subject's reflection can be seen in a body of water, capture that reflection in your shot (see Figure 5-13).

FIGURE 5-13

Take advantage of reflections in water to add an artistic or creative flare to what might other-wise be visually boring shots. Tree branches in the foreground were used here to add a more artistic element to the photo, as well as a sense of depth.

You can also creatively use reflections of your intended subject that are cast in a window, mirror, or just about any shiny object. Keep in mind that reflections can add an artistic flare to your images, but be careful of unwanted light that's also reflected directly into the lens that could cause glares.

TIP   In digital photography, what might be considered the opposite of a reflection is a silhouette. This is caused when the primary light source is positioned behind your intended subject (and in front of the iPhone or iPad's lens). When used intentionally, silhouettes can create dramatic and artistic visual effects, especially when taking pictures of subjects in front of a sunset, for example.

To counteract an unwanted silhouette effect, try using the iPhone's flash to lighten up your subject, or add more light in front of your intended subject.

GIVE YOUR PHOTOS A SENSE OF SCALE AND DEPTH

Sometimes, the actual size of a subject in a digital photo can be deceiving, unless something else in the image can be used as a size reference. For example, if you take an extreme close-up of a tiny bug, that bug will look huge in the photo, unless you take a photo of the bug standing on someone's hand or next to an object that people inherently know the actual size of.

If you take photos of a large structure or object, consider having someone stand in front of or next to it to add a sense of scale in the image.

TIP When the tiny or massive size of your subject appears misleading in photos, consider incorporating something additional in the image that adds a sense of scale and that's easily identifiable.

Meanwhile, one easy way to add a sense of depth in your photos is to utilize what's in the background and/or foreground. When doing this, be mindful of what the AE/AF sensor automatically focuses in on, and make sure it's your intended subject. Also, make sure what you decide to include in the foreground or background doesn't become the focal point of the image instead of your intended subject. For example, anything that's brightly colored, reflective, or shiny immediately draws people's eyes to it when they look at your photos. Make sure that your intended subject captures their attention.

MAKE YOUR VACATION PHOTOS AS MEMORABLE AS YOUR ACTUAL TRIP

The concept of taking photos that tell a chronological story becomes more important when you're taking vacation photos, especially if you plan to showcase a group of images in a photo album, scrapbook, collage, photo book, or digital slideshow. As you're shooting photos during your vacation, take plenty of candid shots of the people you're traveling with, but combine those with posed photos as well as photos of the places you visit and the experiences you have.

Depending on where you're vacationing, chances are you'll be able to experience a gorgeous sunrise or sunset. To capture the best sunrise or sunset shots, plan your trip itinerary so that you're at the most popular or most photographic tourist attractions, landmarks, beaches, or locations during a sunrise or just before and during a sunset, to take full advantage of the gorgeous natural lighting.

Turn on the HDR shooting mode, and try to avoid using the zoom capabilities of the iPhone or iPad's camera as you point the lens directly toward the sun. As you do this, try repositioning the AE/AF sensor by tapping on various areas of the view-finder to force the iOS mobile device to capture the natural light in different ways.

TIP   Many photo editing apps offer image filters you can apply after the fact to make the colors in your photos appear even more vivid. Some of these filters, particularly ones that improve an image's brightness and contrast, while boosting colors in the image, work particularly well on sunrise or sunset shots.

For these types of sunset shots, you can add an artistic element to the photos by positioning people in the shot or using other natural objects in the area, such as trees or buildings, which will become visible in your shots as silhouettes (because the primary light source is behind those objects or people and is shining directly into the lens). The silhouettes in Figure 5-14, for example, add a sense of depth to the images when they're positioned in front of the rising or setting sun.

FIGURE 5-14

Incorporate nearby objects, such as trees, into your shots to add a sense of depth, make the photos look more visually interesting, and add some artistic flare.

TIP   Refrain from using the iPhone's flash when taking sunset photos. The optional Pro HDR app is ideal for taking sunset photos because this app does a great job of capturing natural colors in low-light situations.

A handful of apps available from the App Store enable you to enter any location and date, and quickly determine the exact sunrise and sunset times. For example, there's Living Earth - Clock & Weather ($2.99), Sunrise Sunset Pro ($1.99), and Sunset and Sunrise ($1.99), each of which can help you plan your schedule based on local sunrise and sunset times wherever you happen to be.

> **TIP** The Map-A-Pic Location Scout for Photographers app ($4.99) is a useful tool for choosing where you'll want to take pictures, keeping track of where you've taken pictures, and quickly being able to determine sunrise and sunset times for those locations.

WHAT TO DO IF TOO MUCH LIGHT KEEPS YOU FROM SEEING THE iPHONE OR iPAD'S VIEWFINDER

When taking photos outside, one common problem you'll encounter is that the sun reflects off the iPhone or iPad's screen when you're using the Camera app (or another photography app), which makes it almost impossible to see what's appearing within your viewfinder.

From a lighting standpoint, your goal as a photographer is to place your primary light source behind you, so that it shines evenly onto your subject. Doing this, however, often causes the primary light source, such as the sun, to shine directly onto your iOS mobile device's screen. Unfortunately, this issue is not unique to the iPhone or iPad. It happens when using almost any point-and-shoot digital camera.

The best way to prevent this is to try to position yourself (the photographer) in a shaded area, or cup one hand over the iPhone or iPad's viewfinder screen as you hold the device and control the Camera app (or another photography app) with your other hand.

Ultimately, you might have to guesstimate when it comes to framing or compos-ing your shots in the viewfinder if too much light is drowning out the display. In this situation, take a moment to find a shady area, and then view your images after they're taken to ensure you've actually captured your intended subject as planned.

TIP Using the new Control Center feature of iOS 7, you can quickly and manually adjust the iPhone or iPad's screen brightness, which may improve your visibility when in direct sunlight. To do this, place your finger near the very bottom of the screen and swipe your finger upward to access the Control Center (see Figure 5-15).

Next, place your finger on the white dot that's displayed in the Screen Brightness slider and drag it left (to make the screen darker) or to the right (to make the screen brighter).

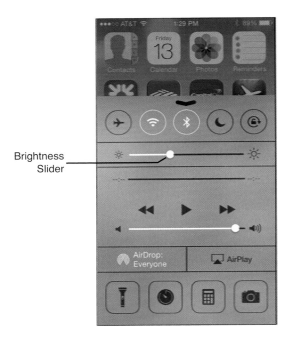

FIGURE 5-15

Adjust the iPhone or iPad's screen brightness manually from the Control Center.

TIP If too much glare from direct sunlight is a problem that occurs frequently when you're taking pictures, consider investing in an optional protective film for your iPhone or iPad's screen that offers glare reduction. Priced between $15.00 and $30.00, BodyGuardz (www.bodyguardz.com), as well as a handful of other companies, offers this type of glare reduction film that you can apply yourself to an iPhone or iPad's screen.

6

VIEW, ORGANIZE, EDIT, AND SHARE PICTURES USING THE PHOTOS APP

Both the Camera and Photos apps come preinstalled with iOS 7. Although the Camera app is used to control the cameras built in to your iPhone or iPad, the purpose of the Photos app is to help you organize, edit, enhance, print, and share the images that are stored in your iOS mobile device.

NOTE If you're serious about digital photography using your iPhone or iPad, or you want an even more powerful toolset to work with as you organize, edit, enhance, share, and print your photos, consider upgrading to Apple's optional iPhoto app. If you've purchased a new iPhone or iPad with iOS 7, the iPhoto app is available for free from the App Store and is the focus of the next chapter. (Otherwise, the app costs $4.99.)

There are also literally hundreds of third-party apps that can be used with or instead of the Camera and Photos apps to provide you with comprehensive digital photography solutions for your iOS mobile device. You'll learn about some of these apps in Chapter 8, "Photography Apps That Enhance Your Picture-Taking Capabilities," and Chapter 9, "Photography Apps That Expand Your Photo Editing and Enhancement Capabilities," respectively.

If you're new to using the Photos app, you'll discover it's designed to help you manage your digital images when they're stored on your iPhone or iPad. Thus, you can use this app to manage images you take using the cameras built in to your iOS mobile device, or work with images that you transfer into or sync with your iPhone or iPad (but that were taken using other photography equipment).

When it comes to sharing and syncing your photos, the nice thing about the Photos app is that it fully integrates with the AirDrop, Mail, Messages, Facebook, Twitter, and Flickr functionality that's built in to iOS 7. In addition, it's fully compatible with Apple's online-based iCloud service, so you can access and manage images stored in the My Photo Stream or Shared Photo Streams that are part of your personal iCloud account. (You learn more about using iCloud to back up, sync, and share photos in Chapter 13, "Discover iCloud's My Photo Stream and Shared Photo Stream.")

ORGANIZE YOUR DIGITAL IMAGES USING THE PHOTOS APP

The iOS 7 edition of the Photos app has been redesigned to offer new ways to easily, and in some cases automatically, organize and sort your images. By default, when you take a photo using the Camera app, in addition to capturing the image itself, your iPhone or iPad also records the time and date when each photo was taken, as well as the location where it was taken. The iPhoto app uses this information, called metadata, to help automatically sort your images.

NOTE Each time you take a new photo using the Camera app, by default, it gets stored in the Camera Roll album (folder), which is readily accessible from the Photos app. When you transfer images into your iOS mobile device, separate folders are automatically created for them.

Meanwhile, at anytime, you can manually create new folders, with custom names, and then move selected images into those folders.

VIEW THE IMAGES STORED ON YOUR iPHONE OR iPAD

The Photos app enables you to sort and organize your images in a variety of ways. If you want to begin by viewing thumbnails of all images stored in your iPhone or iPad, tap on the Photos icon that's displayed at the bottom-left corner of the Photos app screen.

You'll then notice that the Photos app automatically sorts your images using the dates and times they were taken. (If no relevant metadata is included with the images, the date and time the images were transferred into the iPhone or iPad is used.)

NOTE Images are stored (saved) within albums. However, when you access the Years, Collections, or Moments view, the Photos app sorts and displays thumbnails for the images based on the dates and locations each was taken. The image files themselves, however, continue to be stored in their respective albums.

TIP Tapping on the Photos icon offers different viewing modes for quickly perusing thumbnails of your images. To work with a specific album folder, tap on the Albums icon that's displayed in the bottom-right corner of the Photos app screen.

THE YEARS VIEW

After tapping on the Photos icon (see Figure 6-1), you can quickly peruse the thumbnails for all the images stored in your iOS mobile device. The Years view, shown in Figure 6-2, collects all the images taken within a particular year and displays tiny thumbnails for each of them. Next to each year heading, a condensed listing of where the photos were taken is displayed.

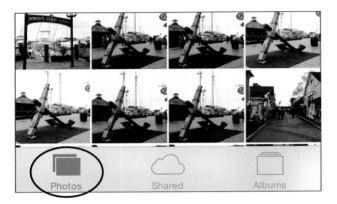

FIGURE 6-1

The Photos icon is displayed at the bottom-left corner of the Photos app.

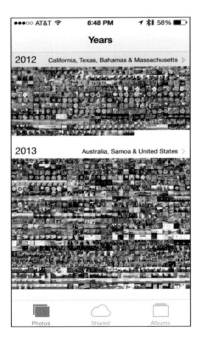

FIGURE 6-2

The Years view in the Photos app displays tiny thumbnails for all images taken within a particular year.

While accessing the Years view, tap on any image thumbnail to switch to the Collections view. However, if you tap on the Year heading or the location names where the images were taken, a Map view is displayed. It shows on a map where photos were shot (see Figure 6-3). As you look at the Map view, the number displayed in the blue circle indicates how many images were shot at that geographic location.

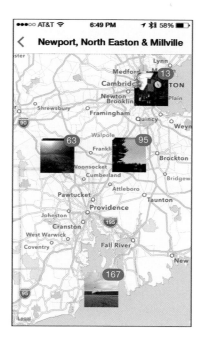

FIGURE 6-3

The Map view displays where photos were taken on a detailed map.

Tap on any of the thumbnails that are displayed on the map to switch to a view that displays slightly larger thumbnails of all images shot at that location, in that year (see Figure 6-4). At this point, tap on any image thumbnail to view a larger version of the image and then be able to work with it using the various tools offered by the Photos app.

> **TIP** When looking at the Map view, to zoom in or out, use a reverse-pinch or pinch finger gesture. To move around on the map, hold your finger on the map and drag it in any direction.

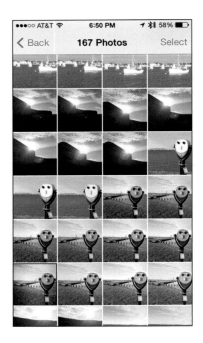

FIGURE 6-4

Tap on an image thumbnail displayed in the Map view to see slightly larger thumbnails of the images taken at that location, within that year.

THE COLLECTIONS VIEW

After tapping on the Photos icon, another way to view your images is using the Collections view (shown in Figure 6-5). This viewing mode automatically sorts images based on date ranges and locations where the images were taken.

From this viewing mode, tap on the heading for any group of photos to switch to the Map view. However, it's also possible to tap on any image thumbnail and switch from the Collections view to the Moments view, which provides slightly larger individual image thumbnails, with images sorted by the specific day they were shot, not by date ranges.

FIGURE 6-5

The Collections view sorts your images by location, based on date ranges, and displays tiny thumbnails for each group of related images.

TIP To switch from the Collections view to the Years view, tap on the Years option that's displayed near the top-left corner of the screen. To switch from the Collections view to the Moments view, tap on any image thumbnail. To switch to the Map view, tap on the Location/Date Range heading that displays above each group of thumbnails.

THE MOMENTS VIEW

Again, after tapping on the Photos icon, the Moments view, shown in Figure 6-6, offers yet another way to view thumbnails of your images displayed based on location and a specific date (as opposed to a date range).

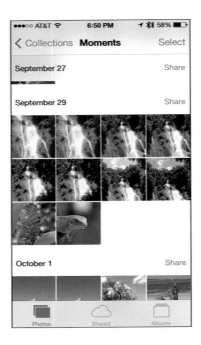

FIGURE 6-6

The Moments view sorts and displays images by location and by a specific date.

As you're viewing the thumbnails displayed as part of the Moments view, you have several options for switching views, including the following:

- Tap on the Collections option that's displayed at the top-left corner of the screen to switch to the Collections view.

- Tap on the Location part of the heading to switch to the Map view.

- Tap on the Date part of the heading to access a Share menu, shown in Figure 6-7, that enables you to either Share This Moment (meaning all images grouped within that Moment) or Share Some Photos (enabling you to pick which images you want to share from a Moments collection).

- Tap on an individual image thumbnail to view a larger version of that single image and be able to work with it using the Photos app's various editing, enhancing, sharing, and printing tools.

- Tap on one of the other two command icons displayed along the bottom of the Photos app screen—Shared or Albums—to switch viewing options altogether.

FIGURE 6-7

This menu enables you to share all images within a Moment, or specifically selected images within that image collection.

TIP   From the Moments view, if you tap on the Share option and select the Share This Moment option, a version of the Photos app's Share menu is displayed. You can then send those images to others via AirDrop, Messages, Mail, iCloud, Facebook, or Flickr, as well as copy or print the images. The share options that become available will depend on how many images are selected. How to use these features is explained later in this chapter.

However, if you tap on the Share Some Photos menu option, the Select Items screen is displayed. From here, tap on the individual thumbnails for the images you want to share to select them. Then, tap on the Share option that's displayed in the top-right corner of the screen. When a thumbnail is selected, a blue-and-white check mark icon appears in the bottom-right corner of the thumbnail.

TIP While using the Moments view, tap on the Select option that's displayed in the top-right corner of the screen to select images from one or more separate Moments. Upon doing this, the Share icon, Add To option, and Trash icon are displayed at the bottom of the screen.

Tap on the Share icon to access the Photos app's Share menu and be able to share the selected images with others, as well as access the Copy and Print commands. Tap on the Add To option to move the selected images from the album they're currently stored in, and place them in another album of your choosing. Tap on the Trash icon to delete the images from the Photos app altogether.

CREATE AND VIEW ALBUMS

Using the Albums view, it's possible to see a directory of separate albums currently stored in your iOS mobile device. To access the Albums view, launch the Photos app and tap on the Albums icon that's displayed at the bottom-right corner of the screen (see Figure 6-8).

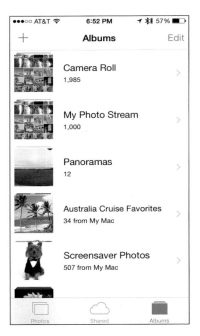

FIGURE 6-8

To view a list of albums that contain your images and that are stored in your iPhone or iPad, tap on the Albums icon.

From the Albums screen, you see listings for each separate album that's stored on your iPhone or iPad. Each listing is composed of one thumbnail, the album's name, and a number that indicates how many images are stored within that album.

To switch from the Albums screen (which lists the individual albums) to a screen that displays all the thumbnails for images stored within a particular album, tap on one album listing.

TIP To create a new album, from the Albums screen, tap on the + icon that's displayed at the top-left corner of the screen. When the New Album pop-up window appears (see Figure 6-9), enter a name for the new album, and then tap on the Save button. You can then manually move images into that newly created album using the Add To option.

FIGURE 6-9

To create a new album, from the Albums screen, tap on the + icon, and then manually enter the name you want to give to the newly created album in the pop-up window that appears.

MOVE IMAGES BETWEEN ALBUMS

To move images from one album into another, tap on the Albums icon at the bottom of the screen and access the album where the images you want to move are currently stored. As you're viewing those image thumbnails, tap on the Select option (found at the top-right corner of the screen), and then tap on each thumbnail that you want to move to select it.

When one or more images are selected, tap on the Add To option that can be found in the bottom-right corner of the screen (see Figure 6-10). Then, from the Add To Album screen, choose which album you want to move the selected images to. Keep in mind that you can only move images into albums created on the iOS mobile device you're using, not into albums that have been imported, transferred, or synced into your iPhone or iPad. Instead of choosing an existing album, tap on the New Album option to create a new album from scratch and move the selected photos into it.

> **TIP** One way to keep images well organized is to manually create albums for specific groups of photos, such as individual vacations, parties, or related groups of photos. Be sure to name the albums with an obvious title, such as Christmas Vacation 2013, Natalie's Birthday, or The Kids.

FIGURE 6-10

Use the Add To command to move images stored in one album into another album.

DELETE OR REORDER AN ALBUM

Albums that were created on the iPhone or iPad you're using can be deleted from that device. To do this, as you're viewing the Albums screen, tap on the Edit option that's found in the top-right corner of the screen. To delete an album (and all of its contents), tap on the circular, red-and-white, negative sign icon that's displayed to the left of an album's listing. Press the Done option (that's displayed in the top-right corner of the screen) to save your changes.

To reorder the album listing displayed on the Albums screen, tap on the Edit option, and then place your finger on a Move icon that's displayed to the right of an album listing. Drag that listing either upward or downward, to the desired location. Press the Done option (that's displayed in the top-right corner of the screen) to save your changes.

> **TIP** Albums that were created on another computer or device, and then transferred or synced to the iPhone or iPad you're using, cannot be deleted or moved from the device you're using. You must manage these albums from the iPhoto app running on your primary (Mac) computer, or using the iCloud-related options on the computer or device from which the album originated. Then, when you make changes to those albums on the Mac or iOS mobile device on which they were created, and then sync that computer or device with the one you're using, the albums on the iPhone or iPad you're using are modified accordingly.

WORK WITH SHARED IMAGES VIA iCLOUD

The Photos app is designed to work seamlessly with your online-based iCloud account. To manage the My Photo Stream collection of images being synced with your iCloud account, or to create, manage, and view images that are part of shared photo streams you've created or that you've been invited to access, tap on the Shared icon that's displayed near the bottom center of the Photos app screen.

From the Shared Streams screen (see Figure 6-11), you can access all photo streams that are stored or accessible via your iCloud account. You can also create new shared photo streams and manage existing shared photo streams.

> **NOTE** Be sure to read Chapter 13 to learn all about how to work with the iCloud-related features when using the Photos app and optional iPhoto app.

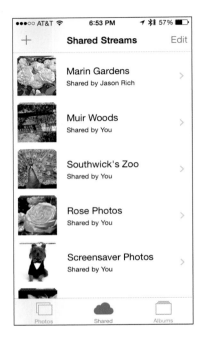

FIGURE 6-11

Tap on the Shared icon at the bottom of the screen to manage the My Photo Stream and shared photo streams associated with your iCloud account.

CAUTION Any changes you make to your My Photo Stream or any shared photo streams from the iOS mobile device you're using will have an almost immediate impact on those images that are also accessible from your other computers and/or iOS mobile devices that are linked to the same iCloud account.

For example, if you delete images from your My Photo Stream, or from a shared photo stream from your iPhone, those images are also deleted from all the other computers and iOS mobile devices that have access to that photo stream. There is no Undo button for this feature.

Likewise, if you create a new shared photo stream on your iPhone, the images within that album become accessible on all of your other computers and iOS mobile devices that are linked to the same iCloud account (assuming all the computers and iOS mobile devices have Internet access).

As you'll discover, to work with any photo stream-related features from your iOS mobile device, a Wi-Fi Internet connection is required.

EDIT AND ENHANCE YOUR IMAGES

In addition to helping you organize and share the images stored in your iPhone or iPad, the Photos app can also be used to view, edit, and enhance each image. To use any of these editing or enhancement tools, first select the image you want to work with. This can be done in a variety of ways. For example, tap on the Photos, Albums, or Shared icon that's displayed at the bottom of the screen, and then tap on the thumbnail for the image you want to work with. When you can see the large version of that image, tap on the Edit option that's displayed at the top-right corner of the screen (see Figure 6-12).

FIGURE 6-12

Select one image at a time to edit or enhance by tapping on its thumbnail, and then tap on the Edit option that's displayed in the top-right corner of the screen.

TIP   When you edit an image, the edited version of it is stored in the album from which it originally came. The edited version of the image replaces the original version. If the image was selected from your My Photo Stream or a shared photo stream (which is stored online, as opposed to on your iOS mobile device), the edited version of that image is automatically stored in the Camera Roll folder on your iPhone or iPad. Depending on how you have your iCloud functionality set up in your iOS mobile device, the edited image can then automatically be synced with your iCloud account.

As you're looking at the image you selected (not its thumbnail) on your iPhone or iPad's screen, tap on the Edit option to begin using the tools built in to the Photos app to edit and enhance the image. When you tap the Edit option, the Edit Photo screen is displayed (see Figure 6-13 for the iPad version).

FIGURE 6-13

The Edit Photo screen offers five editing and image enhancement tools you can utilize on the photo you're currently viewing. These tools are displayed as command icons along the bottom of the screen.

THE PHOTOS APP'S IMAGE EDITING AND ENHANCEMENT TOOLS

The image editing and photo enhancement tools that are built in to the Photos app are basic but powerful. One drawback to these tools is that when you use them, they impact the entire image. It's not possible using the Photos app to edit or enhance only a portion of an image. In addition, the Photos app lacks some editing and image enhancement tools that many other photography apps offer.

> TIP Optional photography apps, including Apple's iPhoto app, along with many offered by third parties (some of which are showcased in Chapter 9) are far more useful when it comes to adding a more professional touch to your images after they've been shot.

Displayed from left to right at the bottom of the Edit Photo screen (refer to Figure 6-13), the tools available include Rotate, Enhance, Filters, Red-Eye, and Crop. As soon as you tap one of these icons, that tool will be used on the selected image.

To immediately undo the edits or enhancements you make on an image, tap on the Cancel option that's displayed at the top-left corner of the screen. To save your edits and enhancements, tap on the Save option displayed at the top-right corner of the screen. In some cases, an Undo option also becomes available that enables you to remove the last edit you made to the image.

> TIP To undo the Enhance feature, before tapping on the Save option, tap on the Enhance icon again to turn it off. To undo a filter effect, tap on the Filters icon again, but this time, select the None option. To undo a red-eye edit, tap a second time on the subject's eyes. To undo a crop, tap again on the Crop icon, and then readjust the crop grid so that it surrounds the entire image.

Keep in mind, while many of the editing and enhancement tools in the Photos app can either be turned on or off, you can mix and match these tools as needed to create a highly personalized image. For example, you can turn on the Enhance tool, crop the image, and also add one special effect filter—all within seconds while viewing an image from the Edit Photo screen.

THE ROTATE TOOL

When editing a photo in the Photos app, upon tapping on the Rotate icon, the entire image rotates 90 degrees counterclockwise and is displayed sideways (see Figure 6-14). Thus, if you tap on the Rotate icon twice, the image rotates 180 degrees (and is then upside down). If you tap the Rotate icon four times, the image returns to its original orientation.

FIGURE 6-14

Each time you tap on the Rotate icon, it rotates the image 90 degrees in a counterclockwise direction.

After rotating the image, tap on the Save option (displayed at the top-right corner of the screen) to save the changes you've made and then return to the Edit Photo screen.

THE ENHANCE TOOL

The capabilities of the Enhance tool offered by the Photos app are somewhat limited. This feature often improves the brightness and contrast of an image and brightens its colors, but it has only an On or Off setting. It's not adjustable, and the enhancements impact the entire image. If an image appears overexposed or under-exposed, for example, the Enhance tool can often help compensate for this and improve the overall appearance of the image. However, in some cases, the impact this tool has on a photo is very subtle.

THE FILTERS TOOL

When taking photos using the Camera app on the iPhone, it's possible to tap on the Filters option and automatically add a special effect filter to your images as you're shooting them. However, whether you're using an iPhone or iPad, from the Photos app, you can add any one of eight special effect filters after the fact, while you're editing a photo.

To select and add a filter, from the Edit Photo screen, tap on the Filters icon. Then, if you're using an iPhone, with your finger, swipe horizontally along the filter icons to scroll through your options. Select the one you want to add by tapping on it. On the iPad, all the filters are displayed along the bottom of the screen (see Figure 6-15).

FIGURE 6-15

Select the filter you want to add to an image. There are eight to choose from via the Photos app.

Your Filter options include None, Mono, Tonal, Noir, Fade, Chrome, Process, Transfer, and Instant. If you tap on the None option, no filter is used. However, if you want to transform your full-color image into a black-and-white image, use either the Mono, Tonal, or Noir filters. Each takes a different approach to removing the colors from your image.

The Fade option subdues the vivid colors displayed in your image, while the Chrome, Process, and Transfer special effect filters alter the colors in an image to create entirely different visual effects. The Instant filter transforms your modern-day digital image into one that looks like it was shot using a Polaroid Instant Camera.

Once you select a filter you want to use by tapping on it, your image is transformed immediately. To save the image, tap on the Apply option that's displayed in the top-right corner of the screen. To remove the filter, either tap on the None or Cancel option. Keep in mind that only one filter can be added to an image using the Photos app; however, if you want access to a broader selection of special effect filters, as well as the option to apply multiple filters to a single image, consider using another photography app when editing your photos.

Figure 6-16 shows the same image as what's seen in Figure 6-15, but with the Tonal special effect filter selected.

FIGURE 6-16

The Tonal filter has been added to transform this full-color image into black and white.

TIP If you use Instagram to share your photos, the official Instagram app offers a wonderful collection of special effect filters, as well as image borders and easy-to-use photo editing tools that can be applied to images taken or stored on your iOS mobile device before they're uploaded to the Instagram service.

Chapter 12, "Share Your Digital Photos Online," offers more information about how to use the Instagram app and online service to share your photos online, directly from your iOS mobile device.

To simply edit your photos using a vast selection of tools and special effect filters (that can be applied to an entire image or a portion of an image), consider using the optional Adobe Photoshop Touch app, which you'll learn more about in Chapter 9.

THE RED-EYE TOOL

Red-eye in photos of people is caused when you use the flash built in to your camera (in this case, your iPhone) and the subject's pupils are not able to adjust fast enough to compensate for the sudden burst of light that's flashed into their eyes when a photo is taken. As a result, bright red dots appear in their eyes within the photos. How close you are to your subject when the iPhone's flash is used, as well as the natural color of the subject's eyes, impacts the severity of the red-eye that winds up being captured within a photo.

NOTE If you're using the True Tone flash that's built in to the iPhone 5s with the Camera app, you'll discover that in many situations, the unwanted red-eye effect is automatically reduced and compensated for. This improved flash system, which is not available in other iPhone models, does not always eliminate red-eye altogether, however.

As you're taking photos, to reduce or eliminate red-eye, consider moving farther away from your subject and then using the zoom. You also can turn on HDR mode and turn off the iPhone's flash altogether (to utilize the existing and ambient light). If you can somehow increase the natural light where you're taking the photo, this too can help reduce red-eye when the flash is used.

However, if you wind up with the unwanted red-eye effect in your photos, which makes the person's eyes look bright red, this can also be fixed after the fact using the Red-Eye tool that's built in to the Photos app. To use this tool, load the photo that showcases the unwanted red-eye, and then tap on the Edit option. Next, tap on the Red-Eye tool. Using your finger or a stylus, tap on the subject's eyes, one at a time, directly over the unwanted red dots. The Red-Eye tool digitally fixes the image.

Unfortunately, the Red-Eye tool does not compensate for a person's natural eye color. It simply removes the unwanted bright red dots and gives your subject's eyes a darker, more natural looking appearance.

THE CROP TOOL

The Crop tool that's built in to the Photos app (and many other photography apps) is used to resize, reframe, and reposition your image after it's been taken. For example, it can be used to remove some unwanted background in an image after it has been shot, to simulate the zoom, to readjust the focal point of an image, or to change the image's dimensions.

From the Edit Photo screen, tap on the Crop tool to access it. Upon doing this, a crop grid is superimposed over your image (see Figure 6-17). Notice that the corners of the grid have darker corners. Using your finger, drag any one of these corners inward at a diagonal (toward the center of the image), or drag it upward, downward, or to the side (depending on its current position) to adjust the size and shape of the crop grid.

FIGURE 6-17

The Crop tool can be used to resize, reframe, or reposition an image. What appears in the crop grid is the portion of your image that will automatically be saved.

Whatever portion of your image that appears within the crop grid is what will be saved when you tap on the Crop option (that's found in the top-right corner of the screen).

Move around one or more of the crop grid's corners to reframe and resize your image as you see fit. It's then possible to place your finger near the center of the grid and drag it around to reposition the image itself within the grid.

> **TIP** As you're repositioning an image within the crop grid, it's also possible to use a reverse-pinch finger motion to zoom in on a portion of the image. Using this tool enables you to add a zoom effect to your photos after they've been shot, and enables you to focus in more on your intended subject. Figure 6-18 shows an image before it's been edited using the Crop tool, whereas Figure 6-19 shows that same image after it's been cropped, repositioned, and a reverse-pinch finger gesture was used to zoom in.

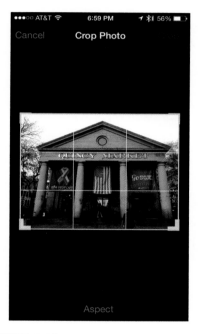

FIGURE 6-18

Here, the Crop tool has been activated but no alterations have been made to the image.

FIGURE 6-19

In the crop grid, you can hold down your finger near the center of the grid to reposition the image within the grid, and/or use a reverse-pinch finger gesture to zoom in digitally.

> **TIP** After you've reframed, resized, and/or repositioned your image using the Crop tool, tap on the Crop option (that's found in the top-right corner of the screen) to save your changes. From the same iOS mobile device, you can always reopen the cropped photo using the Photos app, access the Crop tool, and reedit the image later, even after it's been saved.

When the Crop tool is activated, the Aspect option is displayed at the bottom cen-ter of the screen. Tap on this to manually resize the image or adjust its aspect ratio accordingly, based on how you plan to use the digital image once it's been edited.

Tap on the Original option from the Aspect menu (see Figure 6-20) to retain the image's original, rectangular aspect ratio. However, if you want to change the rect-angular image and crop it into a square shape (for use on Instagram, for example), tap on the Square option.

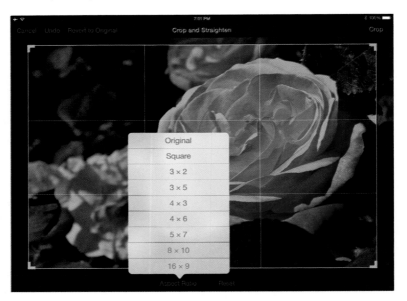

FIGURE 6-20
Adjust the aspect ratio of an image to resize it from the Aspect menu.

If you ultimately plan to create a print of the image in a specific size, such as 4" × 6", 5" × 7", or 8" × 10", select that aspect ratio from the menu. If you change the aspect ratio for a specific print size, but then attempt to make a different size print from that edited digital image, the image showcased in the print is typically dis-torted or does not fit properly within the selected print size.

> TIP Unless you need to create a specific size print, keep the aspect ratio set to Original as you use the Crop tool. Later, after the image is cropped and saved, when you attempt to create prints, you can often temporarily readjust the cropping, if needed, to compensate for the different print dimensions.

SHARE IMAGES FROM THE PHOTOS APP

The Photos app utilizes a wide range of new iOS 7 features to provide iPhone and iPad users with a greatly expanded Share menu. When you're ready to share one or more images with others, copy an image into another app, print an image, or use one of the other photo management tools offered by the Photos app, simply tap on the Share menu option or icon that's displayed.

NOTE What options are available to you from the Share menu depend on how you have your iPhone or iPad set up. For example, if you don't have an email address set up to work with the Mail app, you cannot send images via email from the Photos app. Likewise, if you don't have Facebook, Twitter, or Flickr integration already turned on in Settings, these Share options are not available to you from the Photos app.

Be sure to set up the Mail, Messages, iCloud, Facebook, Twitter, and/or Flickr integration options offered by iOS 7 from within Settings before attempting to share images via the Photos app. To set up Facebook integration, for example, launch Settings and tap on the Facebook option. When prompted, add the email address and password for your existing Facebook account so that your iPhone or iPad can then access your account from various apps, including Photos.

After tapping on the Photos, Shared, or Albums icon (displayed at the bottom of the Photos screen), depending on how you're viewing your images, either a Share option or the Share Menu icon is often available to you, as shown in Figure 6-21, Figure 6-22, and Figure 6-23.

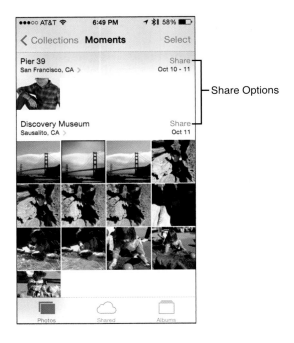

FIGURE 6-21

Shown here are the Share options displayed as part of the Moments view, accessible when you tap on the Photos icon at the bottom of the screen.

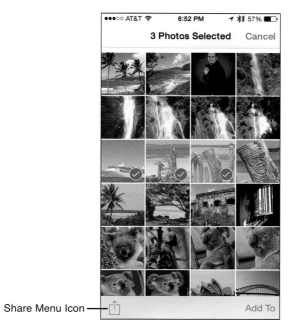

Share Menu Icon

FIGURE 6-22

Upon tapping on the Albums icon, selecting a specific album, pressing the Select option (in the upper-right corner of the screen), and then selecting one or more images in an album, the Share Menu icon becomes visible and active at the bottom-left corner of the screen (iPhone) or the top-left corner of the screen (iPad).

FIGURE 6-23

When viewing a single image, after it's been edited or enhanced, for example, the Share Menu icon is displayed near the bottom-left corner of the screen.

THE SHARE MENU

Again, depending on which iOS mobile device you're using and how you have it set up, the options available from the Share menu will vary. At the top of the Share Menu screen, you see thumbnails for one or more preselected images that are about to be shared. Selected images have a blue-and-white check mark icon displayed in the bottom-right corner of their thumbnail. From this screen, it's possible to select additional images by tapping on their thumbnails.

Below the image thumbnails (on compatible iPhone and iPad models) is the AirDrop option. If this feature is available and turned on, images can be sent wirelessly to other iOS mobile devices in your immediate vicinity. How to use this feature is explained shortly; see the upcoming "Use AirDrop to Wirelessly Share Images" section.

Beneath the AirDrop section of the Share menu is a row of icons representing the available ways you can share the selected image(s) from your iPhone or iPad. Your options may include the following:

■ **Messages**—The Photos app automatically integrates with the Messages app that comes preinstalled on your iOS mobile device. Use this option to send selected images to one or more recipients via text message or Apple's iMessage instant messaging service. Tap on the Messages option and fill in the To field, as prompted (see Figure 6-24). Tap the Send option to send the message with your selected photos embedded.

FIGURE 6-24

Send photos to one or more other people via text message or instant message using functionality built in to the Messages app. This can be done from the Photos app, without having to manually launch the Messages app.

■ **Mail**—Preselect and then email one or more recipients up to five separate images that can automatically be embedded into an outgoing email message from within the Photos app. After tapping on the Mail icon, fill in the To and Subject fields, and if you want, add some text to the body of the outgoing email message. The selected images are automatically embedded in the outgoing email (see Figure 6-25). Tap on the Send option to send the email.

FIGURE 6-25

From the Photos app, fill in the prompts displayed in the New Message screen to send out an email that contains up to five preselected images.

- **iCloud**—Select this option to add the preselected images to an existing shared photo stream (which is accessible from your iCloud account) or to create a new shared photo stream using the preselected images. How to do this is explained in Chapter 13.

- **Twitter**—With only one image selected, you can publish it online as a tweet, so it becomes part of your Twitter feed if you have a Twitter account. To do this, select one image and tap on the Twitter icon. Next, when the Twitter window appears (see Figure 6-26), add a text-based caption to your image. The character counter in the lower-left corner of the text window tells you how many characters your outgoing tweet already contains. You can use up to 140 characters per tweet. If necessary, select which Twitter account you want to send the tweet from by tapping on the Account field. Tap on the Location field to enter a location and to publicly post the location where the photo was taken along with the photo. Tap on the Post option to publish your image on Twitter.

FIGURE 6-26

Tweet one photo at a time and publish it as part of your Twitter feed, directly from the Photos app.

- **Facebook**—Using the Facebook integration built in to the Photos app, it's possible to upload one or more images from your iPhone or iPad directly to your Facebook wall. However, if you want to create albums on Facebook, you must use the official Facebook app. From the Photos app, after tapping on the Facebook icon, fill in the fields displayed as part of the Facebook pop-up window (see Figure 6-27). Tap the Post option to publish the preselected photos online. From the Facebook window, you can add a caption to the photo(s), select in which online album they'll be stored, add a location where the photos were shot, and/or choose who can view the photos on Facebook.

FIGURE 6-27

In the Photos app, select and publish one or more photos at a time directly to your Facebook wall.

- **Flickr**—If you use Flickr as an online service to store and showcase your photos, you can upload one or more preselected images from your iPhone or iPad directly to your Flickr account. This can be done from within the Photos app. Tap on the Flickr icon in the Share menu, and fill in the onscreen prompts. Once again, be sure to configure your Flickr account in Settings before attempting to use this feature.

> **TIP** For more control over how you manage your Flickr account from your iOS mobile device, be sure to install the official Flickr app. To configure your Flickr account to work with iOS 7, and/or to download the Flickr app, launch Settings, and from the main Settings menu, tap on the Flickr option.

Near the bottom of the Share Menu screen are additional command icons that enable you to utilize the selected images in a variety of ways (see Figure 6-28). Depending on how your iOS mobile device is set up, the command icons available from here may include the following:

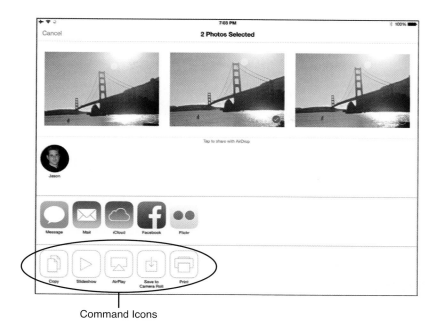

Command Icons

FIGURE 6-28

Near the bottom of the Share menu are a handful of additional command options used to manage photos from the Photos app.

■ **Copy**—Use this command to copy the selected image into iOS 7's virtual clipboard. Then, when using another app, use the Paste command to insert the image into the app you're now using. This is one way to incorporate a photo into a Pages document, Numbers spreadsheet, or Keynote digital slide presentation, for example.

■ **Slideshow**—Display selected images as an animated slideshow on your iOS mobile device's screen, or on an external HD television set if you use an optional cable. You can also use AirPlay (with an Apple TV) to showcase an animated slideshow on a television set. When you choose the Slideshow option, tap on the Transitions option to choose which animated slide transition you want to use as part of your slideshow. You can also add background music. (The music you choose must be stored on your iOS mobile device, in the Music app.)

■ **AirPlay**—Turn on and use this feature to wirelessly display individual images or animated slideshows on an HD television set via an Apple TV device.

- **Save To Camera Roll**—This option enables you to save the image in the Camera Roll folder, which is accessible using the Photos and iPhoto app, as well as many other apps that enable you to access and utilize your images. By default, the Camera Roll folder is where images you take using the Camera app are stored.

- **Assign to Contact**—Insert one selected image to be the profile photo used in a specific Contacts entry. Tap on the Assign to Contact option, from the All Contacts menu, choose which contact entry you want to associate the photo with, adjust the photo from the Move and Scale screen, and then tap on the Choose option to insert that image into the Contacts app and associate it with a specific contact.

- **Use as Wallpaper**—Use the selected image as the wallpaper image on your iPhone or iPad's Lock screen and/or Home screen. Tap on the Use as Wallpaper option, move and scale the image as needed, and then tap on the Set button. Next, select the Set Lock Screen, Set Home Screen, or Set Both option. Your new Lock screen and/or Home screen wallpaper will now be displayed.

- **Print**—If you have an AirPrint-compatible home photo printer linked to your iPhone or iPad, use this command to create prints from your digital images that are stored in your iOS mobile device. Be sure to see Chapter 11, "Create Prints from Your iPhone/iPad Photos," for complete directions on how to do this.

USE THE MAIL APP TO SEND IMAGES

It's also possible to send photos within an email directly from the Mail app. To do this, launch the Mail app and tap on the Compose icon. When the New Message screen is displayed (see Figure 6-29), fill in the To and Subject fields, and then add text to the body of your outgoing email message.

To then embed a photo within that outgoing message, press and hold your finger in the body text area of the New Message window, where you want to insert one or more images. When the menu bar appears just above where you held down your finger, tap on the right-pointing arrow icon, and then tap on the Insert Photo or Video tab (see Figure 6-30). From the Photos menu, locate the image you want to embed within the outgoing email. Upon selecting and tapping on its thumbnail, the image appears in the New Message window.

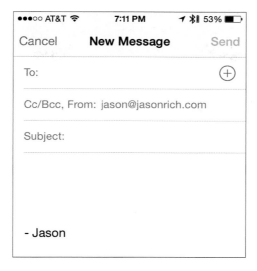

FIGURE 6-29

Launch the Mail app and select the Compose option.

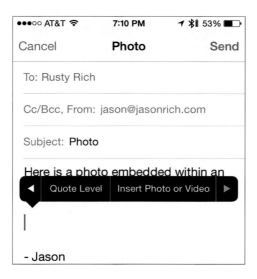

FIGURE 6-30

Tap on the Insert Photo or Video tab, and one at a time, select up to five images to embed within the outgoing email message.

You can repeat this process up to five times to embed five separate images into a single outgoing email message. When you're ready to send the message, tap on the Send option. A pop-up menu appears, asking you to choose a file size for the outgoing images. Your options include Small, Medium, Large, or Actual Size. Not only does this determine the file size of the images being sent, it also impacts what the recipient can do with the image files once received because the resolution of the photos is impacted.

For the maximum flexibility and to retain the highest resolution, leave the images at their Actual Size. This results in larger image files and takes a bit longer for you to upload and for the recipient to download.

TIP   If you're using a cellular Internet connection and trying to conserve use, select the Small option to reduce the amount of data you'll use up to send the images.

USE AIRDROP TO WIRELESSLY SHARE IMAGES

One of the new features added to iOS 7 is the capability to wirelessly send photos and certain other app-specific content to other iPhone or iPad users who are in close proximity to you. This can be done using the AirDrop feature. Keep in mind that this feature works only with the more recent iPhone and iPad models and is not compatible with the AirDrop feature offered for the Mac (as part of OS X Mavericks).

To turn on AirDrop, access the Control Center. To do this, place your finger near the bottom of the iPhone or iPad's screen and flick upward. Next, tap on the AirDrop button. A Control Center menu appears, shown in Figure 6-31, that enables you to turn on this feature, plus decide who you'll be able to use it with. Your options include Contacts Only (meaning people with entries in your Contacts database) or Everyone (meaning any iPhone/iPad user in your proximity).

When AirDrop is turned on, when you access the Share menu in the Photos app, tap on the AirDrop option. Thumbnails representing iPhone or iPad users who are nearby and who have AirDrop on their device turned on are displayed in the Share Menu screen (shown in Figure 6-32).

FIGURE 6-31

Turn on or off the AirDrop feature from iOS 7's Control Center.

FIGURE 6-32

When AirDrop is available, icons representing nearby iPhone or iPad users are displayed in your Share menu.

Preselect the images you want to send in the Photos app, and then tap on the person's thumbnail image. A wireless connection between the two devices is established. On the recipient's screen, an AirDrop pop-up window appears, asking whether he or she wants to accept or decline your images (see Figure 6-33). If the recipient taps the Accept button, the images are sent from your iOS mobile device to the recipient's device. This AirDrop pop-up window appears in the center of the screen, regardless of what the other person is currently using the device for.

FIGURE 6-33

When you send someone photos via AirDrop, a pop-up window allowing the recipient to accept or decline the images is displayed on the device's screen.

When the images are transferred, the word Sent appears on your iPhone or iPad, immediately below the other person's thumbnail. If the images are declined by the other person, the word Declined appears below that person's thumbnail.

NOTE   When sent using AirDrop, the images on your iPhone or iPad remain intact; however, the recipient receives a copy of the images on his or her own iOS mobile device.

IMPORT IMAGES INTO THE PHOTOS APP FROM YOUR DIGITAL CAMERA OR ITS SD MEMORY CARD

There are several ways to import individual images or entire albums into the Photos app. For example, images can be imported from iCloud's My Photo Stream or a shared photo stream (see Chapter 13).

TIP If one or more images are embedded within an incoming email, press and hold down your finger on those images, and then select the Save to Camera Roll option. This also works for images received via the Messages app.

To import a collection of images directly from the memory card of your point-and-shoot or digital SLR camera, you need the optional Lightning to USB Camera Adapter ($29.00), Lightning to SD Card Camera Reader ($29.99), or the Apple iPad Camera Connection Kit ($29.99). These adapters are available from Apple Stores, Apple.com, and authorized Apple dealers.

NOTE These adapters work with either the iPhone or iPad. Just make sure you purchase the right adapter, based on whether your iOS mobile device has a Lightning port or a 32-pin Dock Connector port on the bottom of it.

Attach the Lightning to USB Camera Adapter to your iPhone or iPad (if it has a Lightning port on the bottom), and then plug in the USB cable that came with your digital camera. Plug in the opposite end of the camera's USB cable to the camera itself. Turn on your digital camera and set it to Image Transfer mode. When the connection between your iPhone/iPad and your digital camera is established, follow the onscreen prompts offered by the Photos app, which includes an Import All option.

If your iPhone/iPad has a Lightning port on the bottom and your digital camera supports SD memory cards, connect the Lightning to SD Card Camera Reader to your iOS mobile device, and then insert your camera's SD memory card into the card reader. When the connection between your iPhone/iPad and your digital camera is established, follow the onscreen prompts offered by the Photos app, which includes an Import All option.

The Apple iPad Camera Connection Kit is designed for older iPhone and iPad models that have a 32-pin Dock Connector port (as opposed to a Lightning port). This kit comes with two separate adapters: one for connecting your digital camera directly to the iPhone/iPad via the USB cable that came with your digital camera, and the other for plugging in the camera's SD memory card directly to the card reader adapter that plugs into the 32-pin Dock Connector port of your iOS mobile device.

NOTE When images are imported from your digital camera or its memory card into your iPhone or iPad, the Photos app automatically splits the images into separate albums, based on the date the images were shot.

TIP For more information on how to use the optional iPad Camera Connection Kit or one of the adapters described in this section to import image files from your digital camera (or its memory card) into your iPhone or iPad, visit Apple's Support website (http://support.apple.com/kb/HT4101).

APPLE'S iPHOTO APP OFFERS EVEN MORE FUNCTIONALITY

As of November 2013, Apple's more powerful iPhoto app is available to iPhone and iPad users for free via the App Store. If you're a Mac user, you're probably already familiar with the iPhoto app. The iOS version of iPhoto offers many of the same features and functions as its Mac counterpart, including much more powerful image editing and enhancement tools. How to use the iPhoto app is the focus of Chapter 7, "Expand Your Photo Editing Toolbox with iPhoto."

EXPAND YOUR PHOTO EDITING TOOLBOX WITH iPHOTO

With the release of iOS 7, not only did Apple enhance its optional iPhoto app, which was previously sold through the App Store, but it also dropped the price of this feature-packed photography app (if you've purchased a new iPhone or iPad that runs iOS 7) to a very attractive price—free. Otherwise, the price for the app is $4.99. Meanwhile, the Mac version of iPhoto has long been a part of the iLife suite that comes bundled with all new iMacs and MacBooks.

You can use iPhoto to view, organize, edit, enhance, print, and share photos. The iOS 7 edition of iPhoto not only offers compatibility with its Mac counterpart, but it also offers many of the same features and functions as well as some useful tools that are not available from the Photos app or the Mac version of iPhoto.

NOTE The iOS 7 edition of iPhoto is now available for free from the App Store if you've purchased an iPhone or iPad with iOS 7 preinstalled. If you're using an older device, the app is priced at just $4.99. It's ideal for iPhone or iPad photographers who want access to a more robust set of tools for viewing, organizing, editing, enhancing, printing, and sharing their digital photos, but who also want the same integration to Apple's online-based iCloud service that the Photos app offers.

One of the iPhoto app's many features, which the Photos app does not include, is the capability to create a variety of photo projects from your iPhone or iPad that can be used to showcase your digital images. For example, directly from the iPhoto app, it's possible to order prints from Apple's own photo lab, and then have those professionally created prints shipped to you within a few business days. You can easily order prints in a wide range of sizes and pay for them from the iPhoto app.

In addition, the iPhoto app enables you to lay out and design photo books, and then upload them to Apple's own photo lab to be printed. Keep in mind, however, that a wide range of other apps from third parties also offer the capability to create prints, photo books, and other photo projects directly from an iPhone or iPad. You learn more about these apps in Chapter 11, "Create Prints from Your iPhone/iPad Photos."

NOTE iPhoto makes it much easier to organize your photos. In addition to sorting images into customizable albums, and then viewing them by the date and/or location they were taken, iPhoto enables mobile photographers to mark individual photos as favorites, regardless of which album they're stored in. Those favorite images can then all be viewed together. Images can also be flagged and tagged (associated with keywords), making them easier to locate quickly. How to use these features is explained shortly.

As you'll discover, the iPhoto app also works with the Camera app, and most other apps used for taking pictures with the iPhone or iPad's built-in cameras. The iPhoto app also has full access to the Camera Roll album, which is where new photos taken on your iOS mobile device are automatically saved.

> **NOTE** One of the great things about the iOS 7 edition of iPhoto is that it can fully utilize the Retina display that's built in to the latest iPhone and iPad models, including (but not limited to) the iPhone 5s, iPad Air, and iPad mini with Retina display. Thus, when you view your digital images on one of these devices, you'll see them in vivid color and with the most detail possible.

OVERVIEW OF THE iPHOTO APP

When you launch iPhoto for the first time, it automatically imports images stored in your iPhone or iPad that you previously used the Photos app to view and organize. (These images continue to be fully accessible via the Photos app.) When this process is complete, the iPhoto app's Library screen appears (see Figure 7-1).

FIGURE 7-1

The Library screen of the Photos app (with the Albums view selected) enables you to view, manage, and ultimately work with the digital images stored in your iPhone (shown here) or iPad.

iPhoto's Library screen uses the main area of your iPhone or iPad's display to show-case thumbnails of images stored in your device. How these images are organized and displayed depends on which viewing option you have selected. Displayed at the bottom center of the screen are three command icons, labeled Photos, Albums, and Projects.

Tap on the Photos option to view thumbnails of all images currently stored in your iPhone or iPad, grouped together by the month and year they were shot (see Figure 7-2). Using your finger, swipe upward or downward to view each month's collection of photos, starting with the most recent at the bottom of the display.

Year Tabs

FIGURE 7-2

This Photos view is accessible from the Library screen of iPhoto. View thumbnails representing images stored in specific albums (shown here on the iPad). In the right margin, Year tabs are displayed.

TIP As you're scrolling up or down in the Photos view, tiny Year tabs are displayed along the right margin of the screen. Tap on one of these tabs to jump to a specific year, and then view a month-by-month collection of image thumbnails taken within that year.

TIP   After tapping on the Photos icon, tap on the Search icon to quickly search through and view image thumbnails that represent photos that have been flagged, marked as a favorite, edited using iPhoto, or used in a web journal, slideshow, or photo book created with the iPhoto app. From the menu that appears, tap on the appropriate icon to re-sort the image thumbnails.

Keep in mind that you can tap on multiple options from this menu at the same time. For example, you can opt to view images that have been flagged and selected as a favorite, or images that have been both flagged and edited.

Tap on the Albums icon to sort and display thumbnails of the images sorted by the album in which they're currently saved (refer to Figure 7-1). Near the top-left margin of this screen, you see the Library label. Below it are thumbnails that represent each album that's stored on your iPhone or iPad. Below the iCloud label are thumbnails representing the albums stored online, in your iCloud account, including your My Photo Stream and your separate shared photo streams.

NOTE   When you tap on the Albums icon, any shared photo streams you've been invited to view and access by others are also displayed under the iCloud heading.

Tap on the Projects icon to view thumbnails that represent each separate project you've created using the iPhoto app, including photo books, slideshows, and web journals (see Figure 7-3). You learn how to create these various projects later in this chapter.

TIP   To begin creating a new project from scratch, tap on the New Project icon displayed at the bottom-left corner of the screen when the Projects view has been selected. A menu appears, asking whether you want to create a new web journal, slideshow, or photo book. However, if you want to view or edit an existing project, simply tap on its thumbnail in the main area of the Projects screen.

FIGURE 7-3

Each project you create in iPhoto is stored separately. Access any of them by tapping on the Projects icon.

Displayed near the bottom-right corner of iPhoto's Library screen is the Options icon (it looks like three dots lined up in a horizontal row). From this menu, you can turn on or off virtual switches associated with Wireless Beaming, plus adjust other app-related settings, manage Location Services and geotagging capabilities of the iPhoto app, plus choose which of Apple's professional labs you want to be able to place orders with, based on your location.

> **TIP** On the iPad, at the bottom-left corner of the screen, you'll discover a Help icon (shaped like a question mark). Tap on it at anytime to launch iPhoto's integrated Help feature to learn more about specific features and functions. On the iPhone, this same icon appears on many of the app's screens, but not all of them.

VIEW, EDIT, AND ENHANCE YOUR PHOTOS

One of the primary reasons why you'd want to use iPhoto with or instead of the Photos app is to utilize a more expansive toolset for editing and enhancing photos.

After tapping on the Photos or Albums icon, tap on a thumbnail that represents an album you want to view in iPhoto. Upon doing this, you'll see thumbnails for all of the images in the selected album. When the iPhone or iPad is held in Portrait mode, these images are displayed on the bottom portion of the screen (see Figure 7-4). When your iOS mobile device is held in Landscape mode, they're displayed along the left margin (see Figure 7-5). Use your finger to scroll through all images in the selected album as needed.

FIGURE 7-4

This is what you'll see when you select a single image by tapping on its thumbnail, while holding your device in Portrait mode. The number of thumbnails displayed at the bottom of the screen is adjustable.

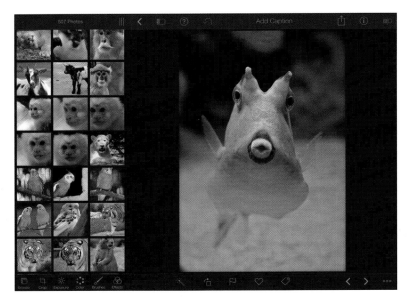

FIGURE 7-5

When you hold your iPhone or iPad (shown here) in Landscape mode, the selected image appears in the main area of the screen (on the right), while thumbnails for the rest of the images in that album are displayed along the left margin of the screen.

The Thumbnail Columns icon (which looks like three horizontal lines) can be moved to decrease or increase the number of thumbnail columns displayed at once. Drag this icon up or down (Portrait mode), or move it left or right (Landscape mode).

> TIP   Displaying two or three thumbnail columns enables you to see more thumbnails at any given time, but this takes up more onscreen real estate than displaying one or no thumbnail columns.
>
> To remove the image thumbnails from the screen altogether, tap on the Show/Hide Thumbnail Grid icon displayed along the top of the screen, between the Back and Help icons on the iPad or the Back and Share options on the iPhone.

> **TIP** To reorder the thumbnails, tap on the heading that displays the number of images in the album. A new menu enables you to sort images by the oldest or newest first, and/or using a Simple or Advanced filter.

Tap on any one image thumbnail to view a larger version of that image in the main area of the screen, and at the same time, you gain access to iPhoto's editing and enhancement tools.

As you're viewing individual images, to zoom in, double-tap on the image itself or use a reverse-pinch finger gesture. To zoom out, double-tap again on the image, or use a pinch finger gesture. Place and hold your finger somewhere on an image and drag it around to move around when viewing a zoomed-in image.

> **TIP** To close an image and return to the Library screen, use a pinch finger gesture when an image is not at all zoomed in. To view additional images in the same album, either tap on a different thumbnail or swipe a finger from right to left, or from left to right, to scroll through images and view them one at a time. On the iPad, you can also use the Forward and Back icons, displayed near the bottom-right corner of the screen as you're viewing an image, to scroll through images in an album.

WORK WITH AN INDIVIDUAL IMAGE

Once you select an individual image to work with in iPhoto, a handful of command icons become accessible along the top and bottom of the screen (see Figure 7-6). From left to right, along the top of the screen on the iPhone, these icons include Back, Show/Hide Thumbnail Grid, Share, Help, Show Original, and Options.

On the iPad, these icons include Back, Show/Hide Thumbnail Grid, Help, Undo, Add Caption, Share Menu, Show Photo Info, and Show Original (see Figure 7-7).

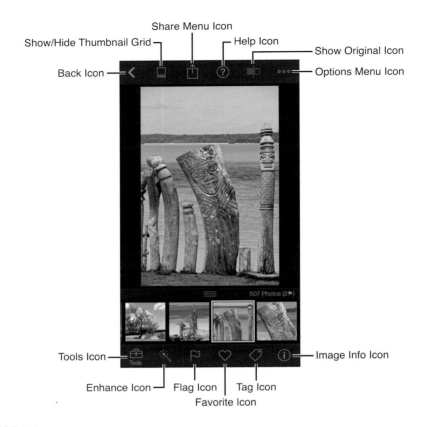

FIGURE 7-6

On the iPhone, a handful of command icons are displayed simultaneously along the top and bottom of the screen when viewing an image.

Here's a summary of what each of these icons and options is used for:

- **Filter/Sort Images**—Tap on the heading that displays the number of images in the selected album to access a menu that enables you to sort the images based on specific criteria.

- **Thumbnail Columns**—Slide this icon to determine how many rows of thumbnail columns are displayed on the screen at once.

- **Back**—Return to the Library screen of iPhoto. Whatever changes or edits made to the images you were viewing and working with are saved.

- **Show/Hide Thumbnail Grid**—Tap on this icon to display or hide the thumbnail grid.

- **Help**—Access iPhoto's interactive Help feature to learn about the app's various commands, features, and functions.

FIGURE 7-7

On the iPad, more command icons are displayed along the top and bottom of the screen than what's seen on the iPhone.

- **Undo**—Tap on this icon to undo or remove only the last edit, enhancement, or change made to an image.
- **Add Caption**—Add a text-based caption to a specific image. Ultimately, the caption you add is linked to that image.
- **Share Menu icon**—Access iPhoto's expanded Share menu, which includes options for sharing the image you're viewing via Mail, Facebook, Flickr, Twitter, Message, iTunes, Beam, or AirDrop. It's also possible to create a project (web journal, slideshow, or photo book) from this menu or export the image to your Camera Roll folder, iMovie, or another compatible app. Options displayed at the bottom of the Share menu enable you to order prints from Apple's photo lab or create prints using a home photo printer that's linked to your iOS mobile device via AirPrint.
- **Show Photo Info**—View information (metadata) that's associated with the digital image. The information displayed here varies, based on whether the image was taken using the camera that's built in to your iPhone or iPad or it was taken using a standalone digital camera, and then imported into iPhoto.
- **Show Original**—Once you've made any edits or enhancements to an image using iPhoto, tap on this icon to toggle between seeing the original (unedited) version of the image and the newly edited or enhanced version.

On the iPhone, displayed in the bottom-left corner of the screen is the Tools icon. Tap on it to reveal six additional icons that enable you to edit and enhance the image you're viewing (see Figure 7-8). On the iPad, these same six command icons are displayed in a row, near the bottom-left corner of the screen. Here's a summary of the tools accessible using each of these icons:

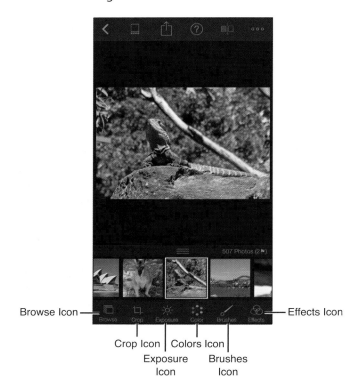

FIGURE 7-8

On the iPhone, tap on the Tools icon to reveal photo editing and enhancing tools offered by iPhoto.

- **Browse**—On the iPhone, tapping on the Browse icon toggles the menu options and command icons that are displayed along the bottom of the screen. On the iPad, tapping on the Browse icon causes the Enhance, Rotate, Flag, Favorite, and Tag icons to be displayed. These icons are replaced by other options when one of the other icons displayed near the bottom-left corner of the screen is selected.

- **Crop**—Use iPhoto's Crop tool on the photo you're currently viewing in the main area of the screen. For more information, refer to the "Use the Crop Tool" section later in this chapter.

- **Exposure**—When you tap the Exposure icon, iPhoto's Exposure slider is displayed at the bottom center of the screen. This slider has three different types of slider options in one that enable you to control the brightness, contrast, and shadows in the image separately. Slide the Brightness, Contrast, or Shadows icon to the left, along the slider, to darken the image. Move one of the icons to the right to lighten the image. Move the Brightness, Contrast, and Shadow icons around on the slider independently to achieve the desired results.

- **Color**—On the iPhone, when you tap on the Color icon, four circular color options are displayed along the bottom of the screen. From left to right, these represent Saturation, Blue Skies, Greenery, and Warmth. Tap on one icon at a time to reveal a slider used to adjust that color-related option. On the iPad, when you tap on the Color option, four separate sliders appear near the bottom center of the screen. Adjust each one separately, as needed.

  After tapping on the Color icon, the White Balance icon is displayed near the bottom-right corner of the screen. Tap on this to reveal the White Balance menu shown in Figure 7-9. This menu contains a series of icons that represent the type of natural or artificial lighting that was captured in the photo, such as direct sunlight, sunlight on a cloudy day, the iPhone's (or a digital camera's) flash, an outdoor shady area, incandescent lighting, fluorescent lighting, or underwater lighting. Choose the appropriate icon to correct the White Balance in a photo.

TIP   To adjust the skin tone on someone's face, tap on the Face Balance icon. To sample a specific gray or white area of a photo, tap on the Custom icon, and then drag the onscreen circular icon that appears to a neutral gray area in the photo and tap on the center of it.

The White Balance Menu

FIGURE 7-9

From the White Balance menu, select the type of lighting that is featured in an image to then adjust the White Balance of an image, if necessary. This allows for more accurate and authentic colors to be displayed.

NOTE When a photo is captured, the image sensor in the digital camera can't always tell when something in the photo is white, due to the natural or artificial lighting. Based on what the iPhone or iPad perceives as white, all of the other colors in an image are then adjusted accordingly. As a result, if what the camera perceives to be white is wrong, all the colors in the photo are also displayed incorrectly. Using the White Balance option to manually indicate the white area of a photo allows for this to be digitally corrected.

- **Brushes**—When editing or enhancing a photo using most of the tools offered within iPhoto (and all the tools offered in the Photos app), the tool in use automatically impacts the entire image. Using the Brushes tools available in iPhoto, it's possible to manually adjust the red-eye, contrast, saturation, and/or sharpness in specific areas of an image. Here's a rundown of the tools available from the Brushes menu:

TIP When you select one of the Brush tools, tap on the Options icon to adjust the brush's size and intensity. On the iPhone, the Options icon is displayed in the top-right corner of the screen. On the iPad, look for it in the bottom-right corner.

Also associated with the Brush tools is the Eraser icon. Tap on this to erase changes made to an image using one or more of the Brush tools. Tap on the Detect Edges icon to apply the Brush tool edits to areas of the photo that showcase the same color and lightness as the color you originally touch in the image.

■ **Repair**—Tap on the Repair option to activate the Repair Brush, and then using your finger, draw on the area(s) of an image that you want to fix. The Repair tool removes what you paint over with your finger, and then blends that area with what's around it.

TIP Use the Repair tool, for example, to remove a blemish from someone's face when editing a portrait. It can also be used to remove a small and unwanted object from a photo.

■ **Red-Eye**—When you take a photo of a person using a flash and the red-eye effect appears in the subject's eyes, use this tool to digitally remove it.

■ **Lighten**—Tap on this option, and then use your finger to paint over areas of the selected image that you want to manually lighten, such as an unwanted shadow. Tap on the Options menu to adjust the Brush settings.

■ **Darken**—Tap on this option, and then use your finger to paint over areas of the selected image that you want to manually darken. Tap on the Options menu to adjust the Brush settings.

■ **Saturate**—Use this tool to boost or enhance the colors depicted within a specific area of the selected image. Tap on the Options menu to adjust this Brush setting before applying it to an image.

■ **Desaturate**—Use this tool to decrease or lighten the intensity and vividness of the colors depicted within a specific area of the selected image.

■ **Sharpen**—If an area of an image appears slightly blurry, use this tool to digitally sharpen a portion of the image.

- **Soften**—To add a slight blur to an area of the selected image, use this tool. For example, if you're editing a portrait and you want to lighten the wrinkles on someone's face or around the eyes, yet make the photo look natural, use the Soften tool.
- **Effects**—Although the Photos app offers eight nonadjustable filters, the iPhoto app offers a vast collection of user-adjustable special effect filters. In addition to being able to select from a broader range of filters, you can adjust the intensity of each filter, plus mix and match filters when editing a single image to create a truly customized effect.

> TIP   First, tap on the selected filter option. Then, when that filter's slider is displayed, as in Figure 7-10, drag your finger left or right to decrease or increase the intensity of the filter's impact on your image.

Effect Filter Slider

FIGURE 7-10

Adjust the intensity of a selected filter using the slider that's associated with it. How you adjust this slider dramatically impacts the look of an image, based on which filter is selected.

> **NOTE** The main special effects filters available in iPhoto include Ink, Warm & Cool, Duotone, Black and White, Drama, Aura, Vintage, Camera Filters, and Artistic. Each offers several customizable adjustments, settings, or options.

On the iPhone, displayed to the right of the Tools icon are the Enhance, Flag, Favorite, Tag, and Show Photo Info icons (shown in Figure 7-11). On the iPad, the Enhance, Rotate, Flag, Favorite, and Tag icons are displayed near the bottom center of the screen. Here's a summary of what these features and functions are used for:

■ **Enhance**—With a single tap, this tool automatically adjusts the contrast, brightness, and saturation in an entire image.

The Flag and Favorite options are selected for this image.

FIGURE 7-11

The Flag, Favorite, and Tag tools can be used to help you later find and sort images. This image has been both flagged and selected as a favorite.

- **Rotate**—On the iPad, tap on this icon to rotate the selected image 90 degrees counterclockwise. Tap twice to rotate the image 180 degrees, three times to rotate the image 270 degrees, or four times to return it to its original orientation. On the iPhone, place two fingers on the screen and use a twisting motion to rotate the image.

- **Flag**—In addition to organizing your images in albums, and then being able to sort and view them by date and location, iPhoto enables you to flag individual images and then quickly locate and view flagged images. When an image has been flagged, a Flag icon appears at the bottom center of its thumbnail (see Figure 7-12), and when viewing a larger version of the image in iPhoto, the Flag icon at the bottom of the screen is bright orange.

> **TIP** When reviewing a collection of photos and choosing which ones to share with others or to create prints from, for example, one quick and easy way to highlight or set apart specific images is to flag them. To flag an image, simply select and view it, and then tap on the Flag icon once. To later remove a flag from an image, view it and again tap the Flag icon.
>
> To view all the images you have flagged, regardless of which album each is stored in, return to the Library screen, tap on the Albums icon, and then, under the Library heading, tap on the thumbnail that represents the Flagged folder. All of the flagged images are then displayed as thumbnails, as if you're looking at an album, even though the flagged images themselves might in fact be stored in different albums.

- **Favorite**—An alternative to flagging an image, in iPhoto you can add individual images to your Favorites list. To do this as you're viewing an image, simply tap on the Favorites (heart-shaped) icon. The functions available related to favorite images work much the same way as flagged images, in that you can later view them all together or quickly find images you manually set apart as one of your favorites.

- **Tag**—The Tag feature in iPhoto offers the capability to assign keyword-based tags to individual photos. It's possible to later search and display images based on individual or groups of tags. For more information about assigning and using tags in iPhoto, see the "Work with Tags to Organize and Quickly Locate Images" section later in this chapter.

- **Show Photo Info**—View information (metadata) that's associated with the digital image. The information displayed here varies, based on whether the image was taken using the camera that's built in to your iPhone or iPad or it was taken using a standalone digital camera and then imported into iPhoto.

Selected Image

Flagged Image

Edited Image

Favorited Image — Tagged Image
Selected Image Is Flagged

FIGURE 7-12

You can tell this image has been flagged because a Flag icon is displayed in its thumbnail.

> **TIP** Displayed near the top-right corner of the screen on the iPhone, and the bottom-right corner of the screen on the iPad, you'll see the Options Menu icon, which offers a handful of additional tools for editing and enhancing, or managing an image. For example, from the Options menu, you can make the selected image the key photo in an album by tapping on the Set as Key Photo option. It's also possible to delete or hide a photo, or copy and later paste Color and Effect settings between images. This can be a huge time-saver if you want to use the same collection of edits and effects on multiple images.

USE THE CROP TOOL

The Crop tool that's built in to iPhoto offers the same functionality as what's offered by the Crop tool in the Photos app, plus it enables users to straighten an image that was accidentally shot at an angle due to not holding the camera (the iPhone/iPad) straight.

When you tap on the Crop tool icon, a white frame appears around the selected image. Using the Gyro Mode dial that's displayed at the bottom of the screen, use your finger to move it left or right to tilt or straighten the image (see Figure 7-13).

FIGURE 7-13

The Crop tool that's built in to iPhoto offers more functionality than similar tools included in other apps, such as the Photos app.

> **TIP**   Another way to tilt or straighten the image is to place two fingers, slightly separated, on the image, and then rotate your fingers to the left or right.

To zoom in and reframe or recompose an image, use a reverse-pinch finger gesture. To zoom out again, use a pinch finger gesture. Once you zoom in or out, to reposition the image within the crop frame, hold down one finger on the image and drag it around.

To resize the image and/or eliminate some of the background, place your finger on any side of the white frame around the image and drag it inward. It's also possible to place your finger at one of the corners of the frame and drag inward, at a diagonal.

> **TIP** When using the Crop tool in iPhoto, to preserve the aspect ratio or select a preformatted aspect ratio to resize the image to specific measurements, tap on the More icon. It looks like three dots displayed in a horizontal row. An Aspect Ratio menu appears, allowing you to choose between a variety of common image sizes. To see all of your options, be sure to swipe horizontally when viewing this menu.
>
> When you select an aspect ratio, to select and lock it, and then be able to resize the crop grid by moving the edges of the frame, tap on the Lock Aspect Ratio icon (which looks like a padlock) after the appropriate aspect ratio is set.

While you're working with the Crop tool and readjusting the white frame around the selected image, hold down your finger anywhere outside the white frame to view the entire image, not just the portion that remains visible in the crop frame.

> **TIP** Using the Crop tool, it's easy to reframe or recompose an image after it's been shot. You can also zoom in on your subject after a picture has been taken to adjust the focal point of the image and incorporate the Rule of Thirds, for example. The Crop tool can also be used to resize an image.

Figure 7-14 shows an original image before the Crop tool was used. In Figure 7-15, the reverse-pinch finger gesture was used to zoom in, and then the image was repositioned within the frame. In Figure 7-16, some of the background of the image was removed by adjusting the crop grid. In Figure 7-17, the aspect ratio of the image was changed from its Original (default) setting to 8" × 10". As you can see, depending on how this tool is used, an image can be dramatically altered in a variety of ways.

FIGURE 7-14

An image before the Crop tool was used.

FIGURE 7-15

To zoom in on the intended subject, a reverse-pinch finger gesture was used. Then, the image was repositioned in the crop grid to incorporate the Rule of Thirds when reframing the shot.

FIGURE 7-16

Here, some of the background of the original image (shown in Figure 7-14) was removed by moving the borders of the crop grid.

FIGURE 7-17

In this example, only the aspect ratio of the original image was changed from its Original (default) setting to 8" × 10".

> TIP   As you're working with a selected image, you can incorporate some or all of the different ways the Crop tool can be utilized. This gives you a tremendous amount of flexibility to reframe or recompose your photos after they've been shot, or to compensate for the fact you accidentally held the iPhone or iPad at an angle when taking a photo.

USE THE BRUSH TOOLS

Instead of using an editing tool that fixes or impacts an entire image, the Brush tools offered by the iPhoto app enable you to edit only a specific area of an image. Plus, as you'll discover, each separate Brush tool offers the ability to adjust a specific element of the image, such as its contrast, the vividness and brightness of colors, and clarity. Using the Repair tool, elements of a photo can also be removed, such as a blemish on someone's face.

The subject shown in Figure 7-18 has unwanted blemishes on his face. Using the Repair tool, these can easily be removed (see Figure 7-19).

Unwanted Blemishes

FIGURE 7-19
Here, the Repair tool was used to remove the unwanted blemishes on the subject's face. This process took less than 15 seconds to complete.

FIGURE 7-18
Using the Repair tool, you can remove unwanted blemishes from your subject's face, or remove an unwanted item from an image.

Unlike some of the other tools built in to iPhoto, the Brush tools require a bit more time and precision to utilize effectively. Sometimes, to achieve the best results, you need to use two or more separate Brush tools in a specific area of an image to achieve natural-looking results.

When you select a specific Brush tool, whether it's Repair, Lighten, Darken, Saturate, Desaturate, Sharpen, or Soften, for example, be sure to customize the tool before you use it to alter your image. This is done by tapping on the Brush Options icon, and then using the slider that's displayed in the Brush Options window to adjust the brush size, for example. Figure 7-20 shows the available Brush Options when the Saturate tool is selected.

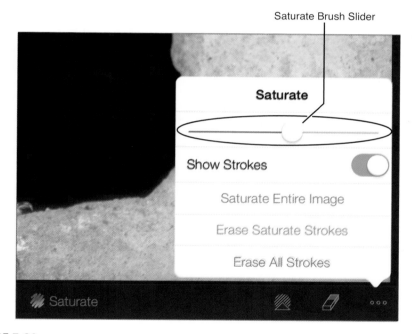

Saturate Brush Slider

FIGURE 7-20

Adjust the size of the virtual brush, as well as other options related to the Brush tool that's selected, by accessing the Brush Options menu.

TIP   The way the Brush tools were designed, they simulate a virtual paintbrush that when editing your images, you apply to a photo using your finger, as if you're finger-painting. Think of the selected Brush tool as a finger paint that's applied directly onto the image by then moving your finger around on the iPhone or iPad's touch screen over the specific areas of the selected image.

For increased precision when using any of these tools, first zoom in on the area of the image you want to edit using a Brush tool, then use the Brush Options menu to adjust the size of the brush and make it smaller. At this point, you might also consider using an optional pen-shaped stylus, instead of your finger, to apply the Brush tool and edit your image.

You learn more about optional stylus accessories that can make certain types of photo editing more accurate in Chapter 10, "Use Optional Accessories to Improve Your Pictures."

From the Brush Options menu, most of the Brush tools offer an option that enables you to quickly apply the selected tool to an entire image, as opposed to a specific area. This speeds up the photo editing process, but then overlaps with what's possible using other editing and image enhancement tools that are built in to iPhoto.

To help you see what areas of an image you've applied a Brush tool to, turn on the virtual switch associated with the Show Strokes option that's found in the Brush Options menu for many of the Brush tools. After applying a Brush tool, if you don't like how your photo looks, tap on the Erase [insert brush name] Strokes or Erase All Strokes option that's also associated with many of the Brush tools in the Brush Options menu.

NOTE It's also possible to tap on the Eraser icon, and then use it the same way you'd use a Brush tool, but to remove Brush tool effects from an area of an image by "finger-painting" over that area of the image when the Eraser is selected.

TIP An additional way to increase the precision of some Brush tools is to tap on the Detect Edges icon. Then, the Brush tool you select is only applied to nearby areas of the image that showcase the same color and lightness as where you initially touch. Again, consider zooming in to see a larger view of the area of an image you want to edit before applying a Brush tool.

As you'll discover, Brush tools give you the most flexibility when editing your images, but they're also the most difficult and time-consuming tools in iPhoto to utilize. With a bit of practice using each Brush tool, and then using some experimentation in terms of which tools work well with each other to achieve specific results, you'll soon be able to utilize professional-level photo editing techniques in the iPhoto app that were previously only available from full-featured photo editing software available on Macs and PCs.

WORK WITH TAGS TO ORGANIZE AND QUICKLY LOCATE IMAGES

As you begin using iPhoto, create a list of what will be commonly used tags, such as Vacation, Kids, Sports, Pets, Friends, Parties, and Christmas. To do this, as you're viewing any single image, tap on the Tag icon displayed near the bottom of the screen. When the Tags menu appears (see Figure 7-21), tap on the Enter New Tag field to create a new tag.

Create a new tag using the virtual keyboard.

Tap on an existing tag to link it with the photo.

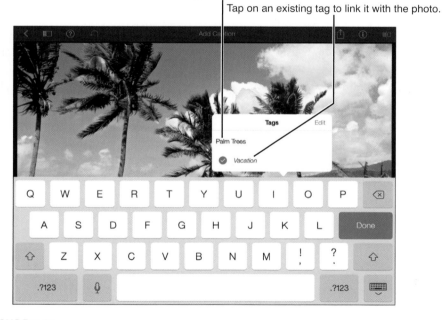

FIGURE 7-21

The Tags menu enables you to create new tags and apply specific tags to specific images. Later, you can search for and sort images based on the tags associated with them.

A tag can be any keyword or short phrase. After a tag is created, it becomes part of the app's personalized Tags menu. Now, as you're looking at photos and opt to add tags, you can quickly tap on one or more of the precreated Tag options. Each photo can have multiple tags associated with it, and you can create as many different tags as you desire.

Later, it's possible to quickly find individual images by doing a tag search. For example, you can search for all images with the tags Kids and Christmas to see your collection of holiday photos featuring your kids that were taken throughout the years.

NOTE   The tags you add to an image become part of the metadata that's stored with each image. If you later transfer an image from iPhoto on your iPhone or iPad to iPhoto on your Mac, the metadata information automatically transfers as well, so you'll be able to find images on your Mac based on keywords (tags) that were assigned to photos while using iPhoto on your iOS mobile device. Likewise, the tags associated with photos on your Mac are accessible when images are transferred, copied, or synced to iPhoto on your iPhone or iPad.

To edit your Tags list, access the Tags menu and tap on the Edit option. You can then delete individual tags or rearrange the order in which tags appear in the menu by placing your finger on a Move icon that's associated with a tag and dragging it upward or downward. By default, tags are displayed in the order they're created.

When an image is tagged, a tag thumbnail is displayed in the bottom center of its thumbnail. As you're viewing a larger version of the image, the Tag icon (displayed near the bottom center of the screen) is highlighted in blue. Tap on the Tag icon again to view which tags are associated with the photo.

TIP   To remove one or more tags from an image, as you're viewing the image, tap on the Tag icon to access the Tags menu. Tap on each tag from the menu that you want to remove. The blue-and-white check mark associated with each selected tag disappears.

SHARE AND PRINT YOUR PHOTOS

As with just about any app you use on the iPhone or iPad, when it comes to sharing app-specific content, look for the Share Menu icon or Share option and tap on it. iPhoto offers an expanded Share menu, as shown in Figure 7-22.

FIGURE 7-22

The Share menu incorporated into iPhoto offers a wide range of options for sharing individual images, groups of images, or projects.

Many of the Share menu options work just as they do when using the Photos app. Refer back to Chapter 6, "View, Organize, Edit, and Share Pictures Using the Photos App," for more information about how to use the Mail, Facebook, Flickr, Twitter, and Message options.

> TIP To wirelessly share photos with other iOS mobile device users who are in close proximity to you, one option is to use the AirDrop feature built in to iOS 7. For information on how to use this feature, refer to Chapter 6.

SYNC PHOTOS VIA iTUNES

You can sync individual photos, groups of preselected photos, or entire albums with your primary computer using the iTunes Sync process. Tap on the iTunes icon that's found in the Share menu. From the iTunes submenu, it's possible to sync just the selected image(s), or choose additional photos to sync by tapping on the Choose Photos option.

After you tap on the Choose Photos option, tap on the thumbnail for each image you want to select. A white check mark appears in each selected image thumbnail. After you've selected all the desired images, tap on the Next option. When the Share to iTunes pop-up menu appears, tap on the Export button. The selected images are then synced with iTunes running on your primary computer the next time it initiates an iTunes sync.

TIP   After tapping on the iTunes option to sync selected photos, and then tapping on the Choose Photos option, you also can select images based on a range. To do this, tap on the Range option. Then, tap on the first image thumbnail and the last image thumbnail you want to select. When you tap the Next option, all image thumbnails between the two selected thumbnails are selected. This is an alternative to tapping on each thumbnail separately.

SHARE PHOTOS USING BEAM

Although the iPhoto app supports AirDrop (which is compatible with the more recently released iPhone and iPad models) as a wireless method for transferring images between iOS mobile devices that are in close proximity, it also supports the Beam feature, which is listed in the app's Share menu.

NOTE   For the Beam feature to work, both iOS mobile devices must be connected to the same wireless network via Wi-Fi, or both devices need to have Bluetooth turned on and be within range of one another. Using this feature, you can begin editing a photo on your iPhone, for example, and then quickly transfer it to your iPad and pick up exactly where you left off.

To use Beam, tap on the Beam option, select the photos you want to send, and then wait for your iOS mobile device to locate other compatible devices. These devices are displayed on the screen. Tap on the device to which you want to send the images. The recipient receives a message in a pop-up window asking if he or she wants to accept the images. If the recipient taps on the Yes button, the images are wirelessly transmitted to the recipient's device and saved.

A Beam Completed message appears on your device when the transmission is finished.

TIP   To export one or more images from iPhoto to your Camera Roll folder, tap on the Camera Roll icon that's displayed under the Apps heading in the Share menu. To select additional images to export, tap on the Choose Photos option.

Likewise, if you want to export images into the iMovie app (assuming iMovie is installed on your iPhone or iPad), tap on the iMovie icon. It's also possible to easily export selected image(s) you're working with in iPhoto into a compatible third-party photography app.

To do this, tap on the Other App icon. Select the image(s) you want to export using the Choose Photo option. Then, when the menu appears displaying the compatible apps you have installed on your iOS mobile device (see Figure 7-23), select the app to which you want to export the selected image(s) by tapping on the app's thumbnail.

FIGURE 7-23

Select a compatible app that's installed on your iPhone or iPad to which you want to export the selected photo(s).

CREATE PRINTS FROM iPHOTO

When it comes to creating traditional prints from your digital images stored in iPhoto, the app offers two main options from within the Share menu. Tap on the

Order Prints option to select prints and print sizes, and then order prints to be created by Apple's own photo lab. After selecting one or more images, the Choose Format & Size screen appears. Tap on Auto-Sized, Traditional, Square, or Poster to see individual print size options and prices for each category. Then, tap on the print size you want to order (see Figure 7-24).

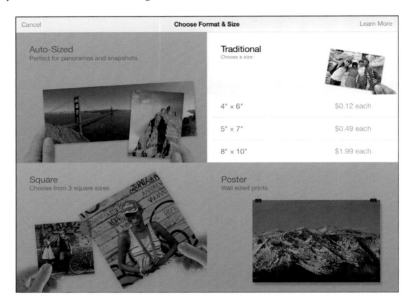

FIGURE 7-24

From directly within the iPhoto app, you can order prints from Apple's own photo lab. Prints can be created in a variety of sizes.

From the Review Your Prints screen, use the virtual switch to turn on or off the Glossy Finish option. Tap on the Price icon to complete your order. Select your Ship To address when prompted. You can enter your own address, or choose any address from an entry in your Contacts database. Review your order details displayed in the Checkout screen, and tap Place Order to finalize your order. Keep in mind that a shipping and handling fee is applied to each order.

TIP   When purchasing prints, select the Glossy finish if you plan to display your prints alone or in a photo album or scrapbook. If the images will be framed behind glass or clear plastic, the Glossy finish is not needed. When a print with a Glossy finished is placed behind glass, it can create unwanted glares or make the image look too shiny.

When prompted, enter your Apple ID password in the Sign In With Your Apple ID window to complete the order. The credit/debit card that's associated with your Apple ID will be charged for the prints. Within a few business days, the prints will be shipped and ultimately arrive at the designated address.

> **TIP** Instead of using Apple's own photo lab to create professional-quality prints, there are a wide range of third-party apps you can use for this purpose. Chapter 11 offers more information about these apps and photo lab options, which include Shutterfly, Costco, and FreePrints. Later in this chapter, you'll also discover how to use an AirPrint-compatible home photo printer to create your own prints from the images stored in your iPhone or iPad.

CREATE WEB JOURNALS TO SHOWCASE YOUR PHOTOS

Web journals are one of the projects that can be created directly from iPhoto on your iPhone or iPad and used as a way to showcase groups of images via the Internet (see Figure 7-25) or on your iPhone or iPad's own screen. To create a new web journal, tap on the Share Menu icon and select the Web Journal option that's found under the Create a Project heading.

> **NOTE** A web journal offers an alternative to using individual prints, a slide-show, a traditional online gallery, a photo album, or a photo book to showcase a group of related images in a visually interesting way. This is a feature that's unique to the iPhoto app.

Next, select the images you want to include in the web journal. These can be images from a particular album or images from several different albums that you've flagged or otherwise preselected. You'll then be asked whether you want to include the selected photos in an existing web journal that's already been cre-ated, and if so, which one, or whether you'd like to create a new web journal from scratch.

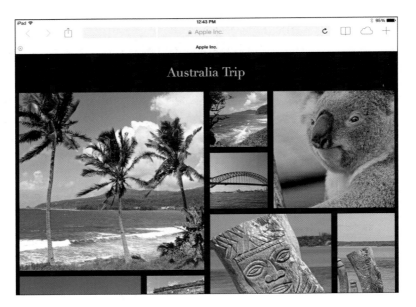

FIGURE 7-25

This web journal was created using iPhoto on an iPad, but then shared online via iCloud and made available to invitees using any web browser (shown here on an iPad running Safari).

> TIP   To create a new web journal from scratch, tap on the New Web Journal option. This can be done from the Share menu or by tapping on the Projects option displayed near the bottom center of the Library screen, and then by tapping on the New Project icon (which looks like a circle with a plus sign in it), followed by the Web Journal option.

If you opt to create a new web journal, the next menu asks you to enter a title for your web journal and select a theme for it. Your theme options include Cotton, Border, Denim, Light, Dark, and Mosaic. Tap on the Create Web Journal to continue.

When iPhoto processes your web journal based on your selected images and the theme option you've selected, a pop-up window appears that says, "Web Journal Created." It also displays the name of the web journal and how many photos it contains. Tap on the Show button to view your web journal.

EDIT A WEB JOURNAL

Simply creating a web journal is easy and takes just a few seconds. However, you can invest a little more time and fully customize its appearance by manually adjusting the size and layout related to how each image is showcased. To do this, as you're viewing the web journal on your iPhone or iPad, tap on the Edit option.

Next, one at a time, tap on each image. A blue border appears around the selected image (see Figure 7-26). You then have the option to resize the image. To drag it to another location, double-tap on the image. When a white left and right arrow appears in the image, use your finger to drag it to a new location in the web journal.

FIGURE 7-26

Control the size and location of each image displayed in a web journal. The image you're working with will have a blue resizable frame around it.

TIP To resize an image, in Edit mode, place your finger on one of the blue dots that appear on the blue frame that surround the selected image and drag it up, down, left, right, or at a diagonal. To add a text-based caption to an individual photo, tap on the Add Caption option that's displayed near the bottom center of the image.

Figure 7-27 shows an image immediately after it was imported into a web journal, whereas Figure 7-28 shows the same image after is was resized, repositioned, and reordered.

FIGURE 7-27

This is how an image looked immediately after being imported into a web journal.

FIGURE 7-28

The same image after it was resized, repositioned, and reordered. This is just a sampling of what's possible.

TIP To truly customize your web journal, while in Edit mode, tap on the More Options icon (which looks like three dots displayed horizontally). From here, you can select a different theme, adjust the grid size, autosort the selected images, and choose a different layout. Tap on the Add icon to incorporate other elements to your web journal.

ADD ADDITIONAL ELEMENTS TO YOUR WEB JOURNAL

Beyond just displaying photos with captions in a collage-like format, by tapping on the Add icon, it's possible to incorporate additional elements to a web journal to make it more visually appealing, better organized, and informative. The Add menu, shown in Figure 7-29, offers 15 different options.

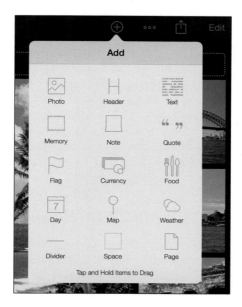

FIGURE 7-29

The Add menu enables you to incorporate a variety of optional elements into a web journal.

For example, tap on the Header option to add additional headlines to your web journal, beyond the main headline that displays the title, and that by default is seen at the top center of the web journal.

By tapping on the Text icon, it's possible to easily add a box in the web journal that can contain text. You can decide on the size of the text box, and then determine how much text will be included, as well as customize the appearance of the text.

Once a text box is created, it can be treated like a photo in the web journal and later repositioned or resized as you desire.

NOTE The Memory option enables you to create a text box, but then displays your text with a different background that looks like a torn sheet of paper. Meanwhile, the Note option gives you the opportunity to include what looks like yellow sticky notes in a web journal. By tapping on the Quote option, your text appears in large quotation marks, which is another way to format and display text in a web journal. Figure 7-30 shows examples of a Text Box, Memory, Note, and Quote after they've been added to a web journal.

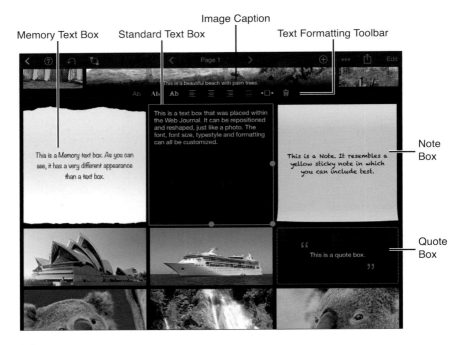

FIGURE 7-30

iPhoto offers a variety of ways to include text in a web journal. When you're creating or editing text, the text formatting toolbar is accessible.

If you do a lot of traveling and ultimately use web journals to show off your vacation photos, tap on the Flag option to embed a graphic of a country's flag. By default, iPhoto utilizes the geotag information associated with your photos and chooses the flag based on where the images were taken. However, by double-tapping on the flag graphic once it's placed, you can turn off the virtual switch that's associated with the Auto selection option, and then manually choose which flag to display.

> **TIP** To display a detailed map and showcase exactly where the selected photos in your web journal were taken, tap on the Add icon, and then choose the Map option. When the map is placed, you can resize the map, plus zoom in or out to determine what information is displayed (see Figure 7-31). To do this, use a reverse-pinch (zoom) or pinch (zoom out) finger gesture.

FIGURE 7-31

Adding a customizable map to your web journals graphically shows where images were taken.

Also from the Add menu, it's possible to add further customizations to the appearance of the web journal. To do this, the Divider, Space, and Page options are available. From the Add menu, drag the Divider option onto your web journal layout and position it where you want it displayed. This drag-and-drop method also works with any of the elements that can be added from the Add menu.

TIP   If you want to give your web journal more of a traditional journal-like feel, tap on the Add icon and then select the Day option. A date graphic is added to your web journal that displays the day, month, and year the images were taken or that the web journal was created. After the Day graphic is placed, double-tap on it to customize the date information (refer to Figure 7-31).

Another way to make your web journal more journal-like is to add a graphic that displays the weather when the photos were taken. To do this, tap on the Add icon and select the Weather option. Then, when the Weather graphic is displayed, double-tap on it to customize the information it displays.

PUBLISH YOUR WEB JOURNAL

After you've done the layout and design work that goes into creating a web journal, it is saved in the iPhone or iPad you're using and can then be viewed at any time on your own device from within iPhoto. However, the true purpose of this feature is to allow you to share groups of images with other people. To achieve this, tap on the Share Menu icon and then choose iCloud, iTunes, Beam, or AirDrop as your sharing method. If you choose iCloud, the process for publishing your web journal is similar to creating and sharing a shared photo stream.

Tap on the iCloud option that's found in the Share menu, and then when prompted, customize the options found in the iCloud menu that's displayed. Your web journal is published online, as part of your free iCloud account. You then have the opportunity to decide exactly who will be invited to view your web journal and whether your invitees will be able to view it using just iPhoto or from any web browser.

NOTE   This process works very much like publishing a shared photo stream, which you learn how to do in Chapter 13, "Discover iCloud's My Photo Stream and Shared Photo Stream."

NOTE   Sharing a web journal using the iTunes, Beam, or AirDrop option works exactly the same way as you'd use these features to share individual photos while using iPhoto. Refer to the "Share and Print Your Photos" section earlier in this chapter.

What's great about the Web Journal feature iPhoto offers is that you can create a professional-looking web journal and share it online with others in less than a minute or two. However, you also have the option of investing a bit more time to fully customize each web journal to create something that looks fantastic and unique.

SHOWCASE DAZZLING ANIMATED SLIDESHOWS USING iPHOTO

Long gone are the days when 35mm slides were used with a slide projector to create and present slide presentations to an audience. Today, slideshows are 100 percent digital. For example, PowerPoint or Keynote can be used to create business-style slideshow presentations that can incorporate your digital images. However, if you want to showcase a group of your digital photos, this can more easily be done from within iPhoto by creating an animated slideshow.

An animated slideshow created in iPhoto can include a group of images that you select, combined with titles, captions, animated slide transition effects, and background music. The end result is a presentation of your images that's visually pleasing and professional looking, but that's also fully customizable.

The slideshow you create can then be presented on your iPhone or iPad's screen. It's also possible to connect your iOS mobile device directly to an HD television set or projector to present your images to an audience. To accomplish this, you need optional adapters from Apple. Using the Apple TV device, it's possible to wirelessly present an animated slideshow on an HD television set or monitor without the need for additional cables or adapters.

You can share the same digital slideshow you create using iPhoto online via iCloud so other iOS mobile device users (who also use iPhoto) or anyone with a web browser, including Mac and Windows PC users, can view it.

> TIP To create a slideshow from scratch using iPhoto, either tap on the New Project icon and select the Slideshow option, or while viewing an image, tap on the Share Menu icon, and then select the Slideshow option that's displayed below the Create a Project heading.

When you opt to create a slideshow, you need to select exactly which photos will be featured. After you select the images, they are displayed as thumbnails on the iPhoto screen. Along the top of the Slideshow editing screen are a handful of command icons used for customizing and presenting the slideshow (see Figure 7-32).

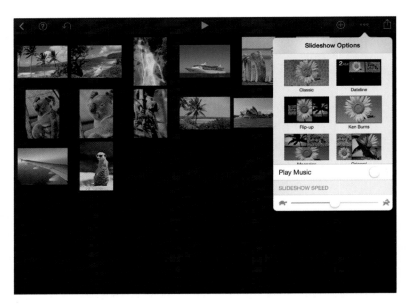

FIGURE 7-32

*From this Slideshow editing screen, you can create, edit, and manage slideshows that feature
your own collection of preselected images. From the menu shown, choose the desired slide transitions and adjust other customizable options.*

From left to right on the iPhone, you see the Back (<), Help, Play, Add, Options,
and Share icons. On the iPad, you find the Back button icon (<), which returns you
to iPhoto's main Library screen, followed by the Help button and the Undo icon.
Displayed at the top center of the screen is the Play icon. Tap Play to view your animated slideshow presentation.

> TIP   To reorder the slides in your presentation, from the Slideshow editing
> screen, place your finger on an image thumbnail and drag it to a new location.

> TIP   As a presentation is playing, tap on the screen to access onscreen controls,
> which include a Back icon (to return to the Slideshow editing screen), Time slider,
> Volume Control slider, as well as Rewind, Pause, and Fast Forward icons.

To add additional photos to your slideshow, tap on the Add icon. However, if you want to edit or delete a photo, double-tap on an image's thumbnail while viewing the Slideshow editing screen, and then tap on the Edit or Trash Can option.

Displayed near the top-right corner of the Slideshow editing screen is the Slideshow Options Menu icon. Tap on this to choose your animation slide transition, whether you want to include background music as part of your presentation, and to set your slideshow speed (which determines how much time each slide is seen before transitioning to the next slide).

TIP The Slideshow Options menu includes a dozen different slide transition formats to choose from. Simply tap on your option (refer to Figure 7-32). Then, move the Slideshow Speed slider left to slow down the speed at which slides are presented, or move it to the right to increase the slideshow speed.

Adding background music to a slideshow is also an easy process. Any music that's already stored on your iPhone or iPad can be selected and used as slideshow background music, including music purchased from the iTunes Store or music composed using GarageBand.

TIP To add music to your slideshow, access the Slideshow Options menu and turn on the virtual switch that's associated with the Play Music option. When the Music field appears in the Slideshow Options menu, tap on it to select one of the preinstalled instrumental music tracks built in to the iPhoto app, or tap on the My Music option to select music that's currently stored in the Music app. Choose a music selection that helps set the mood, based on the types of images you're showcasing.

After your slideshow is created and saved in iPhoto, you can view or present it from within iPhoto or opt to share it with others via iCloud, Beam, or AirDrop. The slideshow can also be synced using the iTunes Sync process and viewed on your Mac or PC. All of these options are accessible by tapping on the Share Menu icon that's displayed at the top-right corner of the Slideshow editing screen within iPhoto.

NOTE Be sure to read Chapter 12, "Share Your Digital Photos Online," as well as Chapter 14, "Other Ways to Share Your Digital Photos," to learn more about the different ways you can share a slideshow with others and/or present a slideshow to an audience.

Keep in mind that you can create digital slideshows that feature your photos using the Photos app, as well as many third-party apps. Each offers a different set of tools and features, as well as a different collection of themes and slide transitions, for example, that allow you to fully customize your presentation.

DESIGN YOUR OWN PHOTO BOOKS

Creating a photo book, which will ultimately be professionally printed as a book and shipped to you from the printer, is yet another way to showcase and share a group of images. In recent years, the on-demand photo book printing process has advanced tremendously, while the cost to create these books has dropped significantly.

NOTE Chapter 14 discusses a handful of additional options, services, and apps that can be used to create professional-looking photo books either directly from your iPhone or iPad or using the images taken with the camera(s) built in to your iOS mobile device(s).

When you opt to create a photo book from within the iPhoto app, the book you design on your iPhone or iPad's screen will ultimately be uploaded to Apple's own photo book printing service, be printed and bound as a book, and then shipped to the address you provide typically within a week or so.

NOTE Regardless of whether you use Apple's photo book printing service or another service from a company such as Shutterfly or Blurb, for example, the cost of your book will vary based on whether you choose to create a hardcover or softcover book, how many pages the book contains, and the trim size of the book. In some cases, the paper quality you select, the number of books you order, and other customizable options also impact pricing.

The benefits to creating a photo book using iPhoto include that you can design, upload, and order the photo book directly from your iOS mobile device, plus it's possible to pay the printing and shipping costs using the credit/debit card that's already associated with your Apple ID account. Additionally, there's no need to first export your images out of the iPhoto app, and then import into another app to design the photo book.

> **CAUTION**   Using the iPhoto app to create photo books offers a few draw-backs as well. For example, other photo book printing companies offer more options, such as the ability to choose between hardcover or softcover books, which are available in many different trim sizes. The various other photo book printing companies also offer their own collection of page templates (some of which can be fully customized), as well as different paper quality options. You'll also discover third-party companies that offer lower photo book printing prices than what Apple charges.
>
> For example, the TimeBox app offers a quicker and cheaper way to create photo books that offer fewer customizable options, whereas the Blurb.com photo book service offers many more customizable options for creating a higher-quality photo book.

From within iPhoto, the photo book creation and ordering process is relatively straightforward. When you tap on the Create Project icon, the Photo Book menu appears. From here, you select the book's trim size; your options include 8" × 8" or 10" × 10". You also select an overall theme for the book.

When you then tap on the Create Photo Book option, the My Photo Book screen appears (see Figure 7-33). This includes empty page templates that compose what, by default, will be a 20-page printed book. Using the menu options and command icons displayed on the My Photo Book screen, you can then customize each page template, change the order of pages, and ultimately insert your photos into each template.

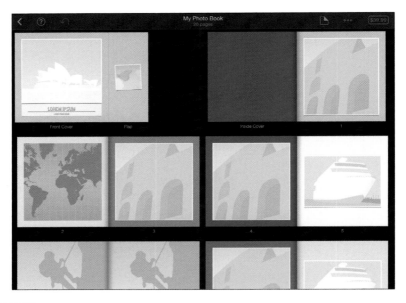

FIGURE 7-33

This is one of the screens you'll see when creating or editing a photo book. Shown here are the page thumbnails that currently make up a 20-page book.

TIP   As you're looking at the My Photo Book screen, tap on a page template to select it. Then, you can move that page to a different location by dragging it on the screen. It's also possible to zoom in or out on the page thumbnail using a reverse-pinch or pinch finger gesture.

To edit and customize a page template and add photos to it, double-tap on the template. It is then displayed utilizing the entire screen, with command icons displayed along the top of the screen (see Figure 7-34).

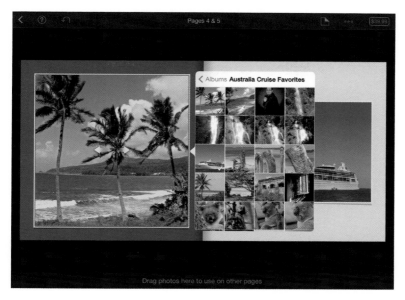

FIGURE 7-34

As you're putting together your photo book, you can work with and customize one page, or one two-page spread at a time.

> TIP   Along the bottom of the screen is a storage area where you can drag and drop images that you want to use elsewhere within your photo book. However, as you're looking at a page template, tap on one of the photo frames (placeholders) on the virtual page to access the Add Photo option and select the image you want to place in that location. Once an image is placed, you can then edit, zoom, and reposition it as needed within that frame.

The trick to making a well-designed photo book is to select photos that best tell a story, and then choose an applicable theme and color scheme. Also, make sure the images that feature a subject oriented in a certain direction are always positioned so they're facing into the book's center spine, as opposed to off the page. An example of this appears in Figure 7-35, whereas an example of photos that are oriented in the wrong direction on the page is shown in Figure 7-36.

Two-Page Photo Book Spread

Center Spine of the Book

FIGURE 7-35

Shown here is a two-page layout in a photo book where the images are oriented so they're facing toward the center of the book.

FIGURE 7-36

In this example, the images are oriented so they're facing in the wrong direction, which ultimately takes away from the professional design of the book.

As you're creating your photo book, tap on the New Page icon to add a page to the book and choose the page template you want to use. Keep in mind that iPhoto offers single-page templates as well as multipage spreads to choose from. This enables you to spread one photo, or a selection of photos, across two pages (see Figure 7-37).

FIGURE 7-37

An example of how one image can be spread over two full pages when designing a photo book. This type of layout works particularly well with panoramic shots (that is, landscapes, city skylines, wide-angle shots, and/or photos of large groups).

TIP   On page layouts where the photo doesn't take up an entire page, you can select a background color to be displayed. To do this, as you're looking at a page thumbnail, tap on the Add Page icon, tap on the Background option, and then select your desired background color from the Background menu. From a visual continuity standpoint, it's usually a good idea to use the same background color throughout a photo book, or at least on individual, two-page spreads.

As you go through the process of designing your unique photo book, the iPhoto app continuously displays the price for printing the book, based on the current number of pages and selected options. The price is displayed at the top-right corner of the screen, in a Price button (see Figure 7-38). When you're finished designing your photo book, tap on this Price button to begin the ordering process, which is very much like ordering prints from the iPhoto app.

Photo Book Price Button

FIGURE 7-38

The iPhoto app keeps track of how much printing your photo book will cost. Tap on this Price button when you're finished creating the book and you're ready to order one or more copies of it.

It's important to understand that photo books that are designed using iPhoto can only be printed using Apple's own photo book printing service. If you want to use another photo book printing service, you must either export your photos into another photo book creation app or upload your pictures to an online-based photo book design and printing service.

CAUTION When ordering prints or photo books from the iPhone app, pay attention to any warning messages that appear as you go through the ordering process. You will be notified if the resolution of an image, how an image is sized, or some other aspect of an image isn't suitable for printing, or in the case of photo books, if you've made an error when formatting or designing specific pages or using various templates. Be sure to fix these errors before completing the ordering process.

If you accidentally place an order from Apple's photo lab, but discover a problem within an hour after the order has been completed, it's often possible to access Apple's website to change or cancel the order, before it has been processed.

NOTE Some photo book printing services, including Blurb, allow you to create a printed photo book, and at the same time, order an eBook version of your photo book, which is fully compatible with the iBooks app. Thus, you can store your photo books in your iOS mobile device and view them anytime using iBooks.

MORE REASONS TO USE iPHOTO

In addition to all of the additional features and functions that iPhoto offers beyond what's possible using the Photos app, while still maintaining full compatibility with iCloud, one of the great things about using iPhoto to edit and enhance photos is the Undo option.

Regardless of what feature or function you use to edit or enhance a photo, if the result is not to your liking, simply use the Revert, Remove, or Reset command, or tap on the Undo icon. On the iPhone or iPad, the Revert, Remove, or Reset command can typically be found when you tap on the Options Menu icon to reveal the Options menu related to a particular feature or function. On the iPad, there's also the Undo icon, which can typically be found among the command icons at the top of the screen.

TIP No matter what you're doing in the iPhoto app, to go back to the previous screen, tap on the Back (<) icon that's typically displayed near the top-left corner of the screen. When you do this, unless otherwise notified, your work is automatically saved.

In other words, anytime you're working with a photo, you always have the option of quickly and easily undoing the last thing you did, removing a specific effect, or getting rid of the changes made to an image as the result of using a particular editing tool. Thus, you're totally free to experiment by mixing and matching the use of various iPhoto tools to create the most visually impressive image possible, without running the risk of making mistakes you can't easily recover from.

8

PHOTOGRAPHY APPS THAT ENHANCE YOUR PICTURE-TAKING CAPABILITIES

As you know, the Camera app comes preinstalled with iOS 7 and can be used to control the front- or rear-facing cameras that are built in to your iPhone or iPad.

In Chapter 2, "Snap Photos Using the Camera App," you learned all about how to use the Camera app and its various features. However, available from the App Store are a wide range of third-party apps that offer feature-packed alternatives to the Camera app when it comes to taking pictures with your iOS mobile device.

TIP   To discover more apps that can be used instead of the Camera app, enter the search phrase Camera. From the search results, choose apps that offer photography and picture-taking features that you find useful. Tap on the app's Price button to download and install the app, or tap on the app's title or logo to read a more detailed description of the app.

Many of these third-party apps can be used with the optional clip-on lenses, tripods, external lights, and other accessories that you'll learn more about in Chapter 10, "Use Optional Accessories to Improve Your Pictures." For example, if you want to use the Camera! Awesome app's Interval Timer, or if you want to capture a clear, 360-degree panoramic photo using the Cycloramic app, using an optional tripod to hold your iPhone or iPad still and level would be extremely beneficial.

NOTE   This chapter focuses on third-party apps that can be used as an alternative to the Camera app for taking pictures. Chapter 9, "Photography Apps That Expand Your Photo Editing and Enhancement Capabilities," showcases a handful of apps that can be used instead of the Photos or iPhoto app to edit and enhance the pictures taken with or being stored on your iOS mobile device.

CAMERA APP ALTERNATIVES

This section showcases a handful of third-party photography apps, listed in alphabetical order, which you can use instead of the Camera app.

TIP   With the greater selection of photography features and functions available to you as you're taking pictures using a third-party app, you might discover you're inspired more from a creative standpoint when it comes to capturing your subject(s) in visually interesting ways, and also when it comes to framing and composing your shots.

As you're about to discover, using a third-party picture-taking app often gives you access to extremely useful and powerful photography features, like a self-timer, a larger selection of filters that can be applied in real time to images while you're shooting, different ways to capture light, or the ability to utilize the camera lenses that are built in to your iPhone or iPad a bit differently. All of these additional tools can be used to enhance the professional quality or visual appeal of the photos you take using your iOS mobile device.

NOTE The majority of the third-party photography apps can control the front- and rear-facing cameras that are built in to your iPhone or iPad, as well as utilize the iPhone's built-in flash. Most of these apps automatically store your photos in the Camera Roll folder that's also utilized by the Photos and iPhoto apps for storing photos, and they're compatible with a wide range of third-party photo editing apps. Keep in mind that before third-party apps can access your device's Camera Roll folder, you must initially grant the app permission to do so. This needs to be done only once.

CAMERA PLUS

This $0.99 app adds a handful of useful autofocus modes to the iPhone or iPad's picture-taking functionality, which gives photographers the added ability to high-light their intended subject(s). For example, as you're preparing to take a photo and tapping on your subject to select where the autofocus sensor should lock on to, you can choose from several different AF modes, based on your proximity to your subject and whether you want some of the background to be blurred.

Using the Lumy feature that's built in to the app and continuously displayed in the viewfinder as you're taking pictures, it's possible to make an image brighter using a controllable slider (see Figure 8-1). This is particularly useful when shooting in low-light situations. To quickly reset the brightness setting, double-tap on the slider.

Like the Camera app, the Flash controls for the iPhone appear in the top-left corner of the screen, whereas the Camera Selection icon is found at the top-right corner of the screen. As you're preparing to take a photo and looking through the viewfinder (your iPhone or iPad's screen), it's possible to tap on the Grid icon to superimpose a tic-tac-toe-like grid over the viewfinder to utilize the Rule of Thirds. (This grid does not appear in your actual photos.)

Level Indicator

Brightness Slider

Menu Button

FIGURE 8-1

The viewfinder view of the Camera Plus app. From this screen, you can frame your image, adjust various feature-related settings, and snap your photos.

From the viewfinder screen of the Camera Plus app, tap on the Menu icon that's displayed to the right of the Shutter button to turn on and utilize additional picture-taking features, such as image stabilization, a Burst shooting mode, and/or a self-timer (see Figure 8-2).

TIP   Anytime you (the photographer) are in motion and can't hold the iPhone or iPad perfectly still while taking a picture, activate the Image Stabilization feature to help ensure that you'll capture an in-focus and sharp photo. For example, if you're in a car or on a boat or bus that's moving, use Image Stabilization to compensate for that movement.

FIGURE 8-2

Tap on the Menu icon to reveal the Camera Plus app's menu. From here, you can easily adjust a variety of options by tapping on the displayed command icons.

Another useful feature that's available as you're taking pictures using the Camera Plus app is the Level Gauge. Tap on the icon for this. You'll see it near the top center of the viewfinder screen, and an onscreen Level Gauge is superimposed in the center of the viewfinder (see Figure 8-3). This feature helps to ensure you're holding your iPhone or iPad level as you're taking pictures.

FIGURE 8-3

The app's built-in Level Gauge helps ensure you're holding your iPhone/iPad perfectly level when taking a picture. This is useful if you're standing at an angle or you (as the photographer) are in motion.

Also available from the app's menu screen is the Geotag feature. It's used to add the location where the picture was shot to the image's metadata. Plus, you can manually adjust the resolution of the image as you're shooting (which impacts its file size).

In general, you always want to shoot photos at the highest resolution possible. You can always make a copy of the image later and, while working with the copy, reduce its resolution, shrink its file size, or make other edits.

After you've taken some photos, Camera Plus has several built-in editing and enhancement features that go beyond what's possible using the Photos app's Enhance feature.

> **TIP** Anytime you're using the Camera Plus app, mildly shake the iPhone (or iPad) to quickly launch the Camera mode so you can begin snapping photos. This is a quick way to switch from the app's image Viewing, Editing, or Sharing mode back to the Picture-taking mode, without having to tap anywhere on the screen.

Like the Camera app, Camera Plus immediately displays a tiny thumbnail of the last image you've shot. It's displayed near the bottom-right corner of the screen. Tapping on this thumbnail icon enables you to view and work with images stored in your device's Camera Roll folder. As you're viewing photos, use the Pix'd feature to quickly enhance an image. This feature works just like the Camera app's Enhance feature to automatically adjust things like contrast, brightness, and color saturation within the image to improve its appearance. Beyond using the one-tap Pix'd feature, however, you can tap the Edit icon to access an additional selection of image editing and cropping tools.

From directly within the Camera Plus app, images taken using the app or that are stored in your iOS mobile device can be shared via Facebook, Twitter, Flickr, Instagram, the Messages app, or email (using the Mail app).

> **NOTE** The Camera Plus app can also be used for shooting HD video.

In addition to offering a handful of useful picture-taking and image enhancement features that are not available from the Camera and Photos apps, Camera Plus is surprisingly easy to use, and it offers an intuitive interface that you'll have no trouble getting used to, especially if you're already familiar with the Camera app. For less than $1.00, this app is an excellent investment if you're interested in expanding your iPhone or iPad's picture-taking capabilities.

> **TIP** If there are photos you want to "lock up" within your device, making sure
> they can't be accidentally deleted or viewed by unauthorized people, the Camera
> Plus app offers an in-app purchase (for an additional $0.99), which adds a Lock func-
> tion to the app. It's accessible (by tapping on the lock-shaped icon) when viewing or
> editing an image. Another feature that becomes available with this in-app upgrade is
> the ability to wirelessly beam photos to other iOS mobile devices that are connected
> to the same wireless network.

CAMERA! AWESOME

The free Camera! Awesome app, shown in Figure 8-4, also offers a handful of features not offered by Apple's Camera app. As you're looking at the viewfinder screen
of the Camera! Awesome app, command icons are displayed along the top and bottom of the display.

FIGURE 8-4

*The viewfinder screen of the Camera! Awesome app from SmugMug. This is the screen you'll see
as you're actually taking pictures using this app.*

NOTE   The Camera! Awesome app was developed by SmugMug (www.SmugMug.com), which is a popular online-based photo sharing and image backup service used by amateur and professional photographers alike. A basic SmugMug account, which is not required to use the app, is free. However, premium (fee-based) accounts are also available.

Near the top-left corner of the screen is the gear-shaped Settings icon. Tap on it to reveal the app's Settings menu. From here, you can turn on or off various options that relate directly to picture-taking features, such as the ability to automatically add a geotag (location information) to each picture taken. It's also possible to decide whether a pinch finger gesture will activate the app's zoom feature.

TIP   From the Settings menu, be sure to scroll down and then set up the integration options for the various online-based photo sharing services that you currently use. One of the great features of this app is that you can share images from within the app directly to services, including SmugMug, Facebook, Twitter, Tumblr, Flickr, Picasa, Photobucket, and YouTube (for videos). Tap on the listing for each service you have an account with and, when prompted, enter your username and password for that service.

Also displayed along the top of the screen are the Grid and fx (special effect filter) icons. When you tap on the Grid icon, it's possible to superimpose a tic-tac-toe-like grid over your viewfinder, which is useful when composing your shots. However, the app also offers other composition tools that can be displayed in your viewfinder instead of a basic grid.

When you tap on the fx icon, a menu that offers nine special effect filters is displayed along the top of the screen. As you're taking pictures, select a filter to incorporate into your image in real time (see Figure 8-5).

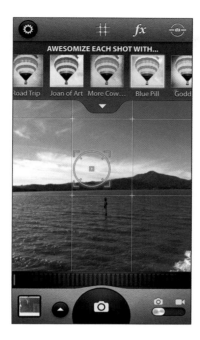

FIGURE 8-5

When taking pictures with the Camera! Awesome app, you can incorporate a filter into your image as you're shooting.

NOTE These same filters can also be added to photos after they've been taken (during the editing process).

Located in the top-right corner of the viewfinder screen is a Level Gauge icon. When you tap on this, a level gauge graphic is displayed in the center of the viewfinder. Use this to determine whether you're holding the iPhone or iPad level as you're taking pictures.

iPAD AND iPHONE DIGITAL PHOTOGRAPHY TIPS AND TRICKS

> **TIP** If you're using the Camera! Awesome app on an iPhone, displayed just below
> the Settings icon as you're looking at the viewfinder screen is the Flash icon. Tap on
> this to set the iPhone's flash to Auto, Off, On, or Flashlight mode. The Flashlight mode
> turns on the iPhone's flash so it emits a steady light, as opposed to working as a tra-
> ditional flash, which activates only when you tap the Shutter button to take a photo.
> Using this mode helps reduce red-eye when taking photos, but it's primarily used
> when shooting video.

Displayed below the level gauge on the viewfinder screen is the Camera Selection
icon. Tap on this to switch between activating the front- and rear-facing cameras
on your iPhone or iPad.

Along the bottom of the viewfinder screen are four additional icons. Look to the
bottom-left corner of the screen for a thumbnail preview window, which shows the
last image taken using the app. To the right of this is a Menu icon (shaped like an
upward-facing arrow). It offers access to several additional picture-taking features,
including an Image Stabilization, Big Button, Slow Burst mode, Fast Burst mode,
Self-Timer, and Interval Timer feature.

Use Image Stabilization to avoid blurs when you're taking pictures and can't hold
your iPhone or iPad perfectly still. The Big Button feature superimposes a large
Shutter Button icon on the screen, making it easier to tap when you're taking pictures. Slow Burst mode enables you to hold down the Shutter button and take multiple photos in quick succession.

> **CAUTION** The Fast Burst feature enables you to capture even more images
> per second when you hold down the Shutter button, but the resolution of these
> images will be lower. In most situations, you're better off using the Slow Burst fea-
> ture when taking pictures that involve a fast-moving subject, so you wind up with
> higher-resolution images.

The Self-Timer feature is adjustable. Set up the iPhone or iPad to snap a photo
between 5 and 60 seconds after you press the Shutter button. Another feature not
found in too many other picture-taking apps is the Interval Timer. This enables you
to set up the iPhone or iPad to have it continuously snap a photo automatically at
a user-selected interval (between 5 and 60 seconds). This continues until you press
the Shutter button again to stop the process.

TIP As you're taking a photo with the Camera! Awesome app, manually activate the Auto Focus feature by tapping on the screen directly over where your intended subject is displayed. This feature works the same way as the Camera app, although the AF sensor box that appears looks slightly different (refer to Figure 8-5).

TIP Displayed just above the Shutter button, near the bottom of the viewfinder screen, is the Zoom slider. Place your finger on this slider and drag it to the right to zoom in on your subject. Move it back to the left to zoom out. From the Settings menu, you also can turn on or off the ability to use the pinch and reverse-pinch finger gestures to adjust this slider.

Like the majority of other apps that serve as an alternative to the Camera app, the Camera! Awesome app enables you to shoot HD video. To switch to Video mode, tap on the Camera/Video selection switch displayed at the bottom-right corner of the screen.

In addition to offering a nice selection of features that enable you to take better pictures using your iPhone or iPad, once you've taken the photos, the Camera! Awesome app offers an equally impressive selection of photo editing, enhancement, and sharing tools. To access them, tap on the Image Preview thumbnail that's displayed in the viewfinder screen.

Instead of an Enhance feature, the Camera! Awesome app includes the Awesomize features. Tap on this icon as you're viewing an image to reveal a menu of editing and enhancement tools, many of which have adjustable sliders associated with them, allowing you to select the intensity of a specific effect, texture, or filter. Built in to the app are also a selection of frames and borders you can add to images before sharing them.

TIP From the app's Edit Photo screen, tap on the Transform icon to access several image cropping and aspect ratio tools, as well as a rotation tool.

NOTE   The ability to mix and match special effect filters, and adjust the intensity of them, is another useful feature that the Camera! Awesome app offers. However, in addition to the filters that are built in to the app, additional filters, textures, frames, and presets can be added through in-app purchases.

A set of nine popular portrait filters are priced at $0.99. All 63 available filters can be purchased for $3.99. For a one-time fee of $9.99, all of the available filters, textures, and frames currently available for the app, or that will be added in the future, become available.

TIP   After you've taken and edited a photo using the Camera! Awesome app, it's possible to share it from within the app, save it to your Camera Roll (or another folder), or export it for use in another app. As you do this, you're given the option to export the original (unedited) image or export the edited version of the image.

Whereas the Photos app enables you to back up your images to your iCloud-based My Photo Stream automatically, the Camera! Awesome app enables you to select which cloud-based service you want to use and then takes advantage of your iPhone or iPad's Wi-Fi or cellular data connection to maintain an archive of the images taken using this app. From within Settings, be sure to turn on the Archive Over Wi-Fi Only feature if you want to conserve your cellular data usage.

Overall, the Camera! Awesome app offers many welcome enhancements and features over the Camera app, and makes available a nice collection of tools for taking, editing, and sharing photos in ways not offered by most other photography apps. It's definitely one of the most feature-packed Camera app alternatives available from the App Store.

CAMERA+

Priced at $1.99, with optional special effect filters offered as in-app purchases for $0.99, the Camera+ app, shown in Figure 8-6, includes a nice collection of photography tools that can be utilized while taking pictures, as well as editing and enhancement tools that can be used after the fact, before you publish or share your pictures.

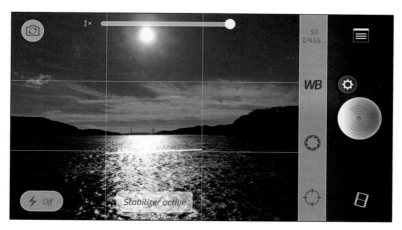

FIGURE 8-6

Shown here is the viewfinder screen of the Camera+ app while the iPhone is being held in Landscape mode with the app's Stabilizer mode active.

More than 10 million copies of this app have been sold worldwide, making it one of the most popular Camera app alternatives available, and with good reason. The Camera+ app's primary goal is to help anyone take better photos. This is done in several different ways.

For example, instead of providing a single Auto Focus and Auto Exposure option, the Camera+ app makes this two separate, but related, settings. This gives you, the photographer, more control over your picture-taking capabilities. Also built in to the app are an Image Stabilizer, Self-Timer, and Burst shooting mode as well as a 6x digital zoom. The onscreen viewfinder includes an optional level gauge.

> **TIP** For added control when taking pictures, access the app's menu and turn on the Live Exposure option. Then, from the viewfinder screen, you can separately set the Auto Focus, Auto Exposure, and White Balance sensors. When you opt to adjust the Auto Exposure, while looking at the viewfinder screen, tap on your subject, or use a slider to make manual adjustments.

As a photographer, you'll often be taking photos in a wide range of situations. To help you consistently capture well-lit and in-focus images, the Camera+ app enables you to select a Scene mode after a photo is taken. Based on the scene you select (there are more than a dozen to choose from), the app automatically adjusts and enhances the image accordingly (see Figure 8-7).

FIGURE 8-7

Choose a scene, and your image is automatically enhanced accordingly, based on how the brightness, contrast, and saturation, for example, should be set for that particular scenario.

In addition, many editing and enhancement tools are available within the app. For example, instead of just being able to rotate an image, the Camera+ app enables images to be flipped horizontally and/or vertically, as well as manually cropped. The Aspect Ratio tool enables images to be resized with ease, while the FX Effects tools include image filters and lighting effects that can be added to photos.

For taking pictures with the iPhone or iPad, and then editing, enhancing, and ultimately sharing them, the Camera+ app is powerful and replicates many of the features you'd find in a standalone point-and-shoot camera.

TIP As you begin using the Camera+ app, be sure to tap on the Menu icon (displayed in the bottom-right corner of the screen) to access a selection of customizable options for turning on or off features utilized while taking pictures, as well as editing, enhancing, and sharing them later.

For example, turn on the capability to use the iPhone or iPad's Volume Up or Volume Down buttons as your Shutter button. Turn on the Grid feature to superimpose a tic-tac-toe-like grid over your viewfinder, turn on the level gauge so it's continuously displayed in the viewfinder, and/or turn on or off the Geotagging feature.

CYCLORAMIC STUDIO 360 PANORAMA

The iPhone is capable of capturing panoramic shots using the Camera app, which is something not possible using the same Camera app on the iPad. These extreme wide-angle shots are ideal for taking photos of landscapes, city skylines, or large groups of people, for example.

The free Cycloramic Studio 360 Panorama app not only offers a different tool for capturing panoramic shots using an iPhone, but it also makes this capability available to iPad users. Taking this concept a step further, however, this app enables you to capture 360-degree panoramic shots with your iOS mobile device, which can then be viewed using this app. Later, if you want to share your 360-degree panoramic shots with others or publish them online, the app enables you to export the images into a short movie clip, which can easily be viewed on services like Facebook, or in a website or blog, for example.

> **TIP** If you're an iPhone 5s user, one awesome feature of the Cycloramic Studio 360 Panorama app is that you can launch the app and then place the smartphone on a flat surface. The app then uses the iPhone's vibration feature to automatically rotate itself around in a circle as it's taking pictures, so the 360-degree shot can be captured automatically.

In addition to the entertainment-oriented uses of this app, many realtors, for example, are using it to capture the inside of houses they're selling as they create detailed listings that will be posted online.

> **TIP** The Cycloramic Studio 360 Panorama app walks you through the process of taking 360-degree panoramic images. In reality, to do this, the app has you take up to 10 separate images while you rotate the iPhone or iPad in a steady and level manner, to the right, in between taking each shot. Use the onscreen guide (see Figure 8-8) to tell you exactly how much to rotate the smartphone or tablet, and be sure to pause when the Stop icon appears on the display during the picture-taking process.

FIGURE 8-8

Taking 360-degree panoramic shots using your iPhone or iPad is easy if you follow the onscreen directions and capture each separate shot as instructed.

After you take a 360-degree panoramic shot, it's possible to preview it on your iPhone or iPad's screen, and then tap on the Instagram, Facebook, or Mail button to share the image. It's also possible to access the app's Photo Editor to enhance the image and/or add special effects.

Along the bottom of the Photo Editor screen, shown in Figure 8-9, you'll find a series of menu icons, labeled Enhance, Effects, Frames, Stickers, Focus, Orientation, Crop, Adjust, Sharpness, Splash, Draw, Text, Red-Eye, Whiten, Blemish, and Meme (used for incorporating text into an image). Each reveals a separate set of tools for editing or enhancing the panoramic or 360-degree panoramic photos taken using the app.

FIGURE 8-9

The Cycloramic Studio 360 app offers a nice selection of photo editing and enhancement tools.

TIP As you're editing a photo, use a reverse-pinch finger gesture on the screen to zoom in on an area of the 360-degree image. You can then hold your finger on the screen and drag it around to reposition the image, or use a left/right swipe motion. Zooming in enables you to see more detail as you're adding effects or editing.

NOTE As an optional in-app purchase ($1.99), it's possible to unlock the 4x HD feature. This enables you to take much higher-quality panoramic or 360-degree panoramic shots, captured at 1250 × 9300 or 2500 × 18600 pixel resolution. Taking higher-resolution images increases their file sizes, but the results are visually impressive because more detail is visible within the images, and the colors appear more vivid.

Once you discover how easy it is to capture panoramic shots and 360-degree panoramic images with your iOS mobile device, and then enhance and share the images, you'll love using this app. It can also be used for taking traditional photos while holding the iPhone or iPad in Portrait or Landscape mode. This enables you to use the app's extensive editing and image enhancement tools on these regular images as well.

HIPSTAMATIC

The Hipstamatic app ($1.99) is also designed to replace the Camera app. What sets it apart is that as you're taking pictures using this app on your iOS mobile device, the app simulates various types of film-based cameras, flash types, and film types. As a result, with very little or no editing, it's possible to create old-fashioned-looking images that can immediately be shared via Facebook, Twitter, Instagram, Tumblr, or Flickr, for example.

The company that developed the Hipstamatic app, shown in Figure 8-10, also has its own photo lab. Thus, from within the app, it's possible to order traditional prints and have them shipped to your door. An extra fee applies for this service.

FIGURE 8-10

The main viewfinder screen of the Hipstamatic app simulates an old-fashioned film camera.

NOTE   In addition to the effects filters that can be incorporated in real time as you're taking pictures, 10 different "add-on filter packs" are available as in-app purchases. They're priced between $0.99 and $1.99 each, and they expand the types of visual effects that can be added to photos as they're being taken, or after they've been shot and stored in your iPhone or iPad.

As soon as you launch the Hipstamatic app, you'll discover that the viewfinder screen looks like an old, film-based camera. The actual viewfinder is a small window displayed near the center of the app's screen.

> TIP Immediately below the viewfinder is the app's Flash switch. Swipe it left or right to activate the iPhone's flash. A sound effect is used to make the app more closely resemble an old camera.

After you've framed your image in the viewfinder, tap on the Shutter button to snap a photo. In this app, the Shutter button looks like a yellow circle, and it's displayed near the top-right corner of the screen.

Displayed along the bottom of the viewfinder screen are several command icons. Tap on the icon in the bottom-left corner to access Hipstamatic's photo editing, management, and sharing tools. Tap on the Favorite icon (shaped like a star) to choose a camera/film/flash combination that you want the app to simulate, and save it as a quickly accessible favorite.

To switch to a front-facing view of the camera (see Figure 8-11), tap on the curved arrow-shaped icon that's displayed in the bottom-right corner of the screen. This same icon can be used to switch from the front- to rear-facing view.

FIGURE 8-11

From the app's front-facing view, you can change the virtual camera, lens, flash, and film type you'll be shooting with. Thanks to optional in-app purchases, your options are extensive.

TIP   From the front view of the Hipstamatic app, it's possible to swap virtual lenses by swiping your finger across the center lens either right or left. The app has a collection of built-in lenses to choose from, but more are available as in-app purchases.

To switch between different types of simulated films, tap on the Film icon that's displayed in the bottom-left corner of the screen (when looking at the front view of the app). To change virtual flash types, tap on the Flash icon. To switch camera types, tap on the Camera Selection icon that's displayed near the bottom center of the screen. Additional "Camera Gear" (also known as in-app purchases) can be acquired by tapping on the Shopping Cart icon.

TIP   After snapping photos using the Hipstamatic app, tap on the Viewing and Sharing icon to view and manage the images taken using this app. As you're about to share individual or groups of images from within the app, you can add your own captions or attach a summary that describes what virtual camera equipment was used to snap the photo(s).

Images taken using the Hipstamatic app are stored in the app but can be exported to your Camera Roll folder from within the app. This enables you to view, edit, print, and share the images from the Photos app or another photography app that's running on your iPhone or iPad.

Hipstamatic is a well-designed app for creative photographers who want to use digital photography "gear" that realistically replicates traditional film-based cameras, 35mm film effects, and various flash types. One interesting feature is that you can mix and match virtual camera gear that would not otherwise have been compatible if you were using actual film-based cameras. The ability to order prints in four different sizes from within the app is also a convenient feature.

TIP   It's important to select the camera type, film type, and flash type (optional) before snapping a photo using the Hipstamatic app. Each option you select dramatically alters the appearance of your images as you're actually taking pictures. It's not possible to add these visual effects after the fact.

PRO HDR

You already know that the Camera app has the HDR (High Dynamic Range) shooting mode built in. When turned on, this shooting mode actually captures several versions of the same image, each utilizing the available light differently, and then merges those images into one. When you want to take "existing light" photos in low-light situations, HDR mode is used. As a result, your pictures appear a bit crisper and the colors are more vibrant and natural, based on ambient light.

If you find yourself wanting or needing to take photos in low-light situations, but don't want to use your iPhone's flash (or you're shooting with the cameras built in to the iPad), the Pro HDR app ($1.99) dramatically expands your picture-taking capabilities. The main viewfinder screen of the app is shown in Figure 8-12. The app also offers a handful of user-adjustable image editing and enhancement tools you can use immediately after photos are taken in order to improve them.

> TIP The Pro HDR app can also be used in well-lit situations and during sunrises or sunsets, for example, to capture brighter and more vivid colors.

FIGURE 8-12

The viewfinder screen of the Pro HDR app.

What's great about this app is that it blends areas of an image that have too much or too little light, ensuring that all of the natural colors within an image are as clear and vibrant as possible, without compromising clarity. Using the image enhancement programming that's built in to the HDR shooting mode of this app, the resolution of images is automatically improved.

NOTE Each time you press the Shutter button, the app takes a few seconds to analyze the available light. It then snaps two separate photos, one at a time, so the picture-taking process using this app takes several seconds. The end result, however, is vastly superior to what you'd get using the HDR mode of the Camera app.

In fact, the photos you wind up taking, based on your iPhone or iPad model, can be equivalent to 12MP resolution. Typically, when taking photos using the rear-facing camera of the iPhone 5s, for example, achieving a maximum of 8MP resolution is possible.

TIP As you're taking photos, you can turn on the app's Auto HDR shooting mode and allow the app to adjust all the picture-taking settings based on the available light. However, for more creative control, switch to the manual shooting mode. This enables you to adjust the exposure of each shot taken, before multiple shots are merged into one. You can also turn off HDR mode altogether and simply use the Pro HDR app to take normal, unenhanced photos.

As you're taking pictures using the Pro HDR app, it's possible to take advantage of the built-in Zoom feature, Grid, or Self-Timer, for example, to give yourself additional tools and further customize how your photos turn out. After images are taken, the app has a built-in Crop tool, allows for text-based captions to be added to photos, and offers a nice selection of optional filters and frames.

When it comes to editing photos, there are manually adjustable sliders for Brightness, Contrast, Saturation, Warmth, and Tint, which give you extra creative control (see Figure 8-13). To increase or decrease the intensity of these effects, simply drag your finger left or right on the appropriate slider.

FIGURE 8-13

Many of the editing tools built in to the Pro HDR app are adjustable using onscreen sliders.

When you're finished editing your image(s), tap on the Save button to save your changes. Then, tap on the Share button if you want to share your images with others via email, text message, Facebook, or Twitter. From the Share menu, tap on the More option to turn on integration with additional online-based services, such as Evernote, Tumblr, Flickr, or Instagram.

Edited images can also be exported from the Pro HDR app and used with any other digital photography app that's installed on your iOS mobile device or used in an app that enables you to import photos, such as Pages, Numbers, or Keynote. If you have an AirPrint-compatible printer linked with your iPhone or iPad, creating prints from within the Pro HDR app is as easy as tapping on the Print button.

NOTE   The Pro HDR app supports both the front- and rear-facing cameras built in to your iPhone or iPad, but you'll wind up with higher-resolution and better-quality images if you use the app with your device's rear-facing camera. Although the app's user interface isn't as well designed as some other photography apps, the capabilities of this app exceed what's possible using many photography apps.

Pro HDR is a versatile photography app for taking, editing, printing, and sharing photos, but the primary reason to use this app is to take full advantage of its
greatly enhanced HDR shooting mode, which is ideal for taking photos in low-light
situations (without using a flash), and for accurately capturing the ambient light
that surrounds your intended subject(s) in daylight.

PROCAM 2

This $2.99 app is also an excellent picture-taking app that can serve as a feature-
packed alternative to the Camera app. In fact, ProCam 2 (shown in Figure 8-14) is
chock full of useful tools for taking and editing photos that can help you enhance
the quality of your images in a wide range of shooting situations.

FIGURE 8-14

*The ProCam 2 app's viewfinder screen enables you to frame and capture images and access
and adjust a vast selection of picture-taking features. It's shown here on an iPhone being held in
Landscape mode.*

For example, ProCam 2 includes more than 25 "live filters." Choose your favorite
(see Figure 8-15), and it can be incorporated into your photos as they're being
taken. Other useful app picture-taking features include the Night mode with a
Timer option, an adjustable Anti-Shake mode, a Self-Timer, a Burst shooting mode,
an Interval shooting mode that's also adjustable, a Face Detection feature, 6x digital zoom, as well as full focus and exposure control.

FIGURE 8-15

The ProCam 2 app has a handful of filters that you can add to your photos in real time, as you're shooting.

Also as you're taking photos, ProCam 2 records the time, date, and location where all photos are shot, allows you to add an optional Copyright stamp, and enables you to superimpose a grid onto the viewfinder. You can also manually adjust the aspect ratio and resolution of photos being taken and on the iPhone, control the flash from within the app.

> **TIP** Using the Night mode takes much of the guesswork out of taking pictures in low-light situations and helps to ensure properly exposed and in-focus images.

Even with all of the features and functions built in to the app that give you added control over your picture taking, the app is surprisingly easy to use. As you're using the app's viewfinder screen to take pictures, along the top and bottom of the screen you'll discover a handful of command icons that can be used to quickly adjust the camera's settings.

In addition to turning on or off certain features, when using ProCam 2, many options are adjustable using onscreen sliders (see Figure 8-16). For example, displayed to the right of the Shutter button is a Menu icon that displays sliders for a handful of customizable functions that can be used while shooting, such as contrast control, white balance adjustments, color saturation, and filter options.

FIGURE 8-16

Use sliders to control certain features of the ProCam 2 app during the picture-taking process. This gives you a tremendous level of control over how your photos turn out.

Tap on the Menu icon that's displayed to the left of the Shutter button to access another menu that offers a handful of adjustable options when taking pictures (shown in Figure 8-17).

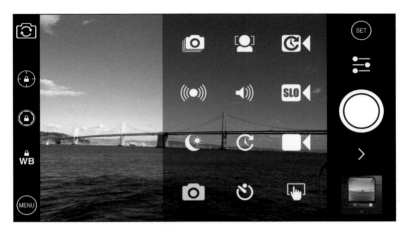

FIGURE 8-17

From this menu, you can turn on or off features such as Burst shooting mode, a self-timer, and image stabilization.

TIP To quickly change shooting options, tap on the arrow-shaped icon that's displayed to the left of the Shutter button, or tap on the other Menu icon that's displayed to the right of the Shutter button.

ProCam 2 is best suited for serious iPhone/iPad photographers who want maximum control over the front- and rear-facing cameras that are built in to their mobile devices as they're taking pictures.

NOTE After each photo is taken using ProCam 2, an image preview thumbnail is displayed on the screen. Tap on this thumbnail to view a larger version of the photo and access the app's Share options. As you'll discover, the objective of this app is to give you the maximum creative control when taking pictures. It's not designed for after-the-fact photo editing. For that, you can rely on other photography apps.

SNAPPYCAM PRO

For a mere $1.99, it's possible to purchase and download the SnappyCam Pro app, shown in Figure 8-18, and dramatically expand your picture-taking and photo editing capabilities when using your iPhone or iPad as a digital camera. For example, this app adds a Burst shooting mode to all iOS mobile devices, not just the iPhone 5s, iPad Air, and iPad mini with Retina display.

FIGURE 8-18

The SnappyCam Pro app's viewfinder screen looks a bit different than other apps. As you can see, the actual viewfinder is displayed in an onscreen window.

NOTE   When used with an iOS mobile device that contains Apple's A7 processor (including the iPhone 5s, iPad Air, and iPad mini with Retina display), the app's Burst shooting mode becomes programmable. Using this feature, it's now possible to capture up to 30 frames per second in full resolution, or up to 120 frames per second at a lower resolution.

Adding a Burst shooting mode enables you to more effectively take pictures when your subject is in motion, and ensures that you can capture that perfectly timed shot. It's especially well suited for taking pictures during sporting events, for example.

> **TIP** By manually adjusting the Burst shooting mode with SnappyCam Pro's self-timer, it's possible to use this app for time lapse photography. For example, you can set up your iPhone or iPad on a tripod and have it automatically take one shot at a time, at any interval, up to one shot per hour.

As you're taking photos using SnappyCam Pro, it's possible to take full advantage of the app's manual-focus mode, or double-tap on the viewfinder screen to activate the app's autofocus feature. To create two separate autofocus sensors on the screen simultaneously, use a reverse-pinch finger gesture, and then double-tap on each of two separate subjects to activate each sensor, one at a time.

To activate the Burst shooting mode, simply hold down the Shutter button, which is located near the bottom center of the screen.

> **TIP** To adjust the app's Zoom feature, use the + and - magnifying glass shaped icons that are displayed near the bottom-right corner of the viewfinder window. To adjust the iPhone's built-in Flash mode, superimpose a grid on the viewfinder screen, or switch between the front- and rear-facing cameras, tap the command icons displayed near the bottom-left corner of the viewfinder window.

As you're taking pictures, tap on the Menu icon that's displayed to the right of the Shutter button to adjust a variety of picture-taking features and functions that are built in to the app, such as the virtual Camera Lens, Shutter Mode, Aspect Ratio, Grid Type, Image Quality, and Geo-Tagging. The menu screen is shown in Figure 8-19.

FIGURE 8-19

The menu screen of the SnappyCam app.

SnappyCam Pro is primarily a picture-taking app and is not designed for after-the-fact photo editing. Images taken using this app are stored in a separate folder in your iPhone or iPad but can easily be exported into the Camera Roll folder, where they can be imported into other apps for editing and sharing. The Export feature also enables you to send photos via email or upload them to Instagram.

Although this app doesn't offer the vast selection of picture-taking features and functions offered by some photography apps, it is a good alternative to the Camera app if you're interested in utilizing a Burst shooting mode and maximizing the capabilities of this feature to take pictures of moving subjects or other time-sensitive actions.

SO MANY MORE PHOTOGRAPHY APPS ARE AT YOUR DISPOSAL

Beyond the photography apps described in this chapter, by visiting the App Store, you can find many other apps that can be used as an alternative to the Camera app for taking pictures with your iPhone or iPad. Some of these apps are designed for general-purpose photography, whereas others are designed to help you successfully take very specific types of photos.

In the next chapter, you'll read about apps that can be used to help you view, organize, edit, enhance, print, and share your images after they've been taken. However, there are two other categories of photography apps you should be aware of. The first are apps that can replace the Camera app for taking pictures, enable you to quickly edit or enhance the pictures, and then upload those images to a specific online service so they can be shared.

The Instagram app is the perfect example of this. Using the Instagram app, you can snap photos; automatically crop them into a square shape; add a filter and/or border as well as your location, caption, and/or keywords; and then upload one image at a time to the Instagram service to share it. The whole process takes just seconds.

> **NOTE** You'll learn more about the Instagram app and online social networking service in Chapter 12, "Share Your Digital Photos Online."

> **TIP** Apple's own Photo Booth app comes preinstalled on the iPad. It too can be used for taking pictures instead of the Camera app. What sets these two apps apart is that the Photo Booth app has eight additional built-in special effect filters that can be used in real time when taking photos, and it's designed so you can take and share whimsical photos of yourself and the people around you.

Another type of photography app transforms your iPhone or iPad into a tool that can remotely control your digital SLR camera (and its settings while you're taking pictures), when the camera is linked to your iOS mobile device wirelessly or via a special cable. In essence, the iPhone or iPad becomes a camera accessory for your high-end, standalone Nikon or Canon digital SLR camera. If you're interested in this type of application, be sure to read Chapter 10.

IN THIS CHAPTER

- Learn about optional photography apps that enable you to view, edit, enhance, and share your photos
- Add filters and other elements to your images after they've been taken

PHOTOGRAPHY APPS THAT EXPAND YOUR PHOTO EDITING AND ENHANCEMENT CAPABILITIES

You already know that the Camera app can be used to take photos by utilizing the front- and/or rear-facing cameras that are built in to the iPhone or iPad. Then, those photos can be viewed, edited, enhanced, printed, or shared from the Photos app. Or, if you want to expand what's possible, instead of using the Photos app that comes preinstalled with iOS 7, you can take advantage of Apple's own iPhoto app (which you learned about in Chapter 7, "Expand Your Photo Editing Toolbox with iPhoto").

Yet another option is to download a third-party photography app that's designed specifically for photo editing and image enhancement. These apps typically include tools and features not found in the Photos or iPhoto apps but that can be used to quickly and dramatically improve the appearance of your images, without first having to transfer them to a PC or Mac for editing. This chapter showcases a handful of third-party apps that can be used for photo editing, image enhancement, and sharing, directly from your iPhone or iPad.

TIP   Beyond the photography apps that are showcased in this chapter, be sure to visit the App Store and enter the phrase "Photo Editor" in the Search field to find hundreds of additional app alternatives you can use to edit, enhance, and/or share your images directly from your iPhone or iPad.

THIRD-PARTY PHOTO EDITING AND IMAGE ENHANCEMENT APPS

In addition to offering photo editing and image enhancement tools not offered by the Photos or iPhoto apps, many of the third-party photography apps that are designed to handle photo editing and image enhancement also include specialized tools for sharing your images using online-based services that aren't necessarily integrated with the Photos or iPhoto apps.

Keep in mind that although many of the third-party photo editing and image enhancement apps are compatible with the iPhone and iPad, doing detailed image editing that goes well beyond applying a precreated filter or frame to an entire image is much easier to do when you're working with an iPad or iPad mini's larger screen (compared with the iPhone).

NOTE   Instead of using the Photos or iPhoto apps and Apple's own iCloud My Photo Stream and Shared Photo Stream features to automatically create an online backup of your images, as well as online albums or galleries that can be shared with others, many third-party photography apps offer integration with other, independent, cloud-based photo sharing and backup services, like Flickr.com, Smugmug.com, Dropbox, Adobe Creative Cloud, and Shutterfly.com. Thus, by using some of these third-party apps, you're given more choices as to where you back up your images in the cloud and how you share your images online.

The following sections detail five popular and powerful photo editing and image enhancement apps that can be used on both images captured using your iOS mobile device or that are transferred into or stored on your iPhone or iPad. In some cases, these apps also have picture-taking capabilities built in, which can be used instead of the Camera app for snapping photos.

ADOBE PHOTOSHOP TOUCH

Adobe Photoshop is one of the most powerful photo editing applications available for Macs and PCs. In fact, it's a rather complex and costly application that most semiprofessional and professional photographers use.

The Adobe Photoshop Touch app ($4.99), however, offers some of the same photo editing and image enhancement capabilities as what was otherwise only possible on a Mac or PC, but allows anyone to use these tools directly on an iPhone or iPad.

What's great about Adobe Photoshop Touch is that it enables you to edit or enhance specific areas in a photo, as opposed to simply applying a filter or effect to an entire image. If you're a Photoshop Creative Cloud (Mac or PC) user, you can automatically sync images between your computer and your iPhone or iPad, and edit images on either platform.

> **TIP** Because Adobe Photoshop Touch allows for intricate editing to be done on specific areas of an image, when you use this functionality, it's best to zoom in on the area of an image you want to work on and then, for added precision, utilize an optional pen-shaped stylus (instead of your finger) when painting, drawing, or using certain tools as part of the editing process.

When you first launch Adobe Photoshop Touch, be sure to take advantage of the onscreen tutorials to help you get acquainted with this rather detailed and complex app, as well as the specific editing and enhancement tools it offers (see Figure 9-1). Tap on the Begin a Tutorial button, and then select which feature or function you want to learn more about. For example, you can quickly learn how to use layers or selections, add dramatic flair to an image, paint with visual effects, replace individual colors within photos, add artistic frames, clean up the background in an image, or blend multiple images together into one.

FIGURE 9-1

Due to its complexity and power, the Adobe Photoshop Touch app has built-in tutorials that explain exactly how to use each editing and enhancement tool that's offered by the app.

As you're ultimately working with your own images, you can mix and match the app's built-in effects.

To begin editing your own images, tap on the Create a New Project icon or the Import Image icon, both of which are displayed near the bottom center of the main app screen.

When you use the Create a New Project option, you can start with a blank canvas of any size. Simply enter the desired width and height of the virtual canvas (which is measured in pixels). However, when you import an image, you can load any digital image that's stored in your iOS mobile device or that's stored online in Adobe's Creative Cloud, Google, or Facebook. It's also possible to import images directly from a standalone digital camera.

After a single image is loaded into the Adobe Photoshop Touch app (see Figure 9-2), all of your editing and image enhancement tools are displayed as icons along the top and in the left and right margins of the screen. Select a tool, and then use your finger or an optional stylus to use that tool on the selected image.

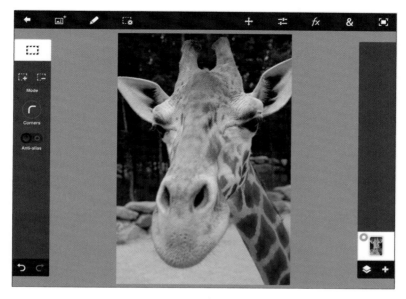

FIGURE 9-2

*Load any digital image (up to 12MP resolution) into the iPhone or iPad version of Adobe
Photoshop Touch to begin editing it.*

For example, tap on the Adjustments icon (displayed near the top-right corner
of the app's screen) to access a menu that contains a dozen easy-to-use tools for
adjusting specific elements of an image, such as saturation, brightness/contrast,
temperature, or color balance.

Tap on the Auto Fix option to quickly enhance an image and automatically adjust
all of these elements with a single tap. However, if you select one of these tools to
work with, a specialized slider displays.

Tap on the fx icon to access 36 different special effect filters that you can instantly
apply to an entire image, and then manually adjust the intensity of the filter using
onscreen sliders (see Figure 9-3). Another option is to tap on the & icon, which
then displays a submenu offering additional photo editing tools that are at your
disposal, such as a Crop, Image Size, Rotate, or Lens Flare.

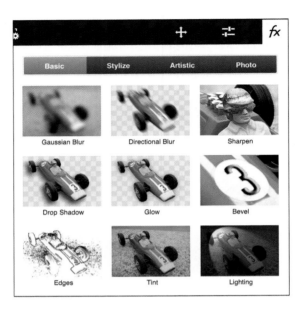

FIGURE 9-3

Adobe Photoshop Touch has 36 special effect filters built in to the app. Mix and match these filters to create truly customized visual effects.

TIP   As you're working with an image, tap on the Full Screen View icon (displayed in the top-right corner of the screen) to showcase only your image, without the added onscreen clutter of menus and command icons. Use a reverse-pinch or pinch finger gesture to zoom in or out as you're viewing the image. Doing this impacts your view of the image, not the image itself. Once you zoom in within a photo, drag your finger on the screen to reposition the image so you can view a specific part of it.

After you've used the various editing tools to edit or enhance your image, be sure to save your work in the Adobe Photoshop Touch app. Then, from the app's main menu screen, tap on the Share icon to upload the image to Adobe Creative Cloud, export the image to your Camera Roll folder (to be stored on your iOS mobile device so it's accessible using other photography apps, including Photos or iPhoto), or export and share the image via the Messages, Mail, Twitter, or Facebook app.

From the app's Share menu, it's also possible to export an image directly to another compatible photography app, such as iPhoto, Shutterfly, or Instagram, or print the image using an AirPrint-compatible printer.

> **TIP** The Adobe Photoshop Touch app is designed for advanced photo editing and image enhancement. Another alternative is the free Adobe Photoshop Express app, which is less feature-packed but much easier to use. It utilizes a series of one-tap filters (there are more than 20 to choose from) as well as image enhancement tools that you can quickly apply to an entire image.

> **NOTE** Both Adobe Photoshop Touch and Adobe Photoshop Express are fully compatible with Adobe's own Creative Cloud online file sharing and image backup service, which can be used instead of Apple's iCloud to back up, sync, and share images online. A free membership to Adobe Creative Cloud includes 2GB of online storage space.

If you're serious about photo editing and want a powerful collection of tools available to you from your iPhone or iPad that rivals what's possible using Adobe Photoshop Creative Cloud on a Mac or PC, you'll definitely want to use the Adobe Photoshop Touch app, providing you're willing to invest the time needed to learn how to use the app and its various features.

This app has a steep learning curve compared with others, but what's possible using this app goes unrivaled, making it a must-have app for serious hobbyists, as well as semiprofessional and professional photographers.

AFTERLIGHT

The Afterlight app ($0.99) is really two apps in one. You can use it instead of the Camera app to actually take photos, plus it doubles as a feature-packed photo editing and image enhancement tool. From the app's opening screen, tap on the Camera icon to begin taking photos, or tap on the Picture icon to begin working with images stored on your iPhone or iPad.

> **TIP** Tap on the gear-shaped Settings Menu icon that's displayed at the bottom-right corner of the screen to customize some of the app's settings. For example, you can set the app to automatically launch in Camera mode, so it's ready to take photos.

The Camera mode works very much like the Camera app. The main area of the screen serves as your viewfinder. The large white circle icon is your Shutter button. Tap on the Grid option to superimpose a tic-tac-toe-like grid over the viewfinder to use as you frame and compose your shots.

> **TIP** As you're using the Afterlight app as a camera, tap on the screen, directly over where your intended subject is located, to activate the autofocus sensor.

Use the Camera Selection icon to switch between the front- and rear-facing cameras built in to your iPhone or iPad. Tap on the Self-Timer icon one or more times to activate and then set the self-timer for 3, 7, or 10 seconds. Tap on the Cancel option to exit out of the Camera mode and return to the app's main menu screen.

When you tap on Afterlight's Photo Editor icon to begin editing your photos, you're given the option to access any photo that's stored on your iPhone or iPad. After you've selected an image, icons that represent your image editing tools appear along the bottom of the screen (see Figure 9-4). From left to right, this includes a Revert Image tool, the Adjustments Menu icon, the Filters Menu icon, an Effects Menu icon, a Crop/Rotation Tools Menu icon, and a Frame and Text Menu icon.

Although each of these tools impacts an entire image, after you select a specific tool, you can adjust its intensity using an onscreen slider. As you'll discover, Afterlight offers dozens of easy-to-use and powerful photo editing and image enhancement tools but does not offer the capability to utilize each tool on specific areas of an image, which is something that Adobe Photoshop Touch offers. You can, however, mix and match photo editing and enhancement tools, plus adjust the intensity of each, which gives you a tremendous amount of flexibility and ability to use your own creativity when working with your images.

After you edit images, you can save them in Small, Medium, or Maximum resolution (which impacts an image's file size) and then export them to your iOS mobile device's Camera Roll folder as well as to Instagram, Flickr, Facebook, Twitter, or other third-party photography apps. You can also share them via email (using the Mail app) or send them as a virtual postcard from within the Afterlight app.

FIGURE 9-4

This is what the main image editing screen of the Afterlight app looks like on the iPad Air.

PHOTO EDITOR-

This free, advertiser-supported app offers a plethora of editing tools that you can use on any digital images stored on your iPhone or iPad. It also has a Camera mode, so you can take pictures using this app (with the front- or rear-facing cameras built in to your iPhone or iPad), and then edit them. To launch the picture-taking function, tap on the Camera Lens icon displayed near the top-left corner of the main app screen.

To load an image into this image editing app, launch Photo Editor-, and then tap on the File (folder-shaped) icon that's displayed in the top-left corner of the screen. Choose an album, and then select one or more images by tapping on their respective thumbnails. When you do this, one at a time, the images appear in the main area of the screen, while a collection of 16 editing and enhancement tool icons appears along the bottom of the screen (see Figure 9-5).

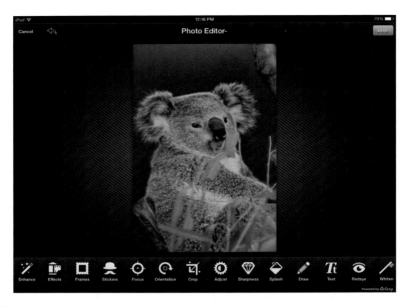

FIGURE 9-5

After you load an image, start by tapping on one of the 16 editing and enhancement tool icons that are displayed near the bottom of the screen.

From left to right, these 16 editing and enhancement tools are as follows:

■ **Enhance**—Tap on this option to reveal a submenu that allows for one-tap image enhancements related to Hi-Def, Illuminate, or Color Fix.

■ **Effects**—With a single tap, apply one of a dozen "Original" effect filters to your entire image. These filters are not adjustable, but you can combine filters to create many unique effects (see Figure 9-6). Tap on the Add Effects button to add a dozen additional filters. (This requires a $1.99 in-app purchase.)

TIP   When you tap on one of these tool icons, the impact it has on the image is immediately displayed. To save the enhancement, tap on the Apply button. To undo the enhancement, tap on the tool icon again. To return to the Editor menu, tap on the Editor button.

FIGURE 9-6

The Photo Editor- app has its own collection of special effect filters you can use to quickly and dramatically alter the appearance of an image.

- **Frames**—Choose from a dozen digital frames that can be added as a border around the image you're editing. You can acquire additional frame sets through in-app purchases.

- **Stickers**—The app comes with a set of 24 virtual stickers that you can place in your images, and then resize and rotate (see Figure 9-7). Additional sticker "packs" are available through in-app purchases.

- **Focus**—Choose what area of the image should be the primary focal point by selecting this tool, and then tapping on a specific area within the image. This autofocuses the image, ensuring that the area you selected becomes the sharpest area of the image. As you go further from the selected point, the image slightly blurs.

- **Orientation**—Tap on this tool to access a submenu that enables you to rotate an image left or right, or flip the image horizontally or vertically.

- **Crop**—Manually crop the image you're working with and/or set its aspect ratio.

- **Adjust**—Access a submenu that enables you to manually adjust the brightness, contrast, warmth, and/or saturation within the image separately using sliders.

FIGURE 9-7

Stickers are a whimsical way to "edit" an image before sharing it.

- **Sharpness**—Use a slider to manually adjust the sharpness of an image, enabling you to transform a slightly blurry image into one that's more in focus. Move the slider to the left to blur an image. This tool applies to the entire image.

- **Splash**—Use this tool to transform a full-color image into black and white, and then to replace the color in only specific areas of the image (if you choose).

- **Draw**—Using your finger, choose a pen thickness and color, and then manually draw on the screen. What you finger-paint on the screen is superimposed over the photo you're editing.

- **Text**—Add a text-based caption or title to your photo. You can also adjust the text size and font color, and then reposition or rotate the text manually. It's not, however, possible to change the font.

- **Redeye**—Use this tool to quickly repair red-eye that appears in a photo as a result of using the flash.

- **Whiten**—If your subject is smiling, tap on this tool and paint over the teeth to whiten and brighten his or her smile.

- **Blemish**—Remove an unwanted blemish from a subject's face. This tool is mainly for editing portraits but can be used to remove small and unwanted objects from an image.

- **Meme**—Add a bold, text-based heading to the top and/or bottom of the image.

> **TIP** Any of the tools built in to the Photo Editor- app can be mixed and matched
> as you're working with an image.

When you're finished editing an image, tap on the Done button. The image is
saved and you have the opportunity to share it via AirDrop or using the Message,
Mail, Twitter, Facebook, or Instagram apps. You also can export the image and use
it with another app when you utilize the Copy command. Finally, you can print to
an AirPrint-compatible printer by tapping on the Print button, which is part of the
Share menu that automatically appears when you tap the Done button.

> **TIP** As you're working with an image, tap on the curved, left-pointing arrow
> icon displayed near the top-left corner of the screen to revert back to the original
> image and remove all edits or enhancements you've added to an image using the
> Photo Editor- app.

Photo Editor- is an extremely easy-to-use app that makes editing and enhancing digital images a quick process. The capability to mix and match editing and
enhancement tools is a huge benefit, although one drawback of this app is that
many of the tools must be applied to an entire image, as opposed to just an area
within an image.

> **NOTE** Because this is a free app, a banner ad is usually displayed along the
> bottom of the app screen. To remove the ads, it's possible to upgrade to the Pro
> version of the Photo Editor- app for $0.99. To do this, tap on the Settings icon and
> choose the Pro Upgrade option.

PHOTOTOASTER

Like Photo Editor-, the PhotoToaster app ($2.99) is easy to use, enables you to
fix or enhance a photo in seconds, and offers a wide range of useful editing and
enhancement tools and filters (shown in Figure 9-8).

FIGURE 9-8

PhotoToaster is a versatile and powerful photo editing and image enhancement app.

What's great about PhotoToaster is that the majority of the available enhancement tools can be painted onto specific areas of an image, which gives you a tremendous level of creative control and flexibility. In addition to the various special effect filters, it's possible to crop, rotate, or straighten an image; adjust the contrast, brightness, and saturation within an image; plus add an optional and selectable frame or border around the image (there are many to choose from).

TIP   If you want to apply a filter, effect, or applicable editing tool to an entire image, before tapping on a filter selection, activate the Global option by tapping on the globe-shaped icon that's displayed near the bottom-left corner of the screen (see Figure 9-9). Otherwise, just tap on the icon for the tool you want to use, and then use your finger to paint that effect within specific areas of an image.

Once you select the Global option, rotate the virtual dial that's displayed in the bottom-left corner of the screen to scroll through filter and effect options.

FIGURE 9-9

Some of the editing tools built in to the PhotoToaster app can be applied to either the entire image or just specific areas of an image. Choose the Global option to apply an effect to an entire image.

When you've finished editing an image, tap on the Share icon displayed in the top-right corner of the screen. When the Save To menu appears, you can opt to save the edited version of the image to your iOS mobile device's Photo Library, email the image, print it using an AirPrint-compatible printer, or upload the image to Facebook, Flickr, Tumblr, or Twitter from directly within the app.

> TIP   To create a virtual postcard that features your edited image, one that you can email to one or more recipients, tap on the Share icon, and then choose the Postcard option from the Save To menu. Also from within the app, it's possible to directly order a canvas print of your image(s), in a wide range of sizes, for between $25.00 and $38.00 per image.

PhotoToaster is a powerful app for editing and enhancing photos. It is more versatile than many optional photography apps, but doesn't offer as much control over individual editing options as the Adobe Photoshop Touch app (which is more complicated to use).

PICSHOP HD PHOTO EDITOR

Priced at $4.99, PicShop HD Photo Editor is also a comprehensive photo editing and image enhancement app that offers a straightforward and well-organized menu interface that walks you through the editing process. The app also has its own Camera mode for taking pictures.

From the main menu, tap on the leftmost Open Images From Menu icon to select the Camera option, or choose an image to edit from your iPhone or iPad's internal storage (Gallery). It's also possible to select an image from your online-based Facebook account.

After you've selected and displayed an image (see Figure 9-10), tap on the Edits button to access the Autofix, Crop, Straighten, Brightness, and Color tools (see Figure 9-11). Then, to add an optional special effect filter to the image, tap on the Filters button. There are 18 special effect filters to choose from. After a filter is applied to an entire image, it's possible to use the onscreen slider to manually adjust the intensity of that filter.

FIGURE 9-10

Shown here is the main image editing screen of the PicShop HD Photo Editor app.

TIP   You can apply multiple filters to an image, but this must be done one at a time. Start by tapping on the Filters button, and then select one of the app's built-in special effect filters (see Figure 9-12).

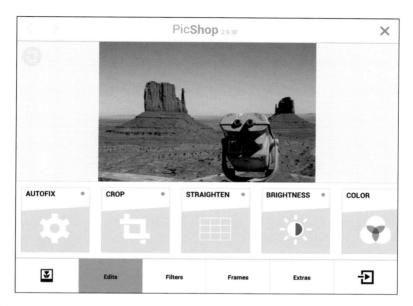

FIGURE 9-11

Most of the image editing tools built in to this app are accessible by tapping on large, well-labeled, onscreen buttons.

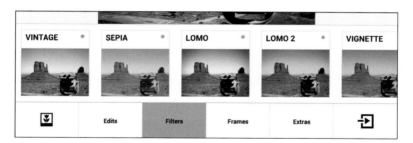

FIGURE 9-12

PicShop offers a nice selection of optional special effect filters, which you can mix and match as you're editing your images.

Next, select an optional frame or border to superimpose around the outer edge of the image you're working with by tapping on the Frames button, followed by the frame option of your choosing.

To create image layers, apply virtual stickers or pointers to your image, superimpose attention-getting shapes over your image, draw with your finger directly on an image, or add a variety of other effects, tap on the Extras button, and then choose the effect you want to add.

TIP   One interesting editing tool built in to PicShop is the Image Layer tool. Use it to blend two different images together into one, and control the opacity of each image as they're being blended. To access this feature, tap on the Extras button, and then select Image Layer. Next, you are prompted to select a second image to blend into the one you're currently working with. After selecting the second image, it's possible to crop it (to use only a portion of the image), plus manually adjust its opacity, and then select its size and placement as it's blended with the original image.

When you've finished editing the image you're working with, tap on the Share button that's displayed at the bottom-right corner of the screen. You can then save your image, send it via email, or upload it directly to Twitter or Facebook.

What's nice about the PicShop HD Photo Editor is the large and easy-to-understand menu buttons, as well as the capability to mix and match enhancement tools and effects to quickly, but dramatically, enhance an image.

TIP   As you're working with an image (prior to saving it), tap the Revert icon to remove all edits or enhancements you've made, or tap the Back icon to undo just your last action.

SPECIALIZED APPS ENABLE YOU TO CREATE UNIQUE SPECIAL EFFECTS

In addition to the many third-party photo editing and image enhancement apps that offer a wide range of different tools, available from the App Store are hundreds of photography apps that enable you to incorporate specific types of special effects into your images. For example, the Photo Reflection HD app ($1.99) enables you to add customizable reflections to your images after they've been taken. MySketch Editor (free) enables you to transform digital images into what look like pencil sketches (see Figure 9-13).

FIGURE 9-13

Use MySketch Editor to make a full-color photo look like a hand-drawn pencil sketch in just seconds.

> **TIP** The Facetune for iPad app ($2.99) is designed specifically for editing por-
> traits of people, and makes it easy to erase blemishes and wrinkles while enhancing
> the visual quality of a portrait.

Use the Photo Mosaica app (free) to create single mosaic images from an entire
album worth of images, or use the Over app ($1.99) to incorporate customized
text and/or professionally designed clip art to your images.

If you want to transform a full-color photo into a visually stunning black-and-
white image, and then be able to work with the monochromatic shades of gray,
black, and white to create vivid effects, the Monokrom Photo Editor app ($0.99) is
extremely useful (see Figure 9-14).

FIGURE 9-14

The Monokrom Photo Editor does more than just transform a full-color photo into black and white. It also enables you to fully customize the black-and-white effect for creative purposes.

Meanwhile, if you want to transform a photo into black and white, but colorize only a specific object or subject within your images, the Color Splash for iPad app ($0.99) makes creating this type of effect easy.

The Pic Stitch app (free) enables you to combine multiple images into one collage image that can be printed, viewed on a computer or iOS mobile device, or shared via any online social networking service. This app offers 232 different collage templates, plus special effect filters that can be added to one or more images within a collage. (Additional filters, frames, borders, and collage templates are available as in-app purchases.) You can also use the InstaStitch app (free) to combine multiple images into eye-catching collages.

> **NOTE** Many of these apps offer optional in-app purchases, which unlock additional tools, filters, and effects that can be used to edit or enhance your images.

MIX AND MATCH PHOTOGRAPHY APPS TO GET THE RESULTS YOU NEED

Based on the places you'll be shooting as well as your intended subjects, the available lighting, and the overall appearance of the shots you're striving to capture, chances are you'll achieve the best results by using a photography app that's best suited to your particular needs during each shooting situation. In other words, get to know how several Camera app alternatives work and what their respective strengths are when it comes to taking pictures, and then choose which app will help you shoot the best images in a particular situation.

Next, from your iPhone or iPad, choose one or more of the photo editing or image enhancement apps that offer the tools you want or need to ultimately give your images the appearance you desire, and that will enable you to achieve your creative vision.

> TIP When it comes to editing your images, you always have the option of first transferring them from your iPhone or iPad to your Mac or PC, and then using full-featured photo editing software, such as Adobe's Photoshop Elements 12 (PC/Mac), Adobe's Photoshop CC (PC/Mac), Google's Picasa (PC/Mac), Microsoft Photo Gallery (PC), Apple's iPhoto (Mac), or Apple's Aperture (Mac), for example, to work with the transferred images using a much broader range of tools.

To help you get the most out of the features and functions available to you from the third-party photography apps, consider using them with various iPhone or iPad photography accessories. Check out Chapter 10, "Use Optional Accessories to Improve Your Pictures," to learn about some of the optional lenses, tripods, lights, and other tools you can use with your iOS mobile device when taking and/or editing photos.

10

USE OPTIONAL ACCESSORIES TO IMPROVE YOUR PICTURES

Taking pictures using the cameras built in to the iPhone and iPad has become an extremely popular use of these mobile devices. When compared with a higher-end point-and-shoot digital camera or a high-end digital Single Lens Reflex (SLR) camera (from Canon or Nikon, for example), the cameras built in to Apple's mobile devices are somewhat limited in their capabilities. Some of these limitations, however, are easily overcome using optional photography accessories.

TIP   Visit the PhotoJoJo online store (http://photojojo.com/store) to see a vast selection of photography-related accessories and specialty tools for the iPhone and iPad. Another great online resource for learning about and shopping for iPhone and iPad photography accessories is Adorama's website (www.adorama.com/iphonetoolshed).

PHOTOGRAPHY-RELATED ACCESSORIES YOU CAN'T DO WITHOUT

In this chapter, you learn about a handful of highly useful accessories, such as clip-on lenses, tripods/stands, and external lights for the iPhone and/or iPad that can dramatically expand your picture-taking capabilities and, in some cases, make it easier to edit or enhance images after they've been shot.

CLIP-ON LENSES FROM OLLOCLIP

The OlloClip company (www.olloclip.com) is a pioneer in iPhone photography accessories, starting with its original 3-in-1 clip-on lens for the iPhone, which offers a zoom, fisheye, and macro lens. Currently, the company offers a variety of clip-on lens products, including a 4-in-1 lens for the iPhone (which includes a wide angle, fisheye, 10x macro, and 15x lens).

Priced at $69.99, this 4-in-1 lens set, shown in Figure 10-1, is available for the iPhone 4/4s or iPhone 5/5s. You can use it with the Camera app and almost any third-party photography app. However, OlloClip has designed its own proprietary picture-taking app, called OlloClip, which is specifically designed for use with the 3-in-1 or 4-in-1 clip-on lens accessories.

TIP   Available for the iPhone 4/4s or iPhone 5/5s, the iPhone Telephoto Lens from PhotoJoJo ($35.00, http://photojojo.com/store/awesomeness/iphone-telephoto-lens) is a clip-on telephoto (zoom) lens that offers 8x to 12x zoom capabilities, plus an integrated tripod (which is needed to hold the iPhone steady). This lens is larger than the OlloClip Telephoto and Circular Polarizing Lens, but it also offers more powerful zoom capabilities.

FIGURE 10-1

The OlloClip 4-in-1 lens easily attaches to an iPhone 4/4s or iPhone 5/5s. Be sure to purchase the right version of the lens for your phone model.

OlloClip also offers its Telephoto + Circular Polarizing Lens ($99.99). The telephoto lens, shown in Figure 10-2, doubles the zoom strength of the built-in Camera app, and what's currently possible using just the camera lens built in to the iPhone. Meanwhile, the polarizing filter side of this clip-on lens dramatically enhances the colors in photos taken outdoors.

A third clip-on lens accessory available from OlloClip is the Macro 3-in-1 lens. This optional lens offers greater depth of field and enables you to take extreme close-up photos using the iPhone. This clip-on lens includes a 7x, 14x, and 21x macro lens and, like all of OlloClip's lenses, uses optical glass for the lens construction, that's housed in a durable, aircraft-grade aluminum casing.

> **NOTE** When not in use, any of the OlloClip lens products can easily be kept in a pocket. Each lens accessory comes with a small microfiber cloth bag and appropriately sized plastic lens caps. As the name suggests, you can attach an OlloClip to an iPhone and have it ready to use in seconds.

FIGURE 10-2

The OlloClip Telephoto + Circular Polarizing Lens is great for taking photos outdoors and in a wide range of situations.

The OlloClip lenses have two potential drawbacks. First, when attached to the iPhone, they cover the phone's built-in flash, which cannot be used with these lenses. Second, most cases and covers designed for the iPhone don't accommodate the OlloClip being attached to the phone, so the phone itself must be removed from the case.

Because the OlloClip is designed to fit snugly over the corner of an iPhone, even the slight thickness added by a clear protective film that's applied to the front and/or back of an iPhone hinders your ability to connect the lens accessory. To compensate for this, OlloClip has designed its own case, called the Quick-Flip Case ($49.99). It enables you to use an OlloClip lens accessory and still keep your phone protected in a hard shell casing.

The Quick-Flip Case, shown in Figure 10-3, also includes a tripod mount and a cold shoe mount, so you can easily connect an optional external light and/or tripod to the iPhone while using the OlloClip for taking pictures.

FIGURE 10-3

The OlloClip Quick-Flip Case is designed for use with one of the OlloClip clip-on lenses, as well as an optional tripod and/or external light source.

NOTE Somewhat similar to the OlloClip 4-in-1 lens for the iPhone is the iPhone Lens Dial ($175.00 to $249.00, http://photojojo.com/store/awesomeness/iphone-lens-dial). Using high-end optical glass, this dial-shaped device slips onto the back of an iPhone 4/4s/5/5s. It offers the choice of a wide angle, fisheye, telephoto, and macro lens. The telephoto lens, for example, almost doubles the zoom capabilities of the iPhone's built-in lens. This device includes two tripod mounts, so you can attach it (and the iPhone) to a tripod with the iPhone positioned in Landscape or Portrait mode.

TIP   Take 360-degree panoramic video shots with your iPhone using the Kogeto Dot ($49.00, www.kogeto.com). This unusually shaped lens attaches to the back of your iPhone. When used with its proprietary Looker app, the Dot enables you to easily capture 360-degree panoramic videos, without having to physically move the iPhone while capturing a video clip. You can then share the videos online or via email, for example.

PORTABLE TRIPODS FROM JOBY

Joby sells a vast selection of portable camera tripods for point-and-shoot digital cameras as well as larger and heavier digital SLR cameras. However, for the iPhone, the company offers its GripTight GorillaPod Stand ($29.95, www.joby.com), which is a tripod with flexible legs that you can place on any flat surface or wrap around a pole, a post, or even a tree branch. Plus, the tips of the legs are magnetic, so it can be attached to almost any metal surface to hold the iPhone perfectly stable and level.

What's nice about the Joby GripTight GorillaPod Stand, shown in Figure 10-4, is that it uses an adjustable easy-mount grip, which accommodates the iPhone perfectly but enables you to attach or detach it from this tripod in seconds. The tripod works with any iPhone model, and can be used with most optional photography accessories.

FIGURE 10-4

The Joby GripTight GorillaPod Stand has flexible legs with magnets on its feet. It firmly holds any iPhone model in place.

THE XSHOT AND LOOQ ONE-HANDED CAMERA EXTENDERS

Taking self-portraits (selfies) or group photos that also feature yourself can be a challenge with the iPhone, unless there's a mirror nearby or you have long arms. Using a one-handed camera extender, however, you can attach your iPhone to one end, extend out this rodlike accessory, and hold it at a good distance and height from your face to capture a well-framed selfie almost anywhere.

The Looq for iOS ($44.99, http://looqsystem.com/looq.htm) weighs just 3.8 ounces and measures 7 inches long by 1.5 inches wide by 6.5 inches high when folded, but expands up to 24 inches long when you're ready to take photos. Built in to this one-handed camera extender is a Selfie button in the handle, so you can remotely press the iPhone's Shutter button when the phone is extended away from your body.

> **TIP** Available for free from the App Store is the Looq app, which is designed specifically for use with the Looq camera extender. It offers most of the features built in to the Camera app, but allows for remote access to them via the device's Selfie button.

The XShot 2.0 ($34.95, http://xshot.com), when used with the XShot iPhone Case, works very much like the Looq, but without the Selfie button. The XShot 2, shown in Figure 10-5, is equipped with a universal tripod mount, which connects to the tripod mount built in to the XShot iPhone Case (sold separately for $19.99). When closed, the XShot 2 one-handed camera extender is only 9 inches long, but it expands up to 37 inches long when in use.

FIGURE 10-5

The XShot 2 is shown here with an iPhone 4s and the optional XShot iPhone Case.

EXTERNAL CONTINUOUS LIGHTING SOLUTIONS AND iPHONE FLASH ALTERNATIVES

If you're shooting with an iPad, or you want to shine more direct light onto your subject than what the iPhone's flash can provide, one option is to use an external, battery-powered, continuous light source that's designed for use with an iOS mobile device. Most of these lights were created primarily for shooting video, but they also work perfectly well as a replacement for a flash when taking pictures with an iPhone or iPad in low light.

The iFlash LED from Cyanics ($12.99, www.cyanics.net) is a tiny LED light that attaches to the bottom of your iPhone 3gs/4/4s via its 30-pin Dock connector port. It uses the iPhone's own battery for power, but greatly increases the strength of the iPhone's built-in flash by shining a continuous light source onto your subject.

The Pocket Spotlight ($30.00, www.photojojo.com) is a portable, continuous light accessory that plugs in to the headphone jack of the iPhone or iPad. It measures 2.5" × 1.5" and includes 32 LED lights that are powered via a rechargeable battery that lasts up to one hour. The light's intensity is adjustable, which gives you tremendous flexibility to light up your subject without causing unwanted shadows or other harsh lighting effects.

Because this is a continuous lighting solution and it works independently from your iPhone or iPad, you can fully utilize the Camera app's AE/AF sensor (or the autoexposure and/or autofocus sensor utilized by any photography app), plus use this lighting accessory with the Camera app's HDR shooting mode.

> **TIP** To add more dramatic lighting effects to your photos, a package of color filters are sold separately ($10.00) that you can place over the LEDs of the Pocket Spotlight.

A similar battery-powered continuous light accessory is available from Bower. The iSpotlight Smartphone LED light includes a clip that attaches to the side or top of any iPhone model, or it can be plugged in to the headphone jack of your iPhone or iPad. Available from Amazon.com ($33.49, www.amazon.com/gp/product/B00DO79NA4), this tool is a 32-bulb LED that offers up to one hour of continuous light each time its internal battery is charged.

A similarly designed continuous light product for the iPhone or iPad is available from Polaroid ($29.99, www.amazon.com/Polaroid-iPhone-Samsung-Blackberry-Motorola/dp/B00DC6PRI4).

TIP Instead of attaching any of these continuous light sources directly to your iPhone or iPad, you can connect them to a portable tripod, and then position two or three of them around your subject (at any desired height) to create a bright and evenly lit environment virtually anywhere, indoors or outdoors. Using multiple lights positioned around your subject can virtually eliminate unwanted shadows and the noise created when shooting in low-light situations without a flash.

A startup company called Brick & Pixel has designed a patented iPhone 5/5s case with a built-in ring flash that surrounds the entire back of an iPhone. Thus, it offers a bright, even light when pictures are taken in low-light situations. Thanks to its design, the flash causes fewer harsh shadows and, when used correctly, won't wash out or overexpose your subject. As you can see, the flash is actually built in to the case (see Figure 10-6).

NOTE The Lightstrap iPhone case ($97.00) was slated to begin shipping in April 2014, but as of December 2013 was in the process of using crowdfunding to raise $245,000 to finance the development and manufacturing of the product. Check the company's website (www.lightstrap.com) for availability.

FIGURE 10-6

The Lightstrap iPhone 5 case uses a rectangular-shaped flash that surrounds the back of this patented iPhone case. The white area of the case is actually the flash.

USE A PRESSURE-SENSITIVE STYLUS WHEN EDITING YOUR PHOTOS

When it comes to editing your digital images on your iPhone or iPad with a third-party app that enables you to paint effects on the screen and/or use other precision tools to enhance your images, using an optional pen-shaped stylus, instead of your finger, can be very helpful. You can purchase a basic pen-shaped stylus that's compatible with the iPhone or iPad from many different companies, for between $10.00 and $40.00. One nice stylus that doubles as a traditional pen is the L-Tech Plus Stealth Ballpoint with Stylus from Levenger ($69.99, www.levenger.com).

A growing number of third-party photography apps, including Adobe Photoshop Touch, are compatible with the Hex 3 Jaja Pressure Sensitive Stylus ($89.99, www.hex3.co/products/jaja). This wireless pen-shaped stylus has a pressure-sensitive Teflon tip, so as you press harder or softer on the iPad or iPhone's screen, the editing, drawing, or painting tool you're using with a compatible app adjusts accordingly. The company also offers the Nota Ultrafine Stylus ($44.95), which is not pressure sensitive.

USE YOUR iPHONE OR iPAD AS A REMOTE SHUTTER BUTTON TRIGGER FOR YOUR DIGITAL SLR CAMERA

In addition to serving as a standalone camera, the iPhone or iPad can connect directly to your high-end digital SLR camera and be used as a programmable remote shutter button trigger. For example, there's the Triggertrap ($30.00, http://photojojo.com/store/awesomeness/trigger-trap), which connects to many Nikon and Canon digital SLR cameras using a special sync cord. You can then use a special app on your iOS mobile device to program or manually activate the camera's shutter button.

TIP The free Wireless Mobile Utility from Nikon enables your iPhone or iPad to control many Nikon digital SLR and CoolPix cameras wirelessly, as long as the iOS mobile device and camera are linked to the same wireless network and the optional Nikon Wireless Mobile Adapter ($59.95) is used. This accessory works with a handful of Nikon's digital SLR cameras and is used to establish a two-way connection between an iOS mobile device and the camera, so the iPhone or iPad can control the picture-taking functionality of the camera, while the camera can wirelessly send digital images to the iOS device.

Canon digital SLR camera users should take a look at Canon's free EOS Remote app. It works with any Canon camera with built-in Wi-Fi capabilities. It too enables the camera to be controlled by an iPhone or iPad while shooting and enables images to be sent wirelessly from a compatible Canon camera directly to an iOS mobile device immediately after they've been shot.

CREATE PRINTS FROM YOUR iPHONE/iPAD PHOTOS

Being able to take awesome-looking photos using your iPhone or iPad enables you to easily capture memories virtually anywhere, without having to carry around a standalone digital camera and an assortment of photography accessories and equipment. After you've shot and edited your images, the next step is to share them.

There are many ways to share digital images, both online and in the real world. One set of options involves sharing your photos online—using a popular social networking service (like Facebook, Instagram, or Twitter), an online-based photo sharing service (like Smugmug.com, Shutterfly.com, or Snapfish.com), via email, or using iCloud's My Photo Stream and Shared Photo Stream features.

> **NOTE** Options for sharing your photos online are covered in Chapter 12, "Share Your Digital Photos Online," and Chapter 13, "Discover iCloud's My Photo Stream and Shared Photo Stream."

Long before there was the Internet, however, photographers created traditional paper-based prints, which can be showcased in picture frames, displayed in traditional photo albums, carried in a wallet, incorporated into a scrapbook, or stored in an old shoebox only to be taken out and viewed when you want to reminisce about past experiences.

> **NOTE** You can also incorporate the photos you take using your iPhone or iPad into professionally printed and bound photo books, or use them to create unique personalized products and gifts, which you'll learn more about in Chapter 14, "Other Ways to Share Your Digital Photos."

The focus of this chapter, however, is on the various methods you can use to create professional-quality prints on photo paper. Keep in mind that when it comes to creating these prints, you have a wide range of options in terms of how they're created.

Prints from your images can be made in a wide range of popular sizes, such as 4" × 6", 5" × 7", 8" × 10", or wallet size, so that they'll easy fit into frames or photo albums. In some cases, prints from your images can also be created in custom sizes or made into poster-size enlargements and printed on materials other than photo paper.

Beyond just choosing print sizes, as the photographer, you can often select the photo paper quality used to create the prints, as well as the photo paper's finish—glossy, semi-glossy, matte, luster, or satin—which also impacts the appearance of your prints.

CREATE PRINTS FROM HOME USING AN AIRPRINT-COMPATIBLE PHOTO PRINTER

The whole DIY (do it yourself) trend continues to be popular, and when it comes to creating prints from the digital images stored in your iPhone or iPad, it's possible to create professional-quality prints at home, from your office, or even while on the go, using an AirPrint-compatible photo printer. Just like a traditional ink-jet printer, a home photo printer can print in full color. Several things set photo printers apart from run-of-the-mill ink-jet printers, however. For example, photo printers use special inks that are designed to adhere to photo paper, display vivid colors, and not smudge or fade over time.

NOTE Many printer manufacturers now offer all-in-one printer solutions, which allow the printer to be used to print any type of document on regular paper, as well as create prints using photo paper. These devices can also be used as a scanner, a copier, and in some cases a fax machine. However, to create the highest-quality prints, you should use a specialized photo printer that's capable of creating prints at a high resolution.

As you'll discover, photo printers typically have adjustable paper trays, allowing for different sizes of photo paper. This makes it easy to quickly create one or several prints at a time, in the size(s) you need, without having to measure and manually cut the photo paper. The more feature-packed photo printers contain two or more separate paper trays, each of which can be stocked with photo paper in a different size.

Meanwhile, one feature that's built in to iOS 7 is called AirPrint. This feature enables your iPhone or iPad to wirelessly connect to a compatible printer for even easier printing of photo files.

Apple has teamed up with many well-known printer manufacturers, including Canon, Epson, Brother, and HP, to create AirPrint-compatible printers, including a handful of high-quality photo printers and all-in-one printers that are competitively priced, starting around $100.00.

TIP For an up-to-date list of AirPrint-compatible printer manufacturers, as well as specific printer models, visit http://support.apple.com/kb/ht4356.

If your plan is to create prints from your digital photos directly from your iPhone or iPad using a photo printer, be sure to invest in an AirPrint-compatible photo printer. Otherwise, you'll probably need to first transfer your images from your iOS mobile device to your Mac or PC, and then print the images from your computer.

Many photo printers that are not AirPrint-compatible, however, are Wi-Fi or Bluetooth compatible. In these cases, special printer-specific iPhone/iPad apps are sometimes available that enable you to print wirelessly, directly from your iOS mobile device. Before purchasing a printer with wireless functionality (that's not AirPrint-compatible), be sure a printing app for that printer make and model is available from the App Store.

The drawback to using a wireless but non-AirPrint-compatible printer is that you can't print directly from the Photos or iPhoto apps (or another third-party photography app). You must first import the image(s) into a special printing app, which adds an extra step to the printing process.

TIP   The benefit to using an AirPrint-compatible photo printer is that you can take, view, edit, and then print images directly from your iPhone or iPad, without having to first transfer them to another computer or online service. The AirPrint function can be used directly from the Photos or iPhoto app, for example, but is also supported by many other third-party photography apps that have a Print feature.

CHOOSE AN AIRPRINT-COMPATIBLE PHOTO PRINTER THAT MEETS YOUR NEEDS

There are several things to consider when choosing an AirPrint-compatible photo printer, including your needs and budget. If you'll be creating many prints on an ongoing basis, you'll want to invest in a higher-speed, better-quality photo printer that has at least two adjustable paper trays. However, if you're on a budget, and you plan to create prints only occasionally, a lower-end and less-expensive home photo printer or all-in-one ink-jet printer will work just fine.

As you're shopping for a photo printer, in addition to AirPrint compatibility, some of the features you'll want to look for include the following:

- The printer's print speed. This is typically measured by how long it takes to create a single 5" × 7" print.
- The number of paper trays the printer has. More than one paper tray reduces the need to swap photo paper each time you want to create a different size print.
- The photo paper sizes that can easily be used with the photo printer. Some are fully adjustable, and can accommodate 4" × 6" to 8.5" × 11" (or even larger) printer paper. Other specialized photo printers can only accommodate one size of photo paper, such as 4" × 6".

- The number of colored ink cartridges that are required to operate the printer, and how much the replacement cartridges cost. Don't be fooled by a low-cost printer that ultimately requires you to invest $50.00 or more each time the ink cartridges need to be replaced.

- The average life of the ink cartridges. In other words, on average, how many 5" × 7" prints, for example, will you be able to create if you start with a set of new ink cartridges. For a full-size photo printer, you should be able to create between 100 and 200 full-color, 5" × 7" prints per set of ink cartridges. Some specialty photo printers have smaller ink cartridges that can create only 50 to 100 prints before you'll need to purchase replacement ink cartridges.

NOTE Many printer manufacturers sell their printers at very low prices but require you to purchase high-priced replacement ink cartridges on an ongoing basis to keep the printer functional. Typically, you'll save money over time if the printer requires a black ink cartridge and just one multicolor ink cartridge. Some higher-end photo printers, however, require six or eight separate colored ink cartridges to be used at once, and each needs to be purchased separately.

The paper tray(s) in a photo printer are often adjustable, so you can insert 4" × 6" or 5" × 7" photo paper into it. To create 8" × 10" prints, for example, you'd use 8.5" × 11" photo paper, and then trim it accordingly.

NOTE Special perforated photo paper is available that makes it easy to trim 8" × 10" prints from 8.5" × 11" photo paper, or create multiple wallet-size prints at once.

In addition to traditional full-size photo printers, there are a handful of specialized photo printers designed for use with iOS mobile devices that are battery powered, portable, and can be used exclusively for creating 4" × 6" size prints. The Smartphone Photo Cube Printer ($159.00), for example, is available from SharperImage.com and a wide range of other online retailers. This printer weighs about three pounds and can create 4" × 6" prints (or panoramic images measuring 4" × 10" or 4" × 16") in one to three minutes per print.

NOTE   Similar to the Smartphone Photo Cube is the VuPoint Photo Cube (www.vupointsolutions.com/photo_cube_compact_photo_printer), which is sold online and through several consumer electronics and office supply superstores. VuPoint also offers a wireless version of its cube printer.

The Smartphone Photo Cube printer uses a special cartridge, which contains photo paper and ink for creating up to 36 4" × 6" prints ($24.99 each). The Smartphone Photo Cube printer connects to your iOS mobile device's Lightning or 32-pin Dock Connector port. In other words, it's not wireless.

CAUTION   Every year, the printer manufacturers release new printer models and discontinue older models. Although you can often save money initially by buying a discontinued printer model, you might ultimately have trouble locating and being able to purchase compatible ink cartridges for an outdated or obsolete printer. Due to ever-changing technology, the lifespan of a photo printer averages around three to four years before it becomes outdated.

Although an AirPrint-compatible photo printer works with any iPhone, iPad, or Mac computer, any non-AirPrint-compatible printer works with your desktop or notebook computer, either wirelessly or via a cable.

NOTE   If a photo printer is not AirPrint-compatible and does not have a special printing app available for it, you first must transfer your images from your iOS mobile device to the photo management software installed on your PC or Mac (such as iPhoto or Aperture), and then edit and print your images from your computer.

SEND IMAGES TO AN AIRPRINT PRINTER FROM YOUR iPHONE OR iPAD

When using the Photos app on your iPhone or iPad to send an image to your AirPrint-compatible printer, be sure to set up the printer and make sure it's turned on and has ink and photo paper installed. Then, from the Photos app, view the image from which you want to create a print, and tap the Share icon (see Figure 11-1).

FIGURE 11-1

To print an image from the Photos app, select the image, and then tap the Share icon. When viewing the Share menu, tap on the Print button.

TIP   You can also view an album, select multiple image thumbnails within that album, and then tap the Share icon to access the Print command. To do this, while viewing the camera roll or thumbnails from another album on the iPhone or iPad, tap on the Select option that's displayed in the top-right corner of the screen. Then, one at a time, tap on the thumbnail for each image you want to select and ultimately print (see Figure 11-2). As each image is selected, a blue–and-white check mark appears in the bottom-right corner of the thumbnail.

When all of the desired images are selected, tap on the Share icon. On the iPhone, it can be found in the bottom-left corner of the screen. On the iPad, it's displayed in the top-left corner of the screen. Next, tap on the Print button. Choose the printer and number of copies per image you want to create, and then tap on the Print option.

FIGURE 11-2

When viewing the contents of an album, tap the Select option, and then choose one or more images that you want to print.

Displayed at the bottom of the Share menu in the Photos app are two rows of command icons. On the iPhone, swipe your finger from right to left along the bottom row of icons to locate the Print icon. Tap on it.

From the Printer Options screen, shown in Figure 11-3, tap on the Printer field, and select the AirPrint-compatible photo printer you want to use. Next, tap on the + or - icon that's displayed to the right of the Copy field to select how many copies of the print you want to create.

Assuming your iPhone (or iPad) can establish a wireless connection to the photo printer, the Print button becomes active near the bottom of the Printer Options screen. Tap on it to send the image from your iOS mobile device to the photo printer.

●●●○○ AT&T 🛜   10:03 AM   ⚹ 98% ▬▬

Cancel   **Printer Options**

Printer Photosmart 6510 series [... ⟩

2 Copies   — | +

Print

FIGURE 11-3

From the Printer options screen, select your AirPrint-compatible printer and how many copies of the print you want to create.

TIP From the optional iPhoto app, tap on the Share icon, and then tap on the Print button from iPhoto's expanded Share menu (see Figure 11-4). From the Print Menu screen, select one or more images to create prints from. Then, from the Printer Options screen, select your AirPrint-compatible photo printer and the number of copies you want to make. Tap on the Print option that becomes active to then send the image file(s) to the printer.

Similar functionality is also built in to some, but not all, third-party photography apps, some of which are described in Chapter 9, "Photography Apps That Expand Your Photo Editing and Enhancement Capabilities."

FIGURE 11-4

The optional iPhoto app has an expanded Share menu that also contains a Print button. It's used to send an image to an AirPrint-compatible printer.

> **TIP** Instead of creating prints using your own photo printer, from the Share menu in the optional iPhoto app, you can order prints from Apple's own photo lab. To do this, tap on the Order Prints button, as opposed to the Print button.

One of the biggest problems consumers have with photo printers is that if the printer goes unused for long periods of time, the printer heads in the printer and/or the ink cartridges clog or dry up. When this happens, you typically need to run the printer's various diagnostic tools one or more times. This often uses up a substantial amount of ink, as well as costly photo paper. To conserve photo paper, when running the printer's diagnostics, use regular copy paper.

> **TIP** If you know you won't be using the photo printer for weeks or months at a time, consider removing the printer's ink cartridges and storing them at room temperature in plastic sandwich bags.

When your photo printer is operating correctly, the cost per print to create individual prints at home from your digital images is slightly higher than what you'd pay for the same prints to be created by a one-hour photo lab.

Depending on the printer make and model, the average cost is between $0.30 and $1.00 per print. The size of the prints being made, the cost of the replacement ink cartridges, and the price of the photo paper you purchase directly impact your average cost per print.

The benefits of using a home photo printer to create prints from images taken with or stored in your iPhone or iPad are that you can create prints in the comfort of your home, anytime you want, and choose the print sizes and quantities you want, without having to wait. You can also easily make edits or enhancements to a digital image and then quickly reprint it to achieve better results.

WHAT YOU SHOULD KNOW ABOUT PHOTO PAPER

To create professional-quality prints, it is necessary to use specialized photo paper with a photo printer. Photo paper is available from consumer electronics stores, office supply superstores, and specialty photography stores, as well as from online merchants.

Photo paper that's designed for consumers typically comes in packs of 25, 50, or 100 sheets and is available in precut 4" × 6", 5" × 7", and 8.5" × 11" sizes. Perforated 8.5" × 11" sheets for creating 8" × 10" and wallet-size prints in groups of four are also available and sold separately.

All photo paper is rated using an industry-standard, star-based rating system (between one and five stars), which determines its quality.

> **TIP** For large-format photo printers, such as the Epson Stylus R2000, photo paper is also available in larger sizes (enabling you to create poster-size prints), but larger-size photo paper often needs to be special ordered online. The Epson Stylus R2000 is an example of a photo printer that requires the use of the free Epson Connect Creative Print app to create prints directly from an iPhone or iPad.

Five-star photo paper is the highest-quality consumer-oriented photo paper available. It's thicker, designed to hold and retain the photo printer's ink better, and won't smudge or fade. As a result, the prints you create showcase brighter and more vivid colors that should last for many years.

CAUTION If the prints you create with a photo printer or using a photo lab are exposed over long periods to direct sunlight or extreme humidity, the colors often fade, bleed, or smudge over time.

TIP Choose photo paper that's ranked between three and five stars. To achieve the best results possible from your photo printer, use the highest-quality photo printer ink possible, along with five-star photo paper.

The final decision you need to make when it comes to photo paper is its finish. Three popular types of paper finishes are readily available, including glossy, semi-glossy, and matte. Higher-end photo paper also comes in a luster or satin finish, but this is typically more expensive and available only online or from photo specialty stores.

Glossy photo paper enables you to create prints that have a shiny, high-gloss, reflective finish. This is typically what's used when you order prints from a one-hour photo lab.

Semi-gloss photo paper has some shine and reflective quality, but much less so than glossy photo paper.

Choose a matte finish if you want prints to have no shine or reflective quality whatsoever. Matte finish prints are best for inserting into a glass covered picture frame or a photo album that uses clear plastic film over each page.

TIP Luster or satin finish photo paper allows prints to showcase a more formal appearance. It's what's often used by professional photographers when creating formal portraits or wedding albums.

Some companies that manufacture high-end photo paper (which can be ordered online or purchased from photo specialty stores) include Hahnemuhle Fine Art paper (www.hahnemuehle.com), Ilford (http://ilfordphoto.com), Harman Professional (www.harman-inkjet.com), and Red River Paper (www.redriverpaper.com).

Keep in mind that each printer manufacturer sells its own branded photo paper and recommends using only its own photo paper in its respective printers. This is not necessary! Any photo paper can be used in any nonspecialty photo printer, as long as the printer's paper tray can accommodate the dimensions of that paper. Thus, you can use Epson photo paper in an HP photo printer, for example (or vice versa), or purchase less-expensive Staples or Office Max branded photo paper and use it in any nonspecialty photo printer from any manufacturer.

HOW TO SAVE MONEY ON PHOTO PRINTER INK

The photo printer manufacturers make money from the sale of their printers but generate huge profits from the ongoing sale of replacement printer ink cartridges for those printers. Each printer manufacturer sells its own line of ink for its specific printer models. In most cases, each photo printer either uses a black ink cartridge and a multicolor ink cartridge, or up to eight different colored ink cartridges at once to create full-color prints.

To save money, you can shop online and often find generic (non-brand-name) ink cartridges that are compatible with your photo printer. However, unlike photo paper rated independently of the actual manufacturer, the quality of these cartridges might or might not be equal to or better than the brand-name cartridges, although they'll typically be much cheaper.

The easiest way to find compatible, non-brand-name ink cartridges for your make and model photo printer is to go online to a price comparison website (such as Nextag.com) and, in the search field at the top of the screen, type the exact make and model of your photo printer, along with the words ink cartridges.

> **TIP** You can also shop online by visiting Amazon.com or eBay.com, and quickly search for multiple online vendors that offer compatible ink cartridges for your printer make and model. Keep in mind that ink cartridges are printer model specific, not just printer manufacturer specific. In other words, ink cartridges for an Epson Stylus Photo 1500W printer do not work with an Epson Stylus R2000 printer.

If you own the Epson Stylus Photo 1500W photo printer, for example, visit www.nextag.com and enter the search phrase Epson Stylus Photo 1500W ink cartridges into the search field. The search results reveal dozens of independent printer ink companies that sell compatible and discounted ink cartridges for this particular printer make and model.

CAUTION Before buying compatible non-brand-name photo printer ink cartridges from an independent company, read the online reviews for both the ink cartridges themselves and the online merchant. Try to determine whether any of your fellow consumers have experienced problems with the ink or the merchant. Also, pay attention to the shipping charges added to your order. In some cases, companies promote low prices for the ink cartridges but charge an exorbitant shipping and handling fee.

HAVE PRINTS CREATED AT A ONE-HOUR PHOTO LAB

Many pharmacies (including Walgreens, Rite-Aid, and CVS), mass-market consumer retail stores (such as Costco, Wal-Mart, and Target), and photo specialty stores all offer one-hour photo processing. The trick, however, is transferring the images stored in your iOS mobile device to these photo labs so the digital images can be transformed into professional-quality prints.

To make this process as easy as possible, many of these one-hour photo labs have their own specialized apps that can be acquired for free from the App Store. Once you launch the app, simply select the image(s) you want to create prints from, choose your desired print size(s), and select how many copies of each print you want.

The app then connects to the Internet and uploads the selected image file(s) from your iPhone or iPad directly to the one-hour photo lab's computer for processing. Within an hour or so, your prints will be ready for pickup at the retail location you select.

TIP When using this type of app to order prints, be sure to select the correct pickup location, especially if the pharmacy or store has multiple locations in your area. The app typically uses your iPhone or iPad's built-in GPS capabilities to determine your location and then helps you pinpoint and select the closest retail location.

This feature is particularly useful if you're on vacation and want to create prints while you're still away. Using one of these apps, you can find the closest Costco, for example, upload your digital images, and then by the time you drive to the store and do some shopping, your prints are ready for pickup (typically within an hour).

Keep in mind that some retailers that have a one-hour photo lab incorporate print-ordering capabilities into their existing proprietary apps, whereas others have standalone (separate) apps for this purpose.

Using a one-hour photo lab to create prints from the digital images taken with or stored on your iPhone or iPad has several advantages. For example, you don't need to invest in a home photo printer or ensure you maintain an ample supply of photo paper and ink. You can also order the print sizes and quantities you want, and have truly professional-quality prints created and ready to pick up within an hour or so. Another advantage is the cost per print is often less than other options, like using a home photo printer.

NOTE In some cases, instead of having a proprietary app, a one-hour photo processing service provides a special website that can be used to upload images. Keep in mind, most of these websites are not compatible with the iPhone or iPad, so it is often necessary to first transfer the image files to your primary computer before uploading them to the one-hour photo lab's website.

TIP The free Kicksend app enables you to select images that are stored in your iPhone or iPad and order standard size prints from the app developer's own photo lab, which are then mailed to you within a few business days. The app also enables you to select the closest one-hour photo lab to your current location that's in a participating Walgreen's, CVS Pharmacy, Duane Reade, Target, or Wal-Mart store; order your prints in the quantities and sizes you want; and then pick them up at the selected location within an hour. The cost associated with print pickup varies based on which lab you select, but prices are extremely reasonable, often starting at $0.19 for a 4" × 6" print.

Although each of these retail chains has its own iPhone/iPad app for ordering prints, the Kicksend app enables you to choose which chain's photo lab you want to use for any given order. After you've entered your credit card details just once, placing an order takes less than one minute. The app also enables images to be shared via email with others, with no file size limitations.

For more information about the Kicksend app, its latest features, and the most current line-up of one-hour photo labs operated by popular retailers that it's compatible with, visit http://kicksend.com/apps.

> **TIP** If you're the parent or grandparent of a newborn child, the free Offspring app enables you to use the cameras built in to your iPhone or iPad to create a digital baby book that chronicles your child's early days, weeks, and months using text, photos, and video. What's great about this app is that it keeps your baby pictures organized by "Moments," so you can chronicle and share funny things your child does, important milestones, and other things you want to remember.
>
> At anytime, the app enables you to share your baby photos and content with others electronically, or you can use the app to create themed photo books that are professionally printed and bound.
>
> The Offspring app is an excellent tool for taking, organizing, sharing, and printing baby photos, plus keeping track of the date, time, and location where each photo was taken. Keywords and/or text-based captions can also be associated with each picture. Visit http://offspringapp.com for more information about this extremely innovative and well-designed app that was designed by parents for parents.

USE THE COSTCO APP TO ORDER PRINTS FROM YOUR iPHONE OR iPAD

To order prints to be created at any Costco location, from the App Store, download the free Costco app. When you launch the app, scroll through the main menu and select the Photo Center option (see Figure 11-5). Next, tap on the Order Prints button and give the app permission to access the photos stored on your iOS mobile device by tapping on the OK button.

From the Image Source screen, tap on the iPhone Photos option to select desired images that are stored on your iPhone or iPad. After selecting the images from their thumbnails, tap on the Order Prints button.

Each selected photo is then displayed as a thumbnail, along with an option to choose how many 4" × 6", 5" × 5", 5" × 7", or 8" × 10" prints you want to create from that image (see Figure 11-6). Tap on the button below each print size heading to increase the number of copies for that print size you want to order.

> **NOTE** Using Costco's app to order prints for pickup at a specific Costco location, prices for prints range from $0.13 each for a 4" × 6" print, to $1.49 each for an 8" × 10" print.

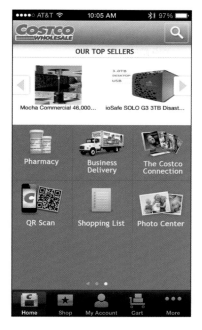

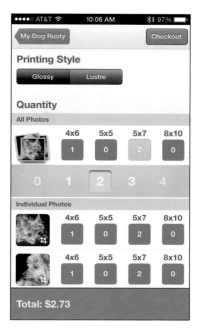

FIGURE 11-5

From the Costco app's main menu screen, select the Photo Center option to begin ordering prints directly from your iPhone or iPad.

FIGURE 11-6

Choose the print size(s) and number of copies you want to create from each digital image.

Displayed near the top-left corner of this screen is a Printing Style option. Tap on either the Glossy or Lustre (matte) option to choose the photo paper finish that will be used when creating your prints.

A running total for your print order is displayed in the bottom-left corner of the screen. When your order is ready to upload, make sure your iPhone or iPad has Internet access, and then tap on the Checkout button.

> **NOTE** If this is your first time using the Costco app to create prints, after tapping on the Checkout button, tap on the Create Account button. When prompted, enter your name, phone number, Costco member number, and email address, and then create a custom password. This needs to be done only once.

The Costco app uploads your images to Costco's Photo Center computer, and your prints are created. A message appears giving you an approximate time they'll be ready for pickup, and at the same time, an order number is created.

Once an order is placed, from the Costco app's Photo Center menu screen, tap on the Order Status button to check on the status of your print order. You can also use the app to create an online backup of images, without immediately placing a print order. To use this feature, from the Photo Center menu screen, tap on the Upload option.

NOTE   Many of the apps from retailers like Walgreens, Wal-Mart, and Target work very much like Costco's when it comes to ordering prints directly from your iPhone or iPad. Some of these apps, however, allow you to only select photos that are stored on your iOS mobile device, whereas others enable you to also select from your photos that are stored online, as part of your Facebook or Instagram account, for example.

ORDER PRINTS FROM AN ONLINE-BASED PHOTO LAB

Instead of using a specialized app to upload your photos to a local one-hour photo lab, an ever-growing number of professional photo labs and photo processing services now offer specialized and proprietary apps that enable you to order prints directly from your iPhone or iPad but have the prints mailed to you within three to five business days (or less if you're willing to pay for expedited shipping).

Using an online-based photo service has several advantages. For example, many of these services can also be used for free online photo sharing. Thus, you can create an online gallery, album, or slideshow to showcase and share your images with friends and family, and also order prints from selected images. Another benefit is that these photo services typically offer a greater selection of print sizes to choose from, as well as more photo paper finish options.

In addition, these photo services often enable you to create products or photo gifts that can be ordered directly from your iOS mobile device. For example, the Shutterfly app enables you to easily design and order iPhone cases, mugs, canvas prints, photo books, poster-size wall décor, photo greeting cards, holiday ornaments, mouse pads (see Figure 11-7), key chains, and other products that can showcase one or more of your favorite photos. This can be done directly from the app.

FIGURE 11-7

Using the Shutterfly app on the iPad, create a mouse pad that features your photo, and have it manufactured and then shipped to you (or any desired recipient).

NOTE Using the iPad version of the Shutterfly app, it's much easier to design and order photo products, although this can be done with the iPhone version of the app as well. Ordering prints from Shutterfly on the iPhone or iPad is a quick and easy process, especially after you set up a free account with the service.

TIP One benefit to using a well-respected and established online photo service, such as Shutterfly, to order prints and photo products is the competitive pricing that's offered and the company's 100 percent satisfaction guarantee. If you don't like how your prints or photo products turn out, you can request a full refund.

Plus, you can often create a free online account with one of these services, and also use it as a free, cloud-based online backup solution for your image collection.

From the App Store, you can find and download specialized apps from a variety of different online photo services that enable you to order prints directly from your iPhone or iPad. Some of these apps include FreePrints, Shutterfly, MotoPhoto, MailPix, and MPix Tap To Print (Miller's Professional Imaging).

> **TIP** Apple's own iPhoto app also enables you to order custom prints from Apple's photo lab and have those prints mailed to you. See Chapter 7, "Expand Your Photo Editing Toolbox with iPhoto," for more information about this feature.

After you install a proprietary app from an online photo processing service, the app walks you through the process of selecting which photos you want to create prints from, choosing the size prints you want, and choosing the quantity of each print. Then, once you set up a free online account, placing future orders takes just seconds because your shipping address and credit card details are already stored in the app.

Based on which online-based photo lab service you use, you'll typically find that the quality of the prints you wind up with is superior to what's possible using a one-hour photo lab for several reasons. First, online photo labs typically use higher-quality photo paper and inks. Plus, although one-hour photo labs are typically fully auto-mated, the online labs often have trained professionals operating the equipment. These people can make manual adjustments, as needed, while your prints are being created, to ensure the highest-quality results possible from your digital images.

> **TIP** When choosing which photo lab to use, focus on the quality of the prints, the selection of printing options offered, pricing, shipping and handling fees, and average processing times. You can easily read online reviews of these various ser-vices while viewing an app's description in the App Store.

12

SHARE YOUR DIGITAL PHOTOS ONLINE

After you've taken photos using the cameras built in to your iPhone or iPad, and you've edited or enhanced the images so they look even better, chances are you'll want to share them with other people. One of the easiest ways to do this is to publish them online.

You have a variety of options when it comes to sharing photos online. For example, you can share individual photos or groups of photos with your online friends using an online social networking service, such as Facebook, Twitter, or Instagram.

NOTE In addition to having their own official (free) apps, Facebook and Twitter integration is built in to iOS 7. As a result, you can upload images directly from the Photos (or iPhoto) app to one of these services, or use the official Facebook or Twitter app, which you'll learn more about later in this chapter. All that's required is that you first set up a free Facebook and/or Twitter account.

Another option is to create an online-based gallery or album and then invite people to access the Internet and view the photos you publish. You can do this using iCloud's Shared Photo Stream feature (you'll learn how to do this in the next chapter) or using an online photo sharing service, such as Flickr.com, Shutterfly.com, Dropbox, or Smugmug.com.

NOTE Flickr.com integration is also built in to the Photos and iPhoto apps. To use it, it's necessary to set up a free Flickr account. To use one of these other independent photo sharing services from your iPhone or iPad, you must install the service's free app (via the App Store) or use a third-party app that works with the chosen service.

A third option that's covered in this chapter is sharing photos via email, directly from your iPhone or iPad, using your existing email address. You can do this from the Photos or iPhoto apps, from a third-party photography app, or from the Mail app, after you've set up your email account to work with your device. (You need to do this only once.)

TIP When sharing photos via email, you can attach up to five images to a single email, and then send that email to one or more recipients. In the outgoing email, it's also possible to include a text-based message.

Keep in mind that, to share photos online, your iPhone or iPad needs access to the Internet via a Wi-Fi or cellular connection. If you have a cellular data plan with a preset monthly allocation, consider using only a Wi-Fi connection to upload, send, or share photos; otherwise, you will quickly use up your monthly cellular data allocation.

CAUTION Depending on how you publish your photos online, they might or might not be public. In other words, make sure you fully understand how a particular online service works, and adjust the related privacy settings to ensure that only the people whom you want to see your images have access to them.

At the same time, to help protect the online privacy of the people featured in your photos, think twice before tagging the photos with people's names.

When you tag someone in a photo, that person's name is associated with that digital image and the information becomes searchable, as well as potentially accessible (viewable) by the public. Those seeking out this information could potentially include an entity such as a prospective employer of the person you've tagged.

Also, decide whether you want to share the location where the photos were taken. In some cases, the various online services publish a geotag (the location where a photo was taken) unless you set the app you're using to turn off this information sharing function.

There are several potential reasons you might want to turn off geotagging when publishing photos; for example, if you're publishing photos in real time when you're supposed to be at work but you're clearly not. You also might want to keep your location a secret if you're publishing photos from your hotel while on vacation but don't want people to know where you're staying. Likewise, if your kids are publishing photos online, or you're publishing photos of your kids, you might not want to disclose where they live or attend school by taking and uploading photos with those locations attached to the images.

SHARE IMAGES THROUGH AN ONLINE SOCIAL NETWORKING SERVICE

If you plan to be active on Facebook, Twitter, or Instagram, for example, you must download and install the official app for each service, and then set up a free account. The app walks you through this process. If you already have an existing account with one or more of these services, after installing its app, sign in using your username and password. Then, depending on which service you use, it's possible to upload one image at a time, or in some cases, groups of preselected images at the same time.

TIP In addition to these online social networking services, many free blogging services enable you to create and publish online galleries and share photos with the masses. Wordpress.com, Tumblr, and Blogger.com are three examples of popular blogging services, each of which has its own free app that walks you through the blog creation and post publishing process.

For sharing specific photos and adding a bit of text to go along with the images, Tumblr is a free and particularly easy-to-use online blogging service. Keep in mind that, when you create a blog, it becomes searchable and accessible by the general public—not just specific people you invite to see it.

PUBLISH PHOTOS ON FACEBOOK

Facebook enables you to publish an individual photo or groups of photos as part of a Status Update on your Wall. This can be done from directly within the Photos app, for example, or just as easily using the official Facebook app. However, using the official Facebook app, you can also create albums that contain groups of preselected images.

TIP When you create an album on Facebook, the album itself has a title and can display a basic description of it. Plus, each image in that album can be tagged with the identity of the people featured in the photos, the location where each photo was taken, the time and date the photo was taken, and a custom caption. In addition, it's possible to adjust the privacy settings for each album, so you can decide who is able to access and view your images.

To learn about and adjust Facebook's privacy settings, from the official app on the iPhone, tap on the More icon, and then tap on the Account Settings menu option. Next, tap on the Privacy Shortcuts option.

If you're using the Facebook app on the iPad, tap on the Menu icon (in the top-left corner of the screen), and then tap on the Account Settings option. From the Settings menu, tap on the Privacy option.

ADD PHOTOS TO YOUR FACEBOOK TIMELINE AS A STATUS UPDATE

You can add photos to your Facebook timeline directly from your iPhone or iPad in several different ways. You can do this from the Photos app (or another compatible app) or directly from the official Facebook app.

From the Photos app, to create a Status Update for Facebook that includes photos, follow these steps:

1. Launch the Photos app.

2. Either select the individual image you want to post, or open the album that contains a group of images you want to publish on Facebook as part of a Status Update. When an image is selected, a blue-and-white check mark appears in the bottom-right corner of the image's thumbnail (see Figure 12-1).

> **TIP** When an album is open in Photos, as you're looking at the thumbnails that represent the images in that album, tap on the Select option to choose one or more of those images to share.

Selected Images ───

FIGURE 12-1

Open an album, tap the Select option, and then tap on the thumbnails for the images you want to publish on Facebook.

3. Tap on the Share icon to reveal the Photos app's Share menu.

4. Tap on the Facebook icon (see Figure 12-2).

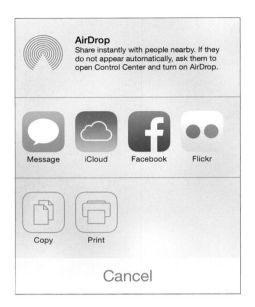

FIGURE 12-2

From the Share menu, tap on the Facebook option.

5. When the Facebook window opens, enter the text you want to associate with your Status Update. The preselected photos are already linked to the Status Update (see Figure 12-3).

6. Tap on the Album field to determine where you want the images to be uploaded in your Facebook account.

7. Tap on the Location field to manually add (and display) the location where the images were taken.

8. Tap on the Audience field to decide who will be able to view the images.

9. When you're ready to publish the Status Update, tap on the Post option.

FIGURE 12-3

Enter the necessary information in the Facebook window to create your post.

To publish photos to your Facebook timeline as a Status Update, using the official Facebook app, follow these steps:

1. Launch the Facebook app on your iPhone or iPad.

2. From the News Feed screen, tap on the Status option (see Figure 12-4).

3. When the Update Status window is displayed (see Figure 12-5), enter your text-based Status Update message in the Write Something field, and then tap on the Camera icon to add one or more images.

Status, Photo, and
Check-In Options

FIGURE 12-4

From the News Feed screen of the Facebook app, tap on the Status option.

FIGURE 12-5

Enter text in the Write Something field of the Update Status window.

4. On the iPhone, select the images you want to include in your Status Update, or tap on the Camera icon to snap a photo from within the Facebook app. On the iPad, tap on the Take Photo or Video button to shoot a photo or video directly from the Facebook app and then publish it on Facebook. Or, tap on the Choose from Library option to select one or more images that are already stored on your mobile device.

5. If you select the Choose from Library option, from the Photos window, find and select the image(s) you want to publish. When an image appears in a Preview window, tap on a subject's face to add a tag to the image, and then tap on the Use option to add it to your Status Update.

6. To include your location or link the people you're with to the posting, tap on the Location or Add Friends icon, respectively.

7. To publish multiple photos at once, repeat step 5. When all of the images you want to publish are selected, tap on the Post option that's displayed near the top-right corner of the Update Status window.

8. The images and the text you entered to be your Status Update are uploaded to Facebook and published almost immediately. Your sharing settings in Facebook determine who can view your images (which are part of your Status Update).

TIP From the Update Status window, tap on the globe-shaped Privacy icon (in the bottom-right corner of the window) to determine who can see the Status Update. Your options include Public, Friends, Friends (Except Acquaintances), Only Me, or people from a specific Friends List that you've pre-created.

ADD PHOTOS TO YOUR FACEBOOK TIMELINE AS A CHECK-IN

To publish photos to your Facebook timeline as a Check-In Update (which includes your location displayed on a map), using the official Facebook app, follow these steps:

1. Launch the Facebook app on your iPhone or iPad.

2. From the News Feed screen, tap on the Check In option.

3. When the Check In window appears, select your location.

4. When the Update Status window appears, enter your text-based Check In message, and then tap on the Camera icon to add one or more images.

5. Tap on the Take Photo or Video button to shoot a photo or video directly from the Facebook app and then publish it on Facebook, or tap on the Choose from Library option to select one or more images that are already stored on your mobile device.

6. If you select the Choose from Library option, from the Photos window, find and select the image(s) you want to publish. When an image appears in a Preview window, tap on a subject's face to add a tag to the image, and then tap on the Use option to add it to your Check In update.

7. To publish multiple photos at once, repeat steps 5 and 6. When all the images you want to publish are selected, tap on the Post option displayed near the top-right corner of the Check In window.

8. The images and the text you entered to be your Check In update are uploaded to Facebook and published almost immediately. Your sharing settings in Facebook determine who can view your images (which are part of your Check In and/or Status updates).

TIP   From the News Feed screen of the official Facebook app, you can also tap on the Photo option to upload one or more photos as part of a status update. When you tap on the Photo option, an Update Status window appears. Fill in the Write Something field with related text, and then tap on the Take Photo or Video button or the Choose from Library button. Follow the steps outlined in steps 6, 7, and 8 that are described above.

TIP   When using the Facebook app to take a photo, which you'll ultimately post online, after snapping the photo, tap on the Done option. From the Camera Roll window that displays the images you've taken, select the image you just shot. From the image edit screen, shown in Figure 12-6, you can use the tools displayed near the bottom of the screen to crop, enhance, or add a special effect filter to the image. The Facebook app includes 14 special effect filters to choose from, any of which will dramatically alter the appearance of your photo.

Tap on the Tag icon to tag specific people in the image. Tap the check mark icon in the top-right corner to save your changes. Next, tap on the Compose icon (in the bottom-right corner of the screen) to return to the Update Status window.

Enhance Tool

Crop Tool

Filters Tool

FIGURE 12-6

Before publishing a photo from the Facebook app, you can use the app's photo editing and enhancement tools to crop, enhance, or add a filter to the image.

PUBLISH AN ALBUM ONLINE IN YOUR FACEBOOK ACCOUNT

To create an online album, which contains a group of images that you want to share online via Facebook, you must use the official Facebook app. Follow these steps to create and publish a new online album:

1. Launch the official Facebook app.

2. From the iPhone, tap on the More icon and select the Photos option. On the iPad, tap on the Menu icon and then tap on the Photos option.

3. Near the top of the screen are three command tabs: Photos of You, Albums, and Synced. Tap on the Albums tab.

4. When the Photos screen appears, thumbnails representing all the albums you currently have stored online in your Facebook account appear. Tap on one of these thumbnails to open an existing album, or tap on the Create Album (plus sign) icon to create a new album.

5. If you opt to create a new album, the Create Album window appears (see Figure 12-7). Fill in the Album Title field, and then add text in the field that says, "Say something about this album." Next, tap on the Location icon if you want to add your location to the post, or tap on the Privacy icon to select who will be able to view the album online. Tap on the Save option to create the album, which is empty. It is now listed in the Photos screen, along with the other existing albums.

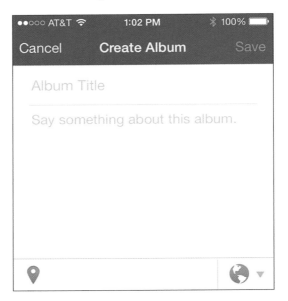

FIGURE 12-7

While using the Facebook app, it's possible to create a new album in your online-based Facebook account, and then populate that album with images you select that are stored on your iOS mobile device.

6. To now add images stored on your iPhone or iPad to an existing album (even an empty one), from the Photos screen, tap on the thumbnail that represents the album you want to use to open it.

7. Tap on the Add Photos (plus sign) icon to select the images you want to upload from your iOS mobile device to the online album. Fill in the optional Add a Caption field, and/or tap on the Take Photo or Choose from Library Option.

8. If you selected Take Photo, snap the photo(s) you want to add using the picture-taking functionality of the Facebook app, which works very much like the Camera app. Or, to select images already stored on your iPhone or iPad, tap on the Choose from Library option. Select an album, and then select one or more images.

9. As you select images, you can add tags by tapping on the subjects in an image's preview. Tap on the Use option to select the image. One at a time, select all of the images you want to add to the Facebook album.

10. Tap on the Upload option to upload the images from your iPhone or iPad to Facebook. The images remain stored on your smartphone or tablet but are also copied to your online-based Facebook account and stored with the album you selected.

> **TIP** Facebook enables you to create as many public or private albums as you desire, and each album can have any number of images stored in it.

> **CAUTION** When you upload images to Facebook, this online service automatically reduces the resolution and file size of the images, making them faster to upload, display, and download. Although Facebook is ideal for sharing photos with your online friends, it is not a service you should use to back up or archive your images.

SHARE ONE IMAGE AT A TIME ON TWITTER

Images can be shared online via Twitter by attaching them to outgoing tweets (messages). This can be done in the Photos app, using the official Twitter app, or using a third-party app that's designed for managing one or more Twitter accounts, such as Twitterific.

> **TIP** Before attempting to share images via Twitter with your followers, you must create a Twitter account, and then set up your iPhone or iPad to work with that account. To do this, launch Settings, tap on the Twitter option, and then tap on the Add Account option. When prompted, enter your username (@username) and password, and then tap on the Sign In button. To first create a new Twitter account, tap on the Create New Account button.

SHARE A PHOTO ON TWITTER USING THE PHOTOS APP

To share one photo at a time with your Twitter followers from within the Photos app, follow these steps:

1. Launch the Photos app.

2. Select the image you want to share with your Twitter followers in the form of a tweet.

3. When you're viewing the image on the screen, tap on the Share button to reveal the Photos app's Share menu.

4. Tap on the Twitter icon.

5. When the Compose Tweet window is displayed (see Figure 12-8), the photo you selected is already attached to the outgoing message. Enter some optional text to accompany the photo. A tweet can include up to 140 characters; however, the inclusion of a photo uses some of those characters, so you only have around 100 characters to work with for your text-based message.

FIGURE 12-8

The Compose Tweet window is used from the Photos app to create and publish a tweet via the Twitter service.

6. If you have multiple Twitter accounts, tap on the Account field to select from which account you want to send the tweet.

7. If you want to include your location in the outgoing tweet, tap on the Location field.

8. When your tweet is ready to publish, tap on the Post option. Within seconds, the image and your text-based tweet are published online and accessible to your Twitter followers, as well as the general public.

> **TIP** When composing a tweet, it's possible to include hash tags in the text-based message to highlight a topic, subject, or keyword, which becomes searchable by the general public. You can include multiple hash tags (#keyword) per tweet. You also can publicly address a specific person in a tweet by adding their Twitter username (@username) within the message.
>
> As an example, look at the tweet in Figure 12-8. Anyone who does a Twitter search for @JasonRich7, or the keyword #zoo, #birds, or #animals, can easily find and view this tweet.

SHARE A PHOTO ON TWITTER USING THE TWITTER APP

To compose and publish a tweet that contains a photo using the official Twitter app, follow these steps:

1. Launch the official Twitter app and sign in to your account.

2. Tap on the Compose Tweet icon.

3. In the What's Happening? field, enter a text-based message that will accompany your tweet. (This can include hash tags or a website URL, for example.)

4. Tap on the Camera icon to use the Twitter app and snap a photo, or tap on the Picture icon to attach a photo that's currently stored on your iOS mobile device.

5. If you opt to select a photo you've already taken, images from your Camera Roll folder appear. Tap on the thumbnail for the image you want to share. If you opt to take a photo, this can be done using the picture-taking capabilities built in to the Twitter app. It works very much like the Camera app.

6. From the Edit Photo window, shown in Figure 12-9, tap on the Enhance icon to automatically enhance an image with a single tap. This auto-adjusts the brightness, contrast, and saturation, for example. Tap on the Filter icon to choose from one of the Twitter app's built-in special effect filters. There are nine filters to choose from. Tap on the Crop icon to crop and reposition your image.

Filters Tool

Enhance Tool

Crop Tool

FIGURE 12-9

From the Twitter app, you can edit and enhance an image before sharing it online.

7. After you've edited your image, tap on the Done option.

8. Upon returning to the Compose Tweet window, if you want to add the location where the image was taken, tap on the Location icon. To change the Twitter account you're using to send the tweet from, tap on your username or profile icon. Otherwise, to publish the tweet online, tap on the Tweet option.

NOTE Even if you've already set up your Twitter account to work with iOS 7 from within Settings, when you begin using the official Twitter app for the first time (or a third-party Twitter-related app), you must still sign in to your existing Twitter account directly from the app.

SHARE IMAGES USING INSTAGRAM

Instagram is a service that works very much like Twitter, but it's designed primarily for sharing one photo at a time with your online followers, friends, and the general public.

To publish photos to Instagram from your iPhone or iPad, use the official Instagram app (free) or a third-party photography app that has Instagram functionality built in. Setting up an Instagram account is free. Keep in mind that when you publish a photo on Instagram, anyone in the general public can access it, although the service also has a direct message feature, which enables you to send single images to specific people.

There are a few things you should know about the Instagram app that make it very useful for sharing photos:

- Instagram uses a square-shaped image format, so any image you opt to share is cropped into a square.

- The Instagram app offers a handful of powerful special effect filters and borders that make enhancing a photo a quick and easy process.

- It's possible to set up the official Instagram app so when you publish a photo onto Instagram, that same image automatically publishes to your Facebook, Twitter, Tumblr, Flickr, and/or Foursquare accounts.

- You can automatically email one or more people a copy of the edited image via the Mail app, directly from the Instagram app.

To select and publish a photo from the Instagram app onto the Instagram service (and one or more compatible services), follow these steps:

1. Launch the official Instagram app.

2. From the main screen, tap on the Picture icon (found at the bottom center of the screen).

3. You can either snap a photo using the picture-taking capabilities of the Instagram app or select a photo that's already stored on your iOS mobile device.

4. If you opt to snap a photo (see Figure 12-10), tap on the Grid icon to turn on or off the onscreen grid that can be superimposed over the viewfinder to assist you in framing your image. Tap on the Camera Selection icon to switch between the front- and rear-facing cameras. Tap on the Flash icon (iPhone only) to turn on or off the flash. Tap on the Shutter button to snap a photo, or tap on the Movie Camera icon to record a short movie clip.

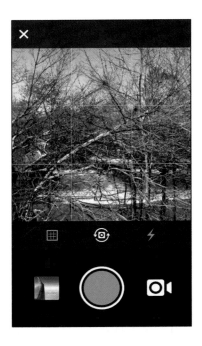

FIGURE 12-10

The official Instagram app enables you to snap photos from within the app, instead of using the Camera app.

5. Tap on the Image Preview icon (displayed near the bottom-left corner of the screen) to select the image you just took, or select one of the images already stored on your smartphone or tablet. Tap on the thumbnail for the image you want to publish.

6. From the Scale & Crop screen (see Figure 12-11), zoom in or out while viewing an image, and reposition the image. Keep in mind that Instagram crops your image into a square shape. Tap the Next option when your selected image has been cropped and properly positioned within the frame.

FIGURE 12-11

From the Scale & Crop screen, you can zoom, crop, and reposition an image, allowing you to adjust to the required square image shape that Instagram uses.

7. Displayed near the bottom of the Edit screen are four command icons for editing your picture (see Figure 12-12). Tap on the Straighten icon to straighten an image or manually make it crooked (for artistic purposes). Tap on the Frame icon to add a border around the image. Tap on the Sharpen icon to sharpen the center of the image (the focal point). Tap on the Brightness icon to adjust the brightness of the image.

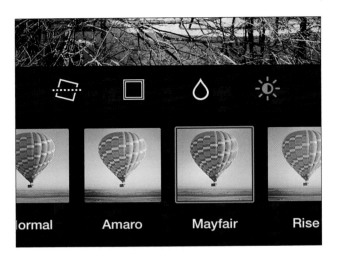

FIGURE 12-12

Use the image editing tools displayed near the bottom of the Edit screen to edit and enhance the selected image before publishing it online.

8. Displayed along the bottom of the screen are the special effect filters built in to the Instagram app. Tap on the Normal (default) option to skip using a filter, or tap on one of the filter thumbnails to add that effect to your image.

9. When you're finished editing the image, tap on the Next button.

10. In the Write a Caption field (see Figure 12-13), add a text-based caption that you want published along with the photo. Just like when using Twitter, in the text portion of the caption, you can include searchable hash tags to highlight a topic, keyword, or subject (#keyword). Adding a caption and/or hash tags is optional.

11. Tap on the Tag People field to add the names of the people who appear in the photo. Keep in mind that, when you add a tag, the names of the people become searchable by the public. (This is optional.)

12. Tap on the Name This Location field to publish the location where the image was taken in the online posting. (This is optional.)

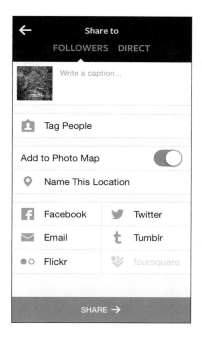

FIGURE 12-13

Before publishing an image, you decide what information (metadata), hash tags, and/or text will be included with it.

13. From the menu near the bottom of the Share To screen, tap on the services to which you want to publish the photo, in addition to Instagram (Facebook, Twitter, Email, Tumblr, Flickr, or Foursquare). You must set up your accounts for each of these services in the Instagram app before using this option.

TIP   Displayed at the top center of the Share To screen are two command tabs, labeled Followers and Direct. Tap on the Followers (default) option to publish your photo on Instagram for your online friends, and potentially the general public, to see. Tap on the Direct option to select a specific Instagram user who you want to share a photo with privately.

14. Tap on the Share button (displayed near the bottom of the screen) to publish your image on Instagram and whatever other services you selected.

SHARE GROUPS OF IMAGES USING AN ONLINE PHOTO SHARING SERVICE

In addition to the online social networking services, there are many free online-based photo sharing services you can use to create and share online albums. Many of these services can also be used for creating an online backup or archive of your images.

To utilize any of these services from your smartphone or tablet, you must install the official app for the service you want to use, plus set up a free online account with that service.

NOTE Any of these services are accessible from the web browser of any PC or Mac, or other mobile device, that's connected to the Internet. Thus, people can view your published images from any computer or mobile device they're using.

Some of the popular online photo sharing services that are compatible with the iPhone and iPad include the following:

- **Adobe Creative Cloud**—www.adobe.com
- **Amazon Cloud Drive Photos for iOS**—www.amazon.com
- **Dropbox**—www.dropbox.com
- **Flickr**—www.flickr.com
- **Shutterfly**—www.shutterfly.com
- **Smugmug**—www.smugmug.com

TIP In addition to having its own app, Flickr integration is built in to the Photos and iPhoto apps. Thus, you can create and upload images from Photos or iPhoto to Flickr, or you can access albums you've stored on Flickr directly from the Photos or iPhoto apps. Using the official Flickr app, however, gives you added control over your online-based account and your online albums.

There are a few advantages to using an online photo sharing service to share and back up your images. First, these services enable you to select and upload groups of images at once and create an unlimited number of albums online, which makes it easier to keep your images organized.

Second, the majority of these services do not automatically reduce the resolution or file sizes of the images you upload. (Facebook, Twitter and Instagram do alter the resolution and file size of uploaded images to speed up upload, download, and display times.) Third, once you create an online album, you can decide exactly who will be able to access and view it.

Fourth, some of these online-based photo sharing services, including Shutterfly and Smugmug, have their own in-house photo lab, so you can order professional-quality prints and photo products from the app and have your order shipped to you (or the desired recipients).

Each of these services has its own proprietary app with its own set of features and functions. Start by visiting the website for a particular service to learn more about it. Then, visit the App Store to download and install the free app so you can access and use the service with your iPhone or iPad.

In general, these services offer a free online-based account. The account typically includes a predetermined amount of online storage space in which you can store your images (usually between 2GB and 5GB). You can purchase additional online storage for an annual fee.

If your goal is to create online-based albums that you'll share with your friends, family, and/or co-workers, for example, be sure to choose a service that enables you to set up privacy settings for each individual album you create. Thus, you can grant individuals access to only certain albums you've created online.

QUICKLY EMAIL UP TO FIVE IMAGES AT A TIME TO SPECIFIC PEOPLE

From your iPhone or iPad, it's possible to compose and send an email message that has up to five separate images as attachments. You can do this from the Photos and iPhoto apps (or many third-party photography apps), as well as from the Mail app. Just as you would when composing any outgoing email message, you must fill in the To and Subject fields. In the main body of the outgoing message, you can also include your own text (in addition to the images).

TIP As you're composing an outgoing email message and attaching images to it, it's possible to select the resolution in which the images are sent. The resolution you choose impacts the file size of each image. Your options include Small, Medium, Large, or Actual Size. To select the image size, tap on the Images option that's displayed to the right of the Cc/Bcc/From field. This option displays the total file size of the outgoing message after one or more photos have been attached to (embedded within) the message.

SEND IMAGES VIA EMAIL FROM THE PHOTOS APP

From the Photos app, to send up to five images to the recipients you select, follow these steps:

1. Launch the Photos app.
2. Open an album and select up to five images.
3. Tap on the Share icon to reveal the Photos app's Share menu.
4. From the Share menu, tap on the Mail icon.

> **NOTE** It's necessary to first set up your existing email account to work with your iPhone or iPad. This is done from within iOS Settings. To do this, launch Settings, tap on the Mail, Contacts, Calendars option, tap on Add Account, select the type of email account you want to add, and then follow the onscreen prompts.

5. When the New Message window appears (see Figure 12-14), fill in the To and Subject fields. The image(s) you've preselected is (are) already embedded in the outgoing email message.
6. Tap anywhere within the body of the image to add your own text.
7. To manually adjust the resolution/file size of the images, tap on the Images option (to the right of the Cc/Bcc/From field). A new Image Size field appears. Tap on the Small, Medium, Large, or Actual Size option.
8. When you're ready to send the message, tap on the Send option. A copy of the outgoing message is saved in your email account's Sent folder.

> **TIP** As you're filling in the To field, if the intended recipients already have an entry in your Contacts database, you can enter that person's first or last name instead of the email address, and the Mail app automatically selects and inserts that person's email address (or enables you to choose which email address for the recipient you should use if a recipient has multiple email addresses).
>
> If you want to send the same message to multiple recipients, tap on the plus sign icon that's displayed to the extreme right of the To, Cc, or Bcc field, and enter one recipient's name or email address at a time.

FIGURE 12-14

The New Message window is used to compose an outgoing email, which includes up to five images, while using the Photos app.

SEND IMAGES VIA EMAIL FROM THE MAIL APP

From the Mail app, sending an outgoing email message that contains up to five images is done the same way as composing and sending a regular message. However, there are just a few extra steps.

After launching the Mail app and tapping on the Compose Message icon, fill in the To and Subject fields as you normally would. Then, place and hold down your finger anywhere in the body area of the outgoing message (while looking at the New Message window). Within two seconds, you see a menu bar appear just above where you held your finger (see Figure 12-15). One of the command tabs on this menu bar is labeled Insert Photo or Video. Tap on it.

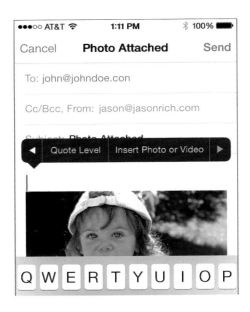

FIGURE 12-15

One at a time, you can embed images into an outgoing email while using the Mail app.

From the Photos pop-up window, select an image to embed in the outgoing email message. To do this, select an album to open, when viewing the thumbnail images in that album, tap your finger on a thumbnail for one image you want to include. A preview of that image appears. Tap on the Use option to continue. That image appears within the body of the email. Repeat this step up to four additional times.

As soon as at least one image is placed in an outgoing message, the Images option appears to the right of the Cc/Bcc/From field. Tap on it to adjust the resolution/file size of the outgoing images.

When you're ready, tap on the Send option to send your email that contains the images you selected and attached to the message. A copy of the outgoing email is saved in your email account's Sent folder.

MORE WAYS TO SHARE PHOTOS ONLINE

In addition to the methods for sharing photos online that were covered in this chapter, using Apple's iCloud service it's also possible to back up and share groups of images using the My Photo Stream and Shared Photo Stream features. You learn how to use these popular iCloud functions next in Chapter 13, "Discover iCloud's My Photo Stream and Shared Photo Stream."

13

DISCOVER iCLOUD'S MY PHOTO STREAM AND SHARED PHOTO STREAM

When it comes to iOS 7 (the operating system that runs on Apple's iPhones and iPads), a key feature it offers can be summed up in one word—integration. In other words, apps can easily and automatically share information with other apps that are installed on your smartphone or tablet, and most of the apps that come preinstalled with iOS 7 (as well as a growing selection of third-party apps) also work seamlessly with Apple's online-based iCloud service.

For example, the Camera app works seamlessly with the Photos and iPhoto apps, and the Photos app works with many other apps, enabling you to easily access and share your digital images. Meanwhile, the Photos and iPhoto apps also work with two core features of iCloud—My Photo Stream and Shared Photo Streams—which are related features, but each serves a unique purpose.

After obtaining a free iCloud account and activating My Photo Stream on each of your iOS mobile devices and Macs, every time you take a new photo using one of the iPhone or iPad's built-in cameras, and that photo is saved in the Camera Roll folder on your device, as long as your mobile device has access to a Wi-Fi Internet connection, that same image automatically uploads to your iCloud account and is stored in your My Photo Stream.

> **NOTE** My Photo Stream is an easy way to share up to 1,000 of your most recently shot images with all of your own Macs and iOS mobile devices, as well as your Apple TV, that are linked to the same iCloud account. Thus, you can automatically and wirelessly access your own images on any of your computers or iCloud-supported mobile devices.

Shared photo streams, however, are separate albums that are stored online in your iCloud account. When creating or managing a shared photo stream, you decide exactly which images it includes. Thus, this is an ideal tool for organizing your favorite images into custom albums, which are then stored online (in the cloud) for backup or archival purposes.

What's great about the Shared Photo Streams feature is that you can also opt to share individual shared photo streams with specific people, and grant them access to your images within a specific shared photo stream, while keeping other shared photo streams restricted. In other words, you decide who has access to specific shared photos streams.

When you share a shared photo stream with one or more other people, if they're Mac or iOS mobile device users, they can view your images as an album from their own Mac using the iPhoto (or Aperture) software, or from their iOS mobile device using either the Photos or iPhoto app. However, you can also invite PC users (as well as non-iOS mobile device users) to view your shared photo stream(s) as online galleries via the Internet. When you do this, each shared photo stream is assigned its own website address (URL), which you can distribute to the people whom you want to be able to view your images.

> **NOTE** You can manage iCloud's My Photo Stream and shared photo streams directly from the Photos or iPhoto app as it's running on your iPhone or iPad. Throughout this chapter, directions are offered for how to use these features with the Photos app (which comes preinstalled with iOS 7). For more information about using these iCloud features with iPhoto, visit www.apple.com/support/ios/iphoto.

CAUTION If your iPhone or iPad does not have Wi-Fi Internet access, you cannot access any photos or albums stored in your online-based iCloud account. Until web access is reestablished, only images stored on your iOS mobile device are accessible from the Photos or iPhoto app.

USE THE MY PHOTO STREAM FEATURE

My Photo Stream creates a collection of 1,000 of your most recently shot (or imported) images and includes them in a single online album for up to 30 days. This album is accessible only by you—or anyone with access to your iCloud account—from any of your own Macs, iOS mobile devices, or Apple TV. It's a collection of images that includes photos taken with your iPhone and/or iPad as well as images imported into or saved on any Macs that are linked to your iCloud account.

Access to My Photo Stream is available anytime the Mac or iOS mobile device you're using has access to the Internet. After each month, you can save the images in My Photo Stream to your Mac as a standalone album. This can be set up to happen automatically using iPhoto. However, if within a single month you add more than 1,000 images to My Photo Stream, you can still save older images to your Mac and have newly added images replace them in your My Photo Stream.

NOTE From the iPhone or iPad, My Photo Stream is accessible from the Photos or iPhoto apps. To view My Photo Stream from the Photos app, launch Photos, tap on the Albums icon (near the bottom of the screen), and then tap on the My Photo Stream folder.

Using My Photo Stream or shared photo streams from an iOS mobile device requires a Wi-Fi Internet connection. These features don't work with a cellular data (3G, 4G, or LTE) connection.

ACTIVATE iCLOUD'S MY PHOTO STREAM ON EACH OF YOUR iOS MOBILE DEVICES

Before your iPhone or iPad can automatically upload new images you take (or that are stored in your smartphone or tablet) to My Photo Stream, or enable you to access My Photo Stream online via the Photos or iPhoto apps, you must turn on this feature.

NOTE It is necessary to separately turn on the My Photo Stream feature on each of your Mac and iOS mobile devices.

When you have an active iCloud account, to turn on My Photo Stream on your iPhone or iPad, from the Home screen, launch Settings and tap on the iCloud option. From the iCloud Control Panel (see Figure 13-1), tap on the Photos option. Then, from the Photos submenu (see Figure 13-2), turn on the virtual switch associated with My Photo Stream.

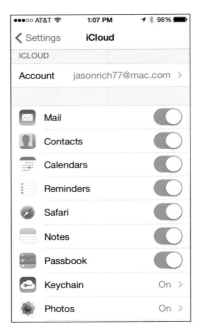

FIGURE 13-1

Access the iCloud Control Panel from within Settings.

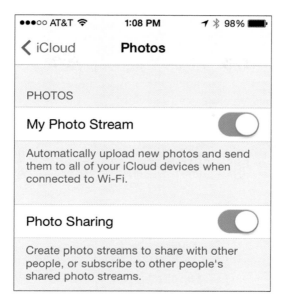

FIGURE 13-2

Turn on the virtual switch associated with the My Photo Stream option to turn on the My Photo Stream feature. The Photo Sharing option (which controls the Shared Photo Stream option) must be turned on separately.

TIP For help initially creating a free iCloud account, visit http://support.apple.com/kb/HT4436. Your iCloud account comes with 5GB of free online storage space. This online storage space is for your personal data and files, excluding photos and iTunes Store and related content purchases. Apple provides, for free, as much online storage space as you need to maintain your My Photo Stream and an unlimited number of shared photo streams.

The allocated 5GB of online storage can be used for other tasks, such as the iCloud Backup feature, storing app-specific data related to Contacts, Calendars, Notes, and Reminders, or syncing and storing documents, data, and files related to the iWork for iOS apps (Pages, Numbers, and Keynote).

My Photo Stream enables any new images you take (or import into a computer or mobile device) to automatically and almost immediately become accessible on all of the computers and/or mobile devices that are linked to the same iCloud account.

MANAGE YOUR MY PHOTO STREAM ALBUM FROM YOUR iPHONE OR iPAD

You can manage the My Photo Stream album that's created each month from your iPhone, iPad, or Mac (using iPhoto or Aperture). However, you can also view it on any HDTV that has an Apple TV device ($99.00, www.apple.com/appletv) connected to it.

From your iPhone or iPad, to manage the My Photo Stream album, first access it using the Photos or iPhoto app. Then, as you're viewing the thumbnails in the My Photo Stream album (see Figure 13-3), tap on the Select option that's displayed on the screen.

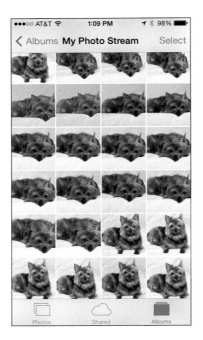

FIGURE 13-3
The My Photo Stream album can be viewed from within Photos (shown here on the iPhone 5s).

Using your finger, tap on one or more image thumbnails you want to select. As each is selected, a blue-and-white check mark appears in the bottom-right corner of the thumbnail.

After images are selected, three options become active—Share, Add To, and Trash (see Figure 13-4). On the iPhone, they're displayed along the bottom of the screen, whereas on the iPad, these same options are displayed in the top-left corner of the screen.

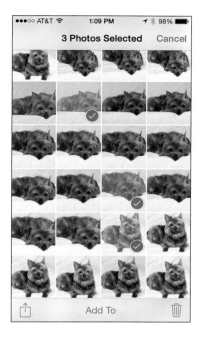

FIGURE 13-4

After selecting one or more images from My Photo Stream, the Share, Trash, and Add To options become available.

Tap on the Share icon to share the selected image(s) with others using any of the options available from the Photos app's Share menu, including AirDrop, Message, Mail, iCloud, Facebook, Twitter (if only one image is selected), or Flickr.

> **TIP** From the Share menu, it's possible to copy the image onto the iPhone or iPad's virtual Clipboard, so you can paste it into another app. You also can save the selected image(s) to the Camera Roll (in your device's internal storage), assign a selected image to a contact, use a selected image as a Wallpaper image (for your device's Lock screen and/or Home screen), or print the image using an AirPrint-compatible photo printer.

Tap on the Add To option to copy the selected image(s) from the My Photo Stream album that's stored online in your iCloud account to an album that's stored on your iOS mobile device. Tap on the Trash icon to delete the selected image(s) from the My Photo Stream album online. When you do this, it is almost instantly removed from the My Photo Stream that's accessible from your Mac, Apple TV, and all of your other iOS mobile devices.

> **NOTE** When using an iPhone or iPad, to edit or enhance a photo that's stored in My Photo Stream, you must download and save it to the internal storage of your mobile device (in the Camera Roll folder). To do this, select the image from My Photo Stream, tap the Share icon, and then select the Save to Camera Roll option. Now, when you access the Camera Roll folder from the Photos or iPhoto apps (or a compatible third-party app), the selected images are available to view and work with.

Keep in mind that after you turn on the My Photo Stream feature, all images you take using your iPhone or iPad are automatically uploaded to My Photo Stream and almost instantly become viewable from all of your other compatible computers and devices. This includes blurry or out-of-focus images as well as images you might or might not want to share with others. Images you import into your iOS mobile device or save from the Internet in your Camera Roll folder, for example, also become part of your shared photo stream.

SHARE SELECTED GROUPS OF IMAGES WITH OTHERS USING SHARED PHOTO STREAMS

Your iCloud account enables you to set up and maintain one My Photo Stream, which is accessible from all of your own Macs, Apple TV, and iOS mobile devices. However, you also have the option of creating and sharing as many shared photo streams as you want, for free, using the Photos or iPhoto apps on your iPhone or iPad. You can also create and share shared photo streams from a Mac (using the iPhoto or Aperture software).

Once again, on each Mac or iOS mobile device with which you'll be using shared photo streams, you must first turn on this feature in Settings. To do this from each of your iPhones and/or iPads that are linked to your iCloud account, launch Settings and tap on the iCloud option to access the iCloud Control Panel. Next, tap on the Photos option. This time, from the Photos submenu (refer to Figure 13-2), turn on the virtual switch that's associated with the Photo Sharing option. You need to do this only once per device, but for shared photo streams to work from your iPhone or iPad, a Wi-Fi Internet connection is required.

After activating shared photo streams on your smartphone or tablet, you can create, view, manage, and share these online-based albums.

CREATE A SHARED PHOTO STREAM

A shared photo stream is a standalone album that contains a group of images that you select and upload to your iCloud account. Each shared photo stream is assigned a unique name. You can then opt to share it with the specific people you want to view your images.

Use the Photos or iPhoto app on your iPhone or iPad to create an unlimited number of shared photo streams. This can also be done from a Mac using the iPhoto or Aperture software. To create a shared photo stream from scratch, make sure your smartphone or tablet is connected to a Wi-Fi Internet connection and launch Photos. Then, follow these steps:

1. Open the album that contains the images you want to include in a shared photo stream. For example, open the Camera Roll album.

2. As you're viewing an album, tap on the Select option.

3. One at a time, tap on the thumbnails that represent the images you want to include in the shared photo stream (see Figure 13-5).

FIGURE 13-5

Select the thumbnails for the images you want to include in a new shared photo stream album.

4. After you've selected all the images you want from a particular album, tap on the Share icon and select the iCloud option.

5. When the iCloud window appears, if you want, fill in the optional Comment field with text that describes the shared photo stream you're about to create. For example, you could write, Nashville Trip—Grand Ole Opry.

6. Tap on the Stream field. Near the top of the Add To Shared Stream window (see Figure 13-6), tap on the (+) New Shared Stream option.

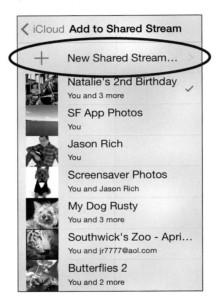

FIGURE 13-6

Tap on the (+) New Shared Stream option to create a new shared photo stream from scratch that will be published online in your free iCloud account.

> **TIP** If you want to add the selected images to an already created shared photo stream album, from the Add to Shared Stream window, tap on the name of the shared photo stream album you want to add the images to, instead of tapping on the (+) New Shared Stream option.

7. From the New Stream window, create a name for the shared photo stream album, and enter it into the Stream Name field. Keep the title short but descriptive, such as **Nashville Trip—Grand Ole Opry**.

8. Tap on the Next option.

9. One at a time, in the To field (see Figure 13-7), enter the email address for the person whom you want to invite to view your shared photo stream. If the person you're adding already has an entry in your Contacts database, instead of manually entering an email address, simply type the first or last name, and the Contacts app inserts the email address (or enables you to choose which email address to use if that contact has multiple email addresses). To include multiple invitees, tap the plus sign (+) icon to the right of the To field.

FIGURE 13-7

As you're creating a new shared photo stream album, you decide exactly who will be able to view it by automatically sending invitees an email invitation.

10. Tap on the Next option.

11. At this point, in the iCloud window, you can edit your optional comment or tap the Post option to create your shared photo stream and upload the pre-selected images to the newly created album.

At the same time the images are uploading to your iCloud account and being stored online in the shared photo stream you just created, your iPhone or iPad automatically sends an email to each of the people you invited to view your photo stream. This email contains the details they'll need to access it online (see Figure 13-8).

Jason Rich   December 24, 2013 1:14 PM
To: jasonrich77@yahoo.com   Hide Details
Reply-To: Jason R. Rich
Subscribe to Jason Rich's "Nashville Trip - Grand Ole Opry"" Photo Stream?

Subscribe to Jason Rich's "Nashville Trip - Grand Ole
Opry"" Photo Stream?

You are invited to view this Photo Stream and post your own photos, videos, and comments.
Other subscribers will see your email address when you join.

✓ Subscribe to this Photo Stream

iCloud

iCloud is a service provided by Apple. My Apple ID | Support | Terms and Conditions | Privacy Policy | Don't Send Me Photo Stream Emails
Copyright © 2013 Apple Inc. 1 Infinite Loop, Cupertino, CA 95014, United States. All rights reserved.

FIGURE 13-8

When you invite someone to access one of your shared photo streams, he or she will receive an email invitation that contains easy directions for accessing your photos.

VIEW AND MANAGE SHARED PHOTO STREAMS FROM YOUR iPHONE OR iPAD

After you've created one or more shared photo streams, as long as your iOS mobile device is connected to the Internet via a Wi-Fi connection, it's possible to access, view, and manage these online-based albums at any time. To do this, launch either the Photos or iPhoto app.

From the Photos app, tap on the Shared command icon that's displayed at the bottom of the screen. As you're viewing the Shared Streams screen, you can either open a shared photo stream to view, or tap on the Edit option to select and delete an entire shared photo stream.

CAUTION If you delete a shared photo stream that you created, it is no longer accessible to you or anyone whom you've invited to view it. The entire album is deleted from your iCloud account. There is no Undo option for this, so proceed with caution.

> **NOTE** If you delete a photo stream you were invited to view but didn't create, it is removed from your iOS mobile device but not from the creator's iCloud account. Thus, you could later access it again using the original invitation email you received (or by requesting a new invitation).

To open, view, and work with a particular shared photo stream, tap on the album thumbnail from the Shared Streams screen. Thumbnails that represent each image appear. You now have several options, as detailed in the following sections.

VIEW AND WORK WITH SINGLE IMAGES

To view an enlarged version of a single image on your smartphone or tablet's screen, tap on the image's thumbnail from any screen in Photos that displays the contents of an album using thumbnails. You can then tap the Edit option and edit/enhance the image (see Figure 13-9).

FIGURE 13-9

Images from a shared photo stream can be edited or enhanced, but must be saved in the Camera Roll folder on the mobile device on which you're editing or enhancing them.

Initially, the image you're viewing is stored online. However, after editing or enhancing it, when you tap on the Save command, it is saved in your device's Camera Roll folder. Thus, it is now stored in the internal storage of your device as a new image. That edited image can now automatically be uploaded to your My Photo Stream because you've made changes to the original and the app now considers it a new image.

As you're viewing a single image from a shared photo stream, you also have the option to "like" an image (by tapping on the Like option, which is associated with a happy face icon), or you can add a comment to the image. Yet another option is to tap on the Share icon, which gives you access to the Photos (or iPhoto) app's Share menu, from which a wide range of options are available.

MANAGE A SHARED PHOTO STREAM'S CONTENT

After accessing a specific shared photo stream that you've previously created, as you're viewing the image thumbnails it contains, tap on the Select option to select one or more of the images. Upon doing this, the Photos or iPhoto app's Share icon becomes active. Tap on it to access the app's Share menu, and you can then share or print the selected images or use any of the other options available from this menu, such as Copy or Save to Camera Roll.

NOTE As you're viewing images in a shared photo stream, they are stored online and are being streamed to your iOS mobile device. To save the images to your mobile device's internal storage in the Camera Roll folder, select the images, tap on the Share icon, and then tap on the Save to Camera Roll option.

If you're working with a shared photo stream that you created, after tapping on the Select option and selecting one or more image thumbnails, the Trash icon also becomes active. Tap on this if you want to delete specific images from the shared photo stream album.

It's also possible to add images to an existing shared photo stream. To do this, select and open an album that contains the images you want to add, select those images, tap on the Share icon, and then tap on the iCloud option. When the iCloud window appears, tap on the Stream field, and select the name of the shared photo stream to which you want to add the images. Tap on the Post option to upload the selected images to the shared photo stream album you chose.

MANAGE WHO HAS ACCESS TO YOUR SHARED PHOTO STREAMS

When you first create a shared photo stream, you can invite specific people to access it. However, at any time later, it's possible to invite additional people to view that shared photo stream album. It's also possible to revoke someone's access.

To manage who has access to your specific shared photo streams, launch the Photos app, tap on the Shared option, and then, from the Shared Streams screen, tap on the thumbnail that represents the album you want to open. When the desired shared photo stream album is open and you're viewing the thumbnails for images in that shared photo stream, tap on the People option (see Figure 13-10). The Edit Photo Stream window appears.

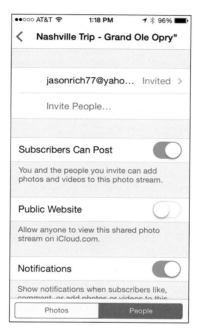

FIGURE 13-10

Access the Edit Photo Stream window to manage who has access to viewing your shared photo stream after it has been created.

Near the top of the Edit Photo Stream window is a list of people you've already invited to view the shared photo stream you're working with. To revoke someone's access to the shared photo stream, tap on his or her name, scroll down to the bottom of the Info window, and then tap on the Remove Subscriber option.

To invite more people to view your shared photo stream after it has been created, tap on the Invite People option. Then, in the To field, one at a time, enter the email addresses or names of the people you want to send invitations to.

MORE OPTIONS AVAILABLE FROM THE EDIT PHOTO STREAM WINDOW

From the Edit Photo Stream window, in addition to managing the people who can access the shared photo stream you're working with, there are three additional options, each with a virtual switch associated with it (refer to Figure 13-10).

Turn on the virtual switch associated with the Subscribers Can Post option if you want the people you invite to view your shared photo stream album to be able to also upload their own images to that album for everyone else who has access to that album (including yourself) to see.

Turn on the Public Website option if you know one or more of the people whom you've invited to view your shared photo stream are not Mac or iOS mobile device users. This enables people to access your shared photo stream as an online gallery using their computer's web browser and by visiting the shared photo stream's unique website address URL.

> **NOTE**   When you turn on the Public Website option, theoretically, anyone who discovers the unique website address assigned to the shared photo stream can access your images. This includes total strangers. The odds of someone stumbling upon your unique shared photo stream URL and accessing it are slim, however. Using the Public Website option is the only way PC users or non-iOS mobile device users can access your shared photo stream via your iCloud account.
>
> By turning on the Public Website feature, iCloud creates an online gallery in the form of a website (see Figure 13-11), which people can access by entering the gallery's unique URL into their web browser. Upon inviting a PC user, for example, to visit your shared photo stream, if the Public Website option is turned on, the PC user receives the website link, as opposed to the ability to access the shared photo stream directly.

By turning on the virtual switch that's associated with the Notifications option, you will receive a notification every time someone posts a comment, likes, or adds photos to your shared photo stream.

FIGURE 13-11

When the Public Website feature is turned on, this is what a shared photo stream's online gallery looks like. (Shown here using the Safari web browser on a Mac.)

> **TIP** Located at the very bottom of the Edit Photo Stream window is a Delete Photo Stream option (displayed in red). Tap on this to delete the entire shared photo stream album from your iCloud account—and instantly revoke everyone's access from viewing its contents. Keep in mind, there is no Undo option for this feature. If you delete a shared photo stream by mistake, you must re-create it from scratch.

OTHER OPTIONS FOR SHARING GROUPS OF PHOTOS ONLINE

Shared photo streams are not your only option for sharing groups of images online or for creating online galleries. Many of the online photo sharing services, such as Flickr.com, Shutterfly.com, Smugmug.com, and others, have iPhone/iPad apps available that enable you to select images stored on your smartphone or tablet, upload them to your free online account with that service, and create an easy-to-access online album or gallery.

In addition, a handful of cloud-based file sharing services, including Dropbox (www.dropbox.com), Amazon Cloud Drive (www.amazon.com), or Microsoft OneDrive (http://onedrive.live.com), enable you to create online albums or galleries and share them with others. To accomplish this, you must set up a free account with the online file sharing service, and then install the service-specific app on your mobile device. For example, the Dropbox, Amazon Cloud Drive Photos, and the Microsoft OneDrive app are available from the App Store.

14

OTHER WAYS TO SHARE YOUR DIGITAL PHOTOS

After you've taken photos with your iPhone or iPad, or you have digital images stored on your iOS mobile device, you can sync those images with all of your other computers and mobile devices, share them with other people online, and showcase them in the real world.

DISPLAY YOUR DIGITAL PHOTOS ON YOUR HD TELEVISION SET

You can use several easy methods to share the images that are stored on your iOS mobile device with others by displaying them on your HD television set. One method is wireless. It involves using the optional Apple TV device ($99.00, www.apple.com/appletv) and the AirPlay feature that's built in to iOS 7.

The second method is also wireless. It involves using iCloud's My Photo Stream or Shared Photo Stream feature. From your iPhone or iPad, create a My Photo Stream or a shared photo stream album, which is ultimately stored in the cloud, in your online-based iCloud account. Then, use Apple TV (which is connected to your TV) to access your iCloud account using its Internet connectivity to display the images stored in your My Photo Stream or the shared photo stream album you select.

The third method utilizes the USB cable that is supplied with your iPhone or iPad, and a special adapter, called the Apple Lightning Digital AV Adapter ($49.00) or the Apple 30-Pin to Digital AV Adapter ($39.99). You must physically connect your iPhone or iPad to your HD television set via the television's HDMI port.

After your iPhone or iPad and HD television set are linked using one of these methods, you can view images that you'd otherwise display on your device's screen in vivid detail on your large-screen HD television set.

You can display images manually, one at a time, or you can easily create animated slideshows (complete with a visual theme, slide transitions, and background music) to display on your television set for yourself or an audience.

DISPLAY DIGITAL IMAGES ON YOUR HD TELEVISION USING APPLE TV

The Apple TV device is optional. It's available from Apple for $99.00, and it connects simultaneously to your HD television set and to the Internet. After an Apple TV is connected to your TV, it can access and play any compatible content acquired from the iTunes Store, including TV show episodes, movies, music videos, or music.

TIP   When using Apple TV to access any images or albums stored in your iCloud account, you must first log in to your iCloud account from your Apple TV device. This needs to be done only once, unless you need to switch between multiple iCloud accounts. To do this, from the Apple TV main menu, select the Settings option. From the Settings menu, select the iCloud option. When prompted, enter your Apple ID/iCloud username and password, and follow the onscreen prompts.

In addition, Apple TV can access and display images stored in your My Photo Stream or shared photo streams, plus play video clips or home movies you've shot and that are stored in your iCloud account.

NOTE Apple has also teamed up with dozens of third-party program producers and television/cable networks to provide free and paid programming via Apple TV channels. Once selected, this on-demand programming streams from the Internet to your Apple TV device and appears on your HDTV. You also have the option of accessing your Netflix or Hulu Plus account from Apple TV and streaming programming from these subscription-based services to your HDTV.

TIP For more information about what Apple TV is capable of, and for directions on how to use its various features, visit www.apple.com/appletv.

DISPLAY IMAGES STORED ON YOUR iOS MOBILE DEVICE ON YOUR HD TELEVISION SET VIA AIRPLAY

If you have your Apple TV device connected to the Internet via a Wi-Fi Internet connection, it's possible to use the AirPlay feature that's built in to iOS 7 and Apple TV's operating system to showcase, wirelessly, the images stored on your iOS mobile device on your HD television screen. This is done using either the Photos or iPhoto app (or any other third-party photography app that supports AirPlay).

To take advantage of this feature, turn on your Apple TV so that the main Apple TV menu is displayed on your television set. Next, from your iPhone or iPad, turn on Wi-Fi, and then launch the Photos or iPhoto app.

Open any album within the Photos or iPhoto app, and select an image to view. As you're viewing a single image, tap on the Share Menu icon. From the Share menu, tap the AirPlay option (see Figure 14-1).

When the AirPlay pop-up window opens, select the Apple TV option (see Figure 14-2). Now, the image you're viewing on your iPhone or iPad is simultaneously displayed on your HD television set. Using finger gestures on your iOS mobile device, swipe left or right to manually scroll through the images in the album (and see them displayed on your television set).

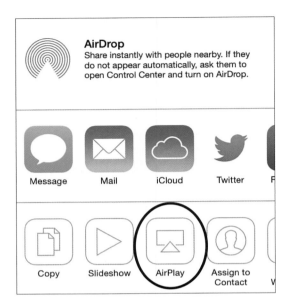

FIGURE 14-1

When your iPhone or iPad has linked with your Apple TV, select the AirPlay option.

FIGURE 14-2

When you tap on the Apple TV option when Apple TV and AirPlay are available, images that are displayed on your iPhone or iPad's screen can be streamed and viewed on your HD television set.

NOTE Although you can zoom in or out when viewing images on your iOS mobile device, this feature does not currently work on the images displayed via Apple TV.

Instead of viewing individual images manually, as you're viewing the thumbnails that represent the images from the album on your iPhone or iPad, tap on the Share icon and select the Slideshow option (using the device's screen).

From the Slideshow Options window displayed on your iOS mobile device, select the Apple TV option (see Figure 14-3). Next, tap on the Transitions option to choose which animated slide transition effect you want to use, and turn on the Play Music option if you want to select and play background music (that's stored on your iOS mobile device).

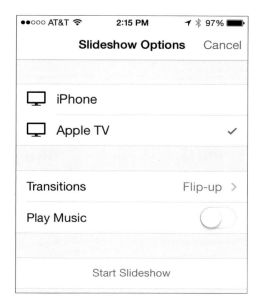

FIGURE 14-3

There are several ways to present a slideshow on your HD television set that features your images.

Tap the Start Slideshow option to begin viewing the slideshow on both your iPhone or iPad's screen and your HD television set. In this case, the images remain stored on your iPhone or iPad and are wirelessly streamed to the Apple TV device. Your Apple TV is not accessing images stored online in your iCloud account. (Although from the Photos app, you can access and display images from My Photo Stream or a shared photo stream album.)

CREATE YOUR OWN APPLE TV SCREENSAVER

When Apple TV and your television set are turned on but not being used to show programming, or if the Apple TV is streaming just music, you can create an animated screensaver that displays your digital images on your television set using a themed, animated slideshow format.

To set up the Apple TV Screensaver feature, access Apple TV's main menu screen and follow these steps:

1. Select the Settings option to access the Apple TV Settings menu.

2. From the Settings menu, select the Screen Saver option.

3. From the Screen Saver submenu, adjust any or all of the five menu options. First, select the Start After option and choose how long your Apple TV should remain inactive before displaying the screensaver. Options range from Never to 30 minutes.

4. Select the Show During Music option and decide whether you want the screensaver to be displayed when Apple TV is playing just music. This includes music you've purchased from the iTunes Store or music that's streaming from iTunes Radio, for example. If you select the Yes option, anytime just music is playing via your Apple TV, the screensaver that features your images is displayed on the television set.

5. Select the Photos option and choose which iCloud album you want to showcase in your Apple TV screensaver. You can select either your My Photo Stream or any of your shared photo stream albums.

6. Choose a theme for your screensaver. Apple created more than a dozen different animated themes to choose from. Each includes different types of slide transitions and graphics.

7. Select the Preview option to see a preview of what your Apple TV screensaver will look like.

8. When all of the options are adjusted and the screensaver is to your liking, exit out of Settings to save your changes and activate the newly created screensaver.

DISPLAY AN IMAGE COLLAGE, ONE IMAGE AT A TIME, OR CREATE AN ANIMATED SLIDESHOW

Using Apple TV and the images stored in My Photo Stream or a shared photo stream album, it's possible to set up Apple TV to display your images one at a time and enable you to manually scroll through them. Alternatively, you can create an animated slideshow to display your images.

NOTE This method for displaying images on your HD television set requires you to first transfer images stored on your iOS mobile device to your online-based My Photo Stream or into an online-based shared photo stream album using one of these iCloud-related features. This can be done directly and wirelessly from your iPhone or iPad.

To display images on your HD television set that were taken using your iPhone or iPad, but that have been since transferred to iCloud, follow these steps:

1. From iCloud's main menu screen, select the iCloud Photos channel.

2. Choose either your My Photo Stream, or one of your shared photo stream albums that are stored online in your iCloud account. They'll all be accessible from your Apple TV.

3. The images from your selected album appear in a collage format on your television set. Using your Apple TV's remote, scroll up or down, or select a single image by pressing the round Select button (in the center of the directional buttons on the remote) to view just that image.

4. When viewing a single selected image, use the Apple TV remote to scroll left or right, and view the remaining images within that album, one at a time, displayed on your screen. Press the Menu button to return to the collage screen.

To display the images from the selected album as an animated slideshow, from the collage screen, press the Slideshow button, which can be found near the top-right corner of the screen. When the Slideshow menu is displayed, customize the various slideshow options before selecting the Start Slideshow option (used to view the animated slideshow on your television screen).

The Slideshow menu options include the following:

- **Shuffle Photos**—Turn on this option to randomize the order in which images from the selected album appear. When turned off, the slides display in the order in which they're stored in the album.

- **Repeat Photos**—Turn on this option if you want the slideshow to continue indefinitely, until you manually turn it off.

- **Default Music**—Select the music you want to play in the background as your slideshow plays. You can select any song(s) stored in your iCloud account that you've previously acquired from the iTunes Store, for example. If you're an iTunes Match subscriber, it's also possible to choose any song(s) from your entire digital music collection. If no music is selected, no music plays when your slideshow runs.

■ **Shuffle Music**—Turn on this feature if you want Apple TV to randomly play music that's stored in your iCloud account, as opposed to specific music you select.

■ **Theme**—Apple TV has more than a dozen different animated slideshow themes to choose from. Select your favorite. This determines what graphics and animated slide transitions appear with your images. Based on which theme you select, additional options, such as how long each slide appears, may become available.

After you've adjusted each of the slideshow-related options, select the Start Slideshow command to begin playing the slideshow on your television screen.

DISPLAY IMAGES FROM YOUR iOS MOBILE DEVICE ON YOUR TELEVISION SET WITHOUT APPLE TV

Instead of investing in an Apple TV device, it's possible to display images from your iPhone or iPad on an HD television set if you connect the two devices via the USB cable that came with your iOS mobile device, along with a special Digital AV Adapter (sold separately).

To use this option, if you own an iOS mobile device with a Lightning Port, purchase the Apple Lightning Digital AV Adapter ($49.00). If you own an older iOS mobile device with a 32-pin Dock Connector port, purchase the Apple 30-Pin to Digital AV Adapter ($39.99). These adapters are available from Apple stores, Apple.com, or Apple authorized resellers.

Next, plug in the appropriate end of the USB cable that came with your iPhone or iPad to the bottom of the iOS mobile device. Plug in the other end of the cable to the Digital AV Adapter, and plug in the opposite end of the Digital AV Adapter to the HDMI In port of your television. On your television set, select the appropriate HDMI In input setting. (This is typically done by pressing the Video Input button on the TV's remote control.) At this point, just about anything that appears on your iPhone or iPad is mirrored, in real time, on your HD television set (with the exception of copyrighted video and certain apps).

After you see everything on both your iPhone or iPad and your television set, launch the Photos or iPhoto app and use any of the app's features to display your images. If you're using iPhoto, for example, you can showcase a web journal or slideshow on your HD television set that's controlled from your iOS mobile device.

TRANSFER IMAGES FROM YOUR iOS MOBILE DEVICE TO YOUR COMPUTER USING iTUNES SYNC

The easiest way to share images between your iPhone or iPad and your computer is to use iCloud or another online-based image sharing or cloud-based service. However, the iTunes Sync option remains viable.

> **NOTE** Keep in mind that since Apple made the iCloud service available, the iTunes Sync process has become somewhat antiquated as a way to sync and share data between your computer(s) and mobile device(s).

iTunes Sync requires that you use the iTunes software installed on your Mac or PC to link that computer with your iOS mobile device. This is done using the USB cable that came with your iPhone or iPad, or you can use the iTunes Wireless Sync process if both your computer and iOS mobile device are linked to the same home wireless network via Wi-Fi.

Launch the iTunes software on your computer, and then connect your iOS mobile device to your computer. When the link is established, check the sidebar of the iTunes software. Your device will be listed below the Devices heading (shown in Figure 14-4).

Click on the device listing. Then, when details about your device appear in the main area of the iTunes screen (on your computer), click on the Photos tab. Next, add a check mark to the Sync Photos From option. From the pull-down menu to the right of this option, select iPhoto or images from a specific folder, such as Pictures. You can then add a check mark to the All Folders option, for example, to sync all images stored on your computer with your iPhone or iPad, or select specific folders or albums. This is done by adding check marks next to the appropriate album or folder listing(s).

Click on the Sync button that appears near the bottom-right corner of the screen to sync the image albums or folders you've selected between your computer and iOS mobile device.

Click on your device in the sidebar.   Photos Tab from the iTunes Summary Screen

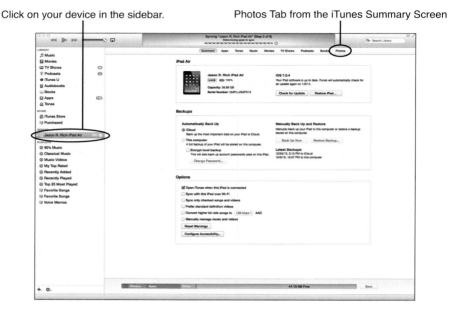

FIGURE 14-4

Click on your device's listing under the Devices heading in the sidebar of the iTunes software.

NOTE Unlike iCloud's My Photo Stream and/or shared photo streams, the iTunes Sync process for syncing photos is a manual process and happens only when you connect your computer with your iOS mobile device. The syncing does not happen automatically when new photos are added to your computer or iOS mobile device.

After you sync the images stored on your iOS mobile device with your Mac, for example, use the iPhoto or optional Aperture software (on your computer) to view, organize, edit, enhance, print, share, and archive your images.

QUICKLY TRANSFER IMAGES BETWEEN iOS MOBILE DEVICES USING AIRDROP

If you're using iOS 7 on any of the latest model iPhones or iPads, when you tap the Share menu, AirDrop is an option for wirelessly sharing digital photos from within the Photos or iPhoto apps with other iPhone, iPad, or iPod touch users who are in close proximity to you.

To turn on the AirDrop feature, access the Control Center by swiping your finger from the very bottom of your iPhone or iPad's screen in an upward direction. From the Control Center window (see Figure 14-5), tap on the AirDrop option.

FIGURE 14-5

Turn on the AirDrop feature from iOS 7's Control Center.

The AirDrop menu contains four options—Off, Contacts Only, Everyone, and Cancel. Tap on Contacts Only to turn on AirDrop but make it so you can share images wirelessly only with people who have an entry in your Contacts database and who are in close proximity to you. Tap on the Everyone option to wirelessly send/receive images from any other iOS mobile device user who is in close proximity to you.

When the Contacts Only or Everyone feature is turned on, to send someone an image from the Photos app, launch Photos and select the photo you want to share via AirDrop. When you're viewing the image, tap on the Share icon to access the Share menu. Tap on the AirDrop option.

> TIP   Instead of selecting just one image, you can select a group of images to send to someone via AirDrop.

All iOS mobile device users who also have AirDrop activated and who are in close proximity are displayed (see Figure 14-6). Tap on the name or profile image of the person you want to send an image to. In this example, an image is being sent from a user's iPhone 5s to their own iPad Air wirelessly using AirDrop.

FIGURE 14-6

From the Share menu, with AirDrop activated, decide who the recipient of the selected image(s) will be, and tap on his or her name or profile photo. Here, an image is being sent from an iPhone 5s to the user's iPad Air.

Within seconds, on the recipient's screen (in this case, the user's iPad Air), an AirDrop pop-up window appears, regardless of what the recipient is doing (see Figure 14-7). A thumbnail of the image and Accept and Decline buttons are displayed. If the recipient taps on the Accept button, that image is transferred wirelessly from your iPhone or iPad to the recipient's device and stored in his or her Camera Roll folder. However, the image remains stored on your device as well.

FIGURE 14-7

The AirDrop pop-up window that appears on the recipient's screen (in this case, the user's iPad Air) after an image sent to their device by another iOS mobile device that's in close proximity.

When the image is received (or if it's declined) by the intended recipient, a message is displayed on your device's screen.

PUT YOUR NEWFOUND KNOWLEDGE TO USE

Taking pictures of what happens around you; of your friends, family, and/or co-workers; as well as the things you experience and the places you visit; is a fun and easy process using apps built in to your iPhone or iPad. Never before has it been so easy to capture memories that you can cherish for many years to come—or share immediately with others, regardless of where you are.

As you now know, after you've taken photos using the cameras that are built in to your iPhone or iPad, you can use apps to view, organize, edit, enhance, print, and share them, plus take advantage of the Internet to showcase your images in many different ways.

Even if you don't consider yourself to be a creative or artistic person, you can easily edit and enhance the photos you take to transform them into eye-catching images that you'll be proud to showcase and share. Keep in mind, many of the image editing and enhancement apps you've learned about and that are available from the App Store offer one-touch special effect filters that you can mix and match to dramatically alter or improve the appearance of an image within a few seconds.

> TIP   Experiment using different special effect filters and/or combinations of filters to quickly give your images a unique, professional, or artistic appearance.

Then, when you're ready to share your images, it's possible to choose from many different ways to accomplish this using the Internet, including email, text message, AirDrop, shared photo streams, online social networking services (such as Facebook, Twitter, or Instagram), online photo sharing services (such as Flickr.com, Smugmug.com, and Snapfish.com), or using cloud-based file sharing services (such as Dropbox, Amazon Cloud Drive, or Microsoft OneDrive).

There are also countless ways to showcase your photos in the real world. As you've discovered, creating prints from your digital images (directly from your iPhone or iPad) is an easy process. Plus, you can create enlargements that are printed on poster-size photo paper, canvas, glass, or other materials using a service like Shutterfly.com, FotoFlot.com, CanvasWorld.com, FotoForms.com, Zazzle.com, or ImageOnGlass.com.

Having your images imprinted on products, like iPhone or iPad cases, mouse pads, mugs, T-shirts, holiday ornaments, or custom printed greeting cards, for example, is also possible, as is creating one-of-a-kind photo books (either directly from your iOS mobile device or by first transferring your images to a Mac or PC). The possibilities are truly limitless, yet typically very affordable.

Almost every month, new and innovative ways to showcase and share your images are being made available right from your iPhone or iPad. We're living in an exciting time, when taking and sharing pictures is easier than ever using the feature-packed smartphone or tablet that you're already carrying around with you.

Using the knowledge you've gathered from *iPad and iPhone Digital Photography Tips and Tricks*, get into the habit of taking photos frequently. Then, decide how you want to sync, archive, showcase, and share them. Most important, have fun taking and sharing your digital photos!

Index

Q-R

MAKE THE MOST OF YOUR SMARTPHONE, TABLET, COMPUTER, AND MORE!

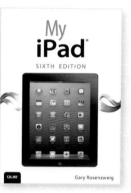

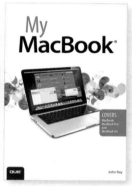

ISBN 13: 9780789751027   ISBN 13: 9780789750440   ISBN 13: 9780789751690   ISBN 13: 9780789749956

Full-Color, Step-by-Step Guides

The "My..." series is a visually rich, task-based series to help you get up and running with your new device and technology and tap into some of the hidden, or less obvious features. The organized, task-based format allows you to quickly and easily find exactly the task you want to accomplish, and then shows you how to achieve it with minimal text and plenty of visual cues.

Visit quepublishing.com/mybooks to learn more about the My... book series from Que.

quepublishing.com

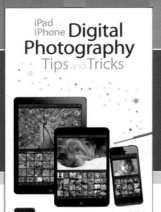

FREE
Online Edition

Safari
Books Online

Your purchase of *iPad and iPhone Digital Photography Tips and Tricks* includes access to a free online edition for 45 days through the **Safari Books Online** subscription service. Nearly every Que book is available online through **Safari Books Online**, along with thousands of books and videos from publishers such as Addison-Wesley Professional, Cisco Press, Exam Cram, IBM Press, O'Reilly Media, Prentice Hall, Sams, and VMware Press.

Safari Books Online is a digital library providing searchable, on-demand access to thousands of technology, digital media, and professional development books and videos from leading publishers. With one monthly or yearly subscription price, you get unlimited access to learning tools and information on topics including mobile app and software development, tips and tricks on using your favorite gadgets, networking, project management, graphic design, and much more.

Activate your FREE Online Edition at
informit.com/safarifree

STEP 1: Enter the coupon code: CNZBIWH.

STEP 2: New Safari users, complete the brief registration form.
Safari subscribers, just log in.

If you have difficulty registering on Safari or accessing the online edition,
please e-mail customer-service@safaribooksonline.com